Baby Doe Tabor

Baby Doe Tabor

THE MADWOMAN IN THE CABIN

Judy Nolte Temple

University of Oklahoma Press : Norman

Also by Judy Nolte Temple

(ed.) *Open Spaces, City Places: Contemporary Writers on the Changing Southwest* (Tucson, 1994)
(under the name Judy Nolte Lensink) *"A Secret to Be Burried": The Diary and Life of Emily Hawley Gillespie, 1858–1888* (Iowa City, 1989)

Library of Congress Cataloging-in-Publication Data

Temple, Judy Nolte, 1948–
   Baby Doe Tabor : the madwoman in the cabin / by Judy Nolte Temple.
      p. cm.
   Includes bibliographical references and index.
   ISBN 978-0-8061-3825-1 (cloth)
   ISBN 978-0-8061-4035-3 (paper)
   1. Tabor, Augusta, d. 1895. 2. Baby Doe, d. 1935. 3. Tabor, Horace Austin Warner, 1830–1899. 4. Pioneers—Colorado—Biography. 5. Leadville (Colo.)—History. 6. Matchless Mine (Lake County, Colo.)—History. 7. Colorado—History— 1876–1950—Biography. 8. Industrialists' spouses—Colorado—Leadville— Biography. 9. Colorado—Biography. 10. Leadville (Colo.)—Biography. I. Title.
   F781.B19T46 2007
   978.8'46030922—dc22
   [B]   2007000700

The paper in this book meets the guidelines for permanence and durability of the Committee on Production Guidelines for Book Longevity of the Council on Library Resources, Inc. ∞

4 5 6 7 8 9 10

Contents

List of Illustrations vii

Preface ix

Acknowledgments xix

Chapter 1. The Legend of Baby Doe 3

Chapter 2. Obsessed with Baby Doe: The Legend Expands 40

Chapter 3. The Wanton: Sex and Power in the Mining Frontier West 73

Chapter 4. The Bad Mother and Good Widow: "Much Madness is divinest Sense" 105

Chapter 5. Entering the Dreamworld: Lizzie Tabor Speaks 140

Chapter 6. Mining the Dreamworld 181

Epilogue. In Her Own Words: "Dreams and Visions" 219

Notes 229

Bibliography 241

Index 247

List of Illustrations

Denver crowd at film premiere of *Silver Dollar*   5

Horace A. W. Tabor   15

Augusta Pierce Tabor   15

Elizabeth Bonduel McCourt, known as "Baby Doe"   16

Denver home of Horace Tabor family   25

Illustrations of young Lily Tabor found in Lizzie's scrapbook   26

"Things Put in Safe" list   29

Silver Dollar Tabor and ex-President Theodore Roosevelt   33

Elderly Baby Doe Tabor in downtown Denver   37

Interior of Matchless mine cabin after Baby Doe's death   44

Postcard illustration of young and old Baby Doe   48

Portrait of Baby Doe by Waldo C. Love   58

Beverly Sills in title role of the opera *The Ballad of Baby Doe*   60

Detail of page from Lizzie Tabor's scrapbook   80

Midlife photograph of Lizzie Tabor   97

Newspaper illustration, "Two Wives of Tabor Met"   106

Newspaper illustration, old Baby Doe praying   107

Draft and revision from "Dreams and Visions"   143

Drawing and vision of blessed Virgin Mary   144

Coded page from Lizzie's scrapbook   145

Childhood photo of Silver Dollar Tabor   160

Lizzie's lament written around a newspaper headline   163

February 1915 coded calendar   169

Photograph of Silver Dollar Tabor as a young woman   173

Photograph of Silver Dollar Tabor as an actress or dancer   173

Multidirectional "Dreams and Visions" account   217

Last known photograph of Baby Doe Tabor   220

Drawing of angel and Matchless Mine Girl   223

Preface

I dreamed that I was in ragged clothes & naked & that men could see my body & that I was part of the time walking around & laying naked on the floor & a child was there and told me a man was looking over the transom at me—July 24, 1912

This book is about a woman who has been regarded with prurient curiosity and disdain for over a century.[1] She is the centerfold of a gaudy mining-frontier legend of home-wrecking "Silver Queen" Baby Doe Tabor. When she was alive, her beauty and bad behavior were so disruptive that she was shunned by polite society, and as she aged, she slowly deteriorated into an elderly madwoman. After she was safely dead, a popular biography punished her again with gruesome detail: "The formerly beautiful and glamorous Baby Doe Tabor, her millions lost many years before, was found dead on her cabin floor at the Matchless Mine in Leadville, Colorado, on March 7, 1935. Her body, only partially clothed, was frozen with ten days' stiffness into the shape of a cross. She had lain down on her back on the floor of her stove-heated, one room home, her arms outstretched, apparently in sure foreboding that she was to die." When I read this tale (for I was one of the curious), I wondered what great wrong Baby Doe had done that she was not only crucified but deserted in poverty and frozen as well. The legend described her distinctly female sins: beauty, gold digging, husband stealing, poor mothering.[2]

Baby Doe's haunting dream of being naked and vulnerable came true. Upon the news of her death, scavengers flocked to see the witch-hermit's home and destroyed it in their search for buried silver. But the silver had long ago been spent, and the Tabors' daughter optimistically named Silver Dollar had died in 1925 under questionable circumstances. There was nothing left in the cabin but scraps of paper in Mrs. Tabor's scrawled handwriting. This woman who had been the victim of others' venomous words left behind a treasure that no one understood: thousands and thousands of her own words. This treasure was buried by bureaucratic maneuvers for the next thirty years, a gestation period in which the legend of Baby Doe Tabor grew without rebuttal. For the first time, this book brings the authentic and insistent voice of Lizzie Tabor to the legend of Baby Doe.

THE LEGEND

I had a wonderful Vision to day. I saw my own face in a looking glass I was very young in my teens—it was just as I looked then & O so beautiful so very bright & young and healthy its brightness was wonderful & I could not tell you how beautiful it was it was so fresh & lovely. I saw it between 3–30 & 4 P.M. September 20–1919

Baby Doe enjoyed incredible wealth as the infamous younger second wife of millionaire "Silver King" Horace Tabor, one of the richest men in the West of the 1880s. But after his bankruptcy and death she lived for nearly thirty years in rags, in a tiny isolated cabin at the Matchless silver mine outside Leadville, Colorado. In her last years she became a public spectacle: dressed in baggy, gender-crossing clothing from which dangled a large crucifix, her feet wrapped in rags, she drew the stares of gossips who recalled her once legendary beauty. Her contemporaries felt she deserved to suffer because she had been the wanton divorcée who entangled Horace Tabor in a tawdry love triangle that led him to divorce his hardworking first wife, Augusta, and to his ultimate ruin. The tragic loss of Baby Doe's daughters, detailed in lurid newspaper articles consumed by the next generation, confirmed that she was also a bad mother. Finally, in old age, she was judged a good widow, but the cost was high: she was also considered a madwoman, who roamed the streets at midnight, talked to spirits, and clung to her crucifix.

I was first mesmerized by the beautiful Baby Doe in 1979 during an illustrated lecture about the western frontier. She was the perfect woman: beautiful, but silent. She was one of the few women mentioned in that western history class, which made her tale all the more compelling. I was also mesmerized by the teller of the tale, the handsome professor, fifteen years older than I, wiser, divorced, much wealthier. Like countless other young women, I fell in love with an older man. Like Baby Doe, I was leaving a failing marriage into which I'd entered with youthful optimism. Like Baby Doe, I experienced shunning—much milder in my era, but still mortifying. This brief relationship gave me empathy for Baby Doe and provoked me to think about her in new ways. She was a young married woman who had the ambition and courage to venture to a western mining town. She left a bad marriage, jettisoned her reputation and Catholic upbringing to pursue love and a second marriage. She honored that love by remaining an independent widow who fought against powerful men on behalf of her daughters. Feeble but proud, she defiantly stayed in her home until death. To those who knew of her through legend and gossip, she was Baby Doe Tabor. To those from whom she demanded respect, she was Mrs. H.A.W. Tabor. To those who loved her during her lifetime, she was Lizzie. Since this is her story and I have grown to love her, I call her Lizzie, as she emerges from behind the legend of Baby Doe, in which she is a beautiful silent object, to become a writing subject who insisted upon a life of agency.

DIGGING BENEATH THE LEGEND

The legend of Baby Doe tells how this troublesome wanton was contained when she retreated up to Leadville as a still-lovely widow. She stayed there at the Matchless mine for over thirty years, shut up in solitude. But in reality Lizzie Tabor would not shut up. She recorded thousands of accounts that she called "Dreams and Visions," which described her nighttime dreams and daytime visions in what I term her Dreamworld. Mrs. Tabor told visitors to her cabin that the hoards of paper she kept in shoe boxes were her memoirs. Unbeknownst to all, Lizzie Tabor had hidden away an even larger treasure trove of her writings—rudimentary diaries, correspondence, bundles of "Dreams and Visions"—in trunks stored for her by nuns. When the contents of the trunks were revealed after Mrs. Tabor's death, these writings were considered so dangerously libelous that the papers were immediately sealed. For more than three decades the papers remained entombed, so threatening were they to powerful Colorado men who feared contamination by association with Baby Doe and her errant daughter Silver Dollar. When people at last had access to the Tabor papers in 1967, they rarely read more than a few "Dreams and Visions" because of their daunting appearance: they were scrawled on deteriorating scraps of paper, contained obscure codes, and lacked coherence. They confirmed the legend that Baby Doe was a madwoman driven crazy by her bad decisions about love, money, and child rearing.

I was first lured into the Dreamworld of Baby Doe in 1980 during a half-day visit to the Colorado Historical Society in Denver. I perused the multi-volume guide to the Tabor papers, for the sizzling legend of Baby Doe burned in my memory. When I discovered that the archives contained her Diary Notes, my heartbeat quickened, for I had always wondered about her side of the story in which she was blamed for ruining Horace Tabor. But I was disappointed when I opened the Diary Notes because they were sporadic rather than daily. I was accustomed to enduring pioneer women's sparse prose about their chickens and children because I found it eventually told a story. Baby Doe's diary was so intermittent that its gaps obscured any narrative. However, as I read Baby Doe's words I heard emerging from beneath the legend a compelling voice that spoke of starvation, not seduction.

Nov 26–1918 Papa Tabors Birthday I owe my room rent & I am in need of food only enough bread for tonight & breakfast. . . . my shoes & stockings only 1 pair are in rags.[3]

After I read the diaries, I progressed to folders entitled "Dreams and Visions" that contained over two thousand fragments. Many were in appalling handwriting that, once deciphered, ranted about visitations from demons, about the Tabor daughters, about the Matchless mine. Despite the fact that the "Dreams and Visions" were carefully dated like diary entries, they defied logic, and I suspected they had probably survived only because their writer was the infamous Baby Doe. I kept reading, however, because everything there interested me: the West, the candor about the body, the mysterious coding, the emotional fervor. I slowly grew accustomed to the fragments' challenges and was drawn into the Dreamworld of Lizzie Tabor. The intense "Dreams and Visions" converted my passing curiosity about "whatever happened to Baby Doe" into a twenty-five-year-long quest to understand a real woman. Patiently digging beneath her legendary persona, I saw that Lizzie's life experiences mirrored those faced by many women—marriage(s), motherhood, widowhood—and that these experiences were tellingly illuminated because of her status as an ostracized "other." Lizzie Tabor's words have evoked in me feelings ranging from repulsion, frustration, empathy, pity, to humility.[4]

Many of Lizzie's dreams recounted omens from God or torments from devil spirits. As a lapsed Lutheran I had no familiarity with passionate religious writing, but as a scholar originally trained in scientific method I believed I could bring "order" to the disorderly "Dreams and Visions."

Archivists had organized the unwieldy scraps into tidy chronological order, which I assumed would provide a narrative. But after several short ventures into the Dreamworld during weeklong research trips, I realized both the limitations of my intellect and the power of Lizzie's voice. Within three days of immersion in her fragments, I began having my own dark dreams. The pleading "Dreams and Visions" demanded attention from my conscious intellect—and from my heart.

One way to stave off the daunting disorder within the Dreamworld was to impose my own order onto Lizzie's text. Making sense of previously disregarded private writings by women, especially their long diaries, was my field of expertise, so I decided during a 1993 research visit to employ the technique of rudimentary content analysis with the aid of my laptop computer. I chose the years 1914 and 1915 because the intensity and volume of "Dreams and Visions" during that period—Lizzie was writing at least three hundred entries a year—signaled that something important was happening. I transcribed the text and indexed pivotal people, places, and colors within Lizzie's perplexing scraps. I had previously skimmed over the repetitive prose, much like the listener who backs away from a madwoman's maniacal repeated story. The slower pace that indexing required made me attentive to how Lizzie talked rather than ranted, attuned me to the internal logic of her Dreamworld, and alerted me to external events to which she obliquely referred. I began to explore the correspondence in the Tabor archives to see if it provided insights and links to her references concerning "Silver's troubles." I searched for "that horrible letter" to which Lizzie referred in a hybrid account that contained her diary-like commentary on the same page as a dream. Although my reassembly of the narrative puzzle illuminated parts of Lizzie's Dreamworld, I realized that a complete transcription of the surviving "Dreams and Visions" was an insurmountable task. I hoped that a broader survey of Lizzie's text would at least provide a sketchy map into her mind. This is when Patty Pokigo, a Women's Studies student at Metro State University in Denver and herself a young widow, agreed to become my research assistant. With invaluable sensitivity to the torments expressed in Mrs. Tabor's "Dreams and Visions," Patty searched the entire remainder of the collection for thematic veins I had identified while indexing and she photocopied particularly rich examples.

I ache at the heart with a burden of unshed tears. My love is like a shut-up fire in a tomb & my children hold the key. Extreme mental anguish. It seems as if I must bleed pity. Only sometimes I would find my eyes wet at the thought of his never-ending kindness.[5]

My closest contact with the emotional fire within the Dreamworld occurred during a five-week-long research trip in 2000. I had given up the notion that a "full text" of Lizzie's writings awaited me in all those files, for Baby Doe's cabin had been vandalized after her death by treasure hunters seeking memorabilia, and it seemed likely that many of the "Dreams and Visions" from Lizzie Tabor's final years had been cast to the icy Colorado winds. I also knew that rational time did not exist in Lizzie's Dreamworld, where she was the young apple of her parents' eye or Horace Tabor's wife (who still flirted with her first husband, Harvey Doe) or a woman fleeing dark spirits. So I changed my research strategy from a chronological one to a topical one determined by reading from Lizzie's text. Patty Pokigo and I organized the fragmentary writings under headings such as "Silver-endangered," "Silver-good," "Matchless mine," and "Religious figures." Lizzie's complex writing warred with this scheme, for within a single vision three topics were interlaced; in one dream Silver could be both horrific and angelic. Yet the twenty-eight stacks of my neatly typed transcripts laid out on the living room floor at first satisfied my need for ordering, editing, and organizing Lizzie's world.

The last half of the "Dreams and Visions" we sorted, however, were Patty's photocopies of Lizzie's labyrinthine handwriting. Lizzie had crammed several dreams onto a single sheet of stationery in order to save paper, drawing lines between her entries. As my scissors followed those very lines that Lizzie had left eighty years ago to guide a future reader, I felt I had become her long-sought amanuensis. Our tidy stacks grew into unruly holographic heaps that flowed into the middle of the room as the puzzle-shaped pieces of Lizzie's transcripts overwhelmed my typed ones. Despite the warm comfort of the room, I felt an uncanny affinity for Lizzie who sat in her chilly cabin, surrounded by growing mountains of papers. I avoided reading any stack of "Dreams and Visions" for too long, lest I be unable to find my way back out of Lizzie's imploring Dreamworld maze. Yet I could not resist the beckoning power of the sheer volume of papers that resembled a book torn asunder by a storm. I returned again and again to the room, hoping that by sitting among those papers I could discern connections, clarity, answers. After repeated forays, I gained some knowledge of symbols and guideposts—and also realized the limits of my ability to decipher much of what

Lizzie meant. I gained respect for her superhuman legacy of writing that both teased me to listen while resisting my attempts to understand it.[6]

I cannot claim to know the core of Lizzie's mind, even though I have more experience with the "Dreams and Visions" than any other living person. What I found in the Dreamworld is not at all what I expected, but I can illuminate some previously unmapped paths. I offer biographical and historical contexts for the "Dreams and Visions" that speak the mind of Lizzie Tabor so that we can grapple with her eccentric autobiographical texts. A second autobiography, that of a culture obsessed with Baby Doe, appears in my analysis of the legends surrounding her alluring figure. My intent in this analysis of the legend and the literary legacy of Baby Doe is to be accessible, so although my work is undergirded by critical theory, I have deployed academic perspectives with a light hand, to avoid burying Baby Doe in an avalanche of scholarly citations. I draw eclectically from the fields of New Western history, gender studies, and life-writing literary theory. This weighty toolkit is necessary for an interdisciplinary study of Baby Doe Tabor, who has fallen between the cracks of serious inquiry. Traditional western U.S. history relies on colorful narrative, and this is where Baby Doe has been stuck for ages. New Western historians for the most part consider Baby Doe a legendary curio unworthy of study. Sophisticated literary theorists, although recently more attentive to writing from the American West, have not considered Baby Doe Tabor as an autobiographer.

ENTERING THE DREAMWORLD

The route I have chosen through the labyrinth of the Dreamworld begins with a gradual introduction to strategically placed selections of "Dreams and Visions" and then moves toward immersion in Lizzie Tabor's writing. Because I have not corrected Lizzie's spelling nor added punctuation in most cases, her "Dreams and Visions" retain their sense of breathless urgency. When I have shortened Lizzie's texts for clarity, I use ellipses to signal my work. We enter the story at the shallow end (the legend) and gradually proceed deeper into the Dreamworld of Lizzie Tabor. I begin with "The Legend" because it is the bait that still draws people to Baby Doe 150 years after her transgressions gained her international notoriety. If the "Dreams and Visions" had been written by an obscure eccentric madwoman, no one would endure them and their relentless pain. It is the living legend that provokes us to listen to Lizzie's story, just as her midnight wanderings intruded the needy, aging Baby Doe Tabor into the minds of Coloradans. To know the lurid details of the legend is to understand what Lizzie Tabor was writing against, for her voice interrupts and complicates that pat legend.

In chapter 2, "Obsessed with Baby Doe: The Legend Expands," I trace the ways in which the Tabor story has been reproduced and commodified. The legend lives on in various tableaus: a sensationalist Hollywood film starring Edward G. Robinson as Horace Tabor; the popular American tragic opera *The Ballad of Baby Doe,* which introduced newcomer Beverly Sills in the title role; Baby Doe on the cover of *Life Magazine*; a theme restaurant chain; a sexually sadistic novel. On occasion I meditate on how the sad story of Baby Doe operates as a cautionary gender tale: don't be too beautiful or other women will hate you; don't challenge social norms or you'll be shunned; don't raise a daughter too sexually independent or she'll break your heart; don't show your face when your beauty fades or you'll become a spectacle; don't age without the protection of a man.

I dreamed that I lost a upper tooth & bloody flesh hung out in chunks & I picked out several of my lower teeth and put them in again & then they seemed alright— December 24, 1912

Chapter 3, "The Wanton: Sex and Power in the Mining Frontier West," explores cultural beliefs about women in the West that form the supporting timbers of the ongoing Tabor fetish. More of Lizzie Tabor's "Dreams and Visions" enter the narrative to deconstruct pivotal moments within the legend. I examine how the mythic Baby Doe provides a lush body onto which historians and biographers have written their own fantasies. Their writings reflect America's obsession with the power of female sexuality, risk-taking masculinity, capitalism, notorious celebrity, abject women. I then analyze the "conversion" of Baby Doe in chapter 4, "The Bad Mother and Good Widow: 'Much Madness is divinest Sense'."[7] I compare Baby Doe with another converted bawdy Irish mining-town caricature, Molly Brown, whose deeds during the *Titanic* tragedy elevated her status while Baby Doe sank into madness. Or was it madness? I explore whether Lizzie's public appearances as unforgettable madwoman Baby Doe might actually have been a performance of penitence. I compare the fates of Baby Doe and two other famous widows—Elizabeth Custer and Jacqueline Kennedy Onassis—to examine the options for women in a patriarchal society where they could either trade upon their husband's fame or be discarded. When even an evanescent writer like Virginia Woolf anticipated fearfully at age forty the prospect of becoming a vague old woman, does the sad end of the Tabor legend foreshadow the fate of most widows who are as isolated in their assisted-living cells as Baby Doe was in her cabin?

In chapter 5, "Entering the Dreamworld: Lizzie Tabor Speaks," we encounter the dreams in all their intensity. Within the madwoman's story—told jumbled together all at once, repeated again and again like a chant—is Lizzie Tabor's voice that contests the simplistic legend in which she was cast as the fast mining-camp Divorcée, Gold Digger, Home Wrecker, Bad Mother, Pariah, Madwoman. The entry point I have selected focuses on Lizzie's daughter Silver, whose sexuality tortured the dreaming mother. I provide crucial context from Lizzie's correspondence and diary to anchor us in reality, for images of Silver madly multiply within the Dreamworld maze. Silver is everywhere: the specter of nightmarish visions, the white-clad Dream Child, the Matchless Mine Girl, the veiled mother of mysterious babies.

> *2/11/20 [a rare case of Lizzie using numerical date notation] Silver sat in chair and all her wrapper as aflame in places many small flame all over her lap I rolled the wrapper up from bottom & put all the fires out & I saved her life. . . . she only looked with her big eyes at me in horror at herself all on fire. . . .*

In the final chapter, "Mining the Dreamworld," I suggest a variety of perspectives for understanding the "Dreams and Visions." When one is equipped to chart its cast of shadowy characters, to spot recurrent patterns, an "interior autobiography" emerges. I examine Lizzie's ability to code-switch between rational and irrational worlds and her dedication to her writing. Lizzie's unconventional text, when placed in the company of other forms of life-writing and literature, suggests that she was not mad but, instead, a most unconventional autobiographer, a pioneer of marvelous realism, or even a religious mystic-in-the-rough.

The epilogue, "In Her Own Words: 'Dreams and Visions,'" contains excerpts from Lizzie's text without any mediating commentary, explication, or context. I leave it to each reader to decide whether Lizzie was a madwoman, a mother driven mad with worry, or a rough-draft religious visionary, perhaps even a mystic. In my ideal scholarly Dreamworld, I would understand the heart of Lizzie Tabor's writings and present them coherently to a sympathetic audience. But most of the "Dreams and Visions" defy logic, contain barriers of ambiguity, even drop off midsentence. They are ultimately unknowable, uncontainable—as was Lizzie Tabor and her nemesis, Baby Doe.

The subtitle of this book, *The Madwoman in the Cabin,* pays homage to a groundbreaking work of feminist literary criticism, *The Madwoman in the Attic: The Woman Writer and the Nineteenth-Century Literary Imagination,* written by Sandra M. Gilbert and Susan Gubar. They identified the recurring specter of a madwoman in literature written by female authors and theorized that it indirectly represented their rage. Thus Bertha Mason Rochester in *Jane Eyre,* the madwoman wife that Rochester confines in an attic room, represents Charlotte Brontë's critique of an era in which women were confined to the role of either angel or monster. Gilbert and Gubar argue that, "by projecting their rebellious impulses not into their heroines but into mad or monstrous women (who are suitably punished in the course of the novel or poem), female authors dramatize their own self-division, their desire both to accept the strictures of patriarchal society and to reject them."[8] This self-division could also manifest itself in the author herself, in the form of anorexia, agoraphobia, or the "aesthetics of renunciation" epitomized by Emily Dickinson, the poet who chose to dress in white. Within the Dreamworld of Lizzie Tabor, the madwoman who chose to dress in rags, this fragmentation arises in contradictory scenes in which she is both an object of lust and a sanctified recipient of redemption, a mother who is embraced by her daughters and scorned by them. *The Madwoman in the Attic* allowed me to accept Lizzie Tabor's writing as that of a mad woman, angry at the confining legend that rendered her speechless. I came to understand Lizzie's bizarre madwoman costume as part of what I term "strategic madness" that demanded community attention to her plight. Like mad Emily Dickinson before her, Baby Doe would not be shut up in conventional prose, and she painstakingly described her enormously rich Dreamworld in such detail that we can enter it—if we dare.

> *Night of Nov 16 or 17–1932 I have seen for a long while at night after I finished my prayers glorious Visions & after I lay down at night I see myself lying down & thousands of folk come just to see me keep passing close to me & stooping over & down as they pull at me all nations & sizes . . . & they walk around my cabin & stare at me & get on my bed & frighten me & I have to get up & to light my lamp.*

Acknowledgments

In the two decades that it took to complete this work, I learned that it takes a village to make a book. I wish to acknowledge the patience, wisdom, and encouragement of the following colleagues and friends: Susan Hardy Aiken, Kent Anderson, Lisa Backman, Peg Zeglin Brand, Suzanne Bunkers, Robert Burns, Fran Buss, Bill Convery, Stephen Cox, Donald DeBats, Sally Deutsch, Barbara Dey, Ruth Dickstein, Myra Dinnerstein, Larry Evers, Joanna Bowen Gillespie, Erica Golo, Steve Grinstead, David Halaas, Kristen Iversen, Robyn Jacobs, Liz Kennedy, Linda Kerber, Barbara Kingsolver, Philip Krider, Rebecca Lintz, Tony Luebbermann, the Lunch Bunch (Bobbie Barg, Dianne Bret Harte, Nancy Fahringer, Helen Ingram, Barbara Kittle, Susan Luebbermann, Lucy Penner, Joan Sandin, Lois Shelton, Marge Sherrill, Georgia Vancza), Gordon and Kari McBride, Judith McDaniel, Kristie Miller, Tom Noel, Stan Oliner, Patty Pokigo, Jeanette Renouf, Hélène Reynolds, Shannon Ritchie, Malcolm Rohrbough, Susan Rosowski, Ruba Sadi, Keith Schrum, Richard and Judy Scott, Clark Secrest, Duane A. Smith, Donna Stein, the University of Arizona Provost's Research Fund, David Wetzel, Jodi Wetzel, Susan Woelzl, Gerardo Wood, James Wood, WOSAC Travel fund, Ellen Zazzarino, and Ann Zwinger.

Two women who dearly loved Lizzie Tabor died before this work reached book form. One was Patty Pokigo, my Denver research assistant, who brought her insights as a widow to Lizzie's writings. When she knew her own death was imminent, Patty thanked *me* for letting her spend hours reading the "Dreams and Visions." Susan Rosowski, past president of the Western Literature Association, read my draft manuscript and wrote me a poignant letter of encouragement just weeks before she died. Her gracious comments on my manuscript and her enthusiasm for my efforts to uncover Lizzie's voice sustained me when the going was rough.

I received extraordinary assistance and support from Rebecca Lintz and Stan Oliner of the Colorado Historical Society. The University of Oklahoma "village" that made this book a reality include (in the order in which I met them): Jean Hurtado, Karen Wieder, Chuck Rankin, Steven Baker, Christi Madden, Pippa Letsky, Tara Malone, Marian Ezzell, and Tony Roberts. While the errors in the book are my responsibility, credit for converting my final draft into a true manuscript goes to Lauren Johnson Bivona, my colleague and friend at the University of Arizona.

Finally, I acknowledge my husband, Rob Temple, with loving gratitude. He believed in this project when I first began my research in earnest in the 1990s and has sustained me through long years of tedious work. He decoded and counted endless "Dreams and Visions," listened patiently to my ideas about Lizzie Tabor, and carried file boxes of my notes and Lizzie's writings into and out of motel rooms en route to Denver during my sabbatical because I did not want to lose them. Rob "held on to the manuscript" through numerous versions and proofreading marathons, for which I am deeply indebted.

Baby Doe Tabor

CHAPTER 1

The Legend of Baby Doe

Matchless Mine Cabin
Our Own Beloved Mr and Mrs. Wallace:
I have longed to write you of all the trials Persecutions our Divine Saviour
has permitted me to endure. . . . I am now as for a long time alone. I am
breaking my heart over that Book and that Picture Show.

The legend of Baby Doe Tabor, like a lode of silver ore, comes from many veins with elusive sources.[1] It is part historically verifiable biography and part myth, a story that confirms desires and taboos through the deeds and misdeeds of heroic figures. This legend, set in the American mining frontier, embodies beliefs about masculinity, female power, money, and sin. Western culture reifies the successful man, yet recurring sagas tell of a smart, beautiful, ambitious, and sexually irresistible woman who brings about his downfall—and ultimately her own demise. The stories of Adam and Eve, Samson and Delilah, Caesar and Cleopatra, even President Clinton and Monica Lewinsky, all contain versions of the femme fatale, of the rule-breaking lovers who trespass moral borders. We devour the lurid details of their glorious if ephemeral freedom from restraint and then follow with satisfaction the tale of their inevitable fall from ill-gotten pleasure. Such legendary lovers form a convoluted link between immorality and immortality. Lizzie had a drawing of Anthony and Cleopatra pasted in her scrapbook, perhaps seeing a parallel between the tragic Egyptian queen who loved unto death and her own short controversial reign as Colorado's Silver Queen.

By the time Mrs. Tabor died in 1935, she had become a legend: the infamous Baby Doe. In obituaries she was called "the Wallis Simpson in the American Empire," an allusion to the gorgeous divorcée who so enchanted the king of England, Edward VIII, and caused an uproar when Edward abdicated the throne in the name of love. The legend of Baby Doe Tabor began during Lizzie's lifetime, nourished by gossips and occasional newspaper articles. Two unauthorized biographies appeared when Mrs. Tabor was seventy-eight and provoked her to protest "that Book and that Picture Show." Popular historian David Karsner wrote the first, titled *Silver Dollar*, in 1932. It was reprinted in at least eleven editions and remained in print until 1970.

Karsner, who had written books about Andrew Jackson and Eugene Debs, made Horace Tabor his main subject; Baby Doe did not enter the story until page 138. The closing chapter on their daughter Silver Dollar, "Death in the Red Lights," must have particularly hurt Lizzie Tabor, who had denied to reporters in 1925 that the young woman found dead in a Chicago flophouse was her errant child. In writing *Silver Dollar*, Karsner drew on newspaper articles, general histories of the mining West, and on his relationships with journalists, an academic, a curator at the Colorado Historical Society, and the heirs of Tabor's first wife, Augusta. But Karsner did not interview Mrs. Tabor. Only after completing his manuscript did he venture up into the mountains to actually meet the elderly widow. In a short "afterword" he described encountering the "strange woman" wielding a shotgun, but on the second day Karsner gained an invitation into Mrs. Tabor's cabin. He wrote, "I attempt no interview with Baby Doe. It would have been folly to do so. The story had been told to me many times by numerous people, probably with more clarity and authenticity than she could remember it and piece it together after passing nearly thirty years in the terrible silence of a solitary shack beside a skeleton mine on the summit of the Rockies."[2] Karsner chose to promote the standard legend of Baby Doe rather than listen to the aged recluse tell her side of her story. Did Karsner even ask Mrs. Tabor about the piles of paper covered with her writing that filled the room? Few realized that Lizzie was doggedly recording her "Dreams and Visions" and writing heartfelt letters from her shack, which was neither solitary nor silent. A second affront to Mrs. Tabor occurred when a film based on Karsner's book and also called *Silver Dollar* premiered on December 2, 1932, in Denver and attracted a huge crowd that hoped to glimpse the legendary Baby Doe herself. Mrs. Tabor had been invited by the producers to attend the premiere, with expenses paid, but she refused this mortification.

Perhaps in response to these hurtful stories, Lizzie Tabor was secretly storing away family documents, including her "Dreams and Visions," in trunks sent to a Denver warehouse and a Leadville Catholic hospital. Her

Denver crowd at the 1932 premiere of the film *Silver Dollar*, based on the Tabor legend. Courtesy Denver Public Library Western History Collection, X-22003.

motive, like that of other "compensatory diarists," as Robert Fothergill terms them, may have been to hide away her own version of her life story for safe keeping in hopes that later generations might be more empathetic to her situation as a grieving widow and mother.[3] For this devout elderly woman, the tell-all memoir or rebuttal interview characteristic of our era would have been unthinkable. Despite her careful planning, Lizzie's writings so carefully stowed away would not be available to readers until thirty-two years after her death. Thus Baby Doe was not only sentenced to three decades of "solitary confinement" in life; she was posthumously silenced for three more decades before her words could confront the hurtful legend. In those decades the legend thrived, fed by voyeuristic public hunger for ever-more salacious details about Baby Doe, and unchallenged by her own voice that would testify to the injustices she bore. One version of the Tabor story purportedly told in Baby Doe's own words was Caroline Bancroft's *Silver Queen*, published in 1950 and still in print today. But this voice, like most of the legend it helped perpetuate, was inauthentic.

I use the term "legend" for a story that is based, however loosely, on the lives and adventures of past people. Within legends, archetypal figures and events appeal to us on deep mythic levels: the sexually uncontrollable woman, the morally weak man, the social eruptions evoked by immoral coupling, the child marked by the sins of the parents. These mythic elements provide what Richard Slotkin calls an "intelligible mask" that hints at the earthly and metaphysical issues that torment us.[4] Can men become powerful enough to escape moral parameters? How do we deal with sexually powerful women? What pathways exist in traditional society for ambitious women? What happens to those who love not wisely but too well? Should justice be tempered by mercy? In the legend, such questions feed the mythic figure of Baby Doe, one that speaks to deeply held cultural notions about sex, power, and wealth. These notions embedded in the legend, I suggest, fuel the mythic engine that keeps alive the sad legend of Baby Doe (see chapter 3).

The legend that follows consolidates a wide range of nonfictional books on the Tabors, some of which form a tawdry genealogy of misinformation, each building upon its predecessors to make Baby Doe's sin and her punishment evermore dramatic.[5] I have included characteristic passages from the so-called biographers to give a flavor of their own voices, voices that can sound like those of hyperbolic gossipers. My analysis of each writer's biases appears later (see chapter 3), so that the momentum of the legend is unin-hibited. However, at certain important junctures in the legend, each writer's view of female power and sexuality influences a turning point in their narrative. For example, they differ over who seduced whom, whether Baby Doe was a spirited pioneer, a sexual predator, a guileless exhibitionist who took "a leaf from Eve's notebook," or simply a woman lucky or unlucky enough to be in the right western boom town at the right time.[6] I signal these telling divergences within the legend by noting that precisely what happened is unclear. Lizzie Tabor's correspondence could have answered many of these mysteries immediately after her death, but her papers were sealed away—and people seemed to like the legend the way it was. I have interspersed, within the virtually voiceless legend, Lizzie Tabor's own words taken from selected "Dreams and Visions" to complement, contradict, and complicate the story. For even though what follows is primarily a fable, it has roots in real-life events that permeated Lizzie's Dreamworld.

THE BELLE OF OSHKOSH BECOMES BABY DOE

Sunday morn May 23–1927 I dreamed Pa and Ma were sitting in a seat of a wagon & I was behind them others were standing around & all over was dark looking & dusky & Ma had on a big dark rich coat of heavy dark fur she looked very large Pa looked so young & bright & gay & had a smart brimed hat on O so young looking & handsome & he talked gaily to me turning around to me all the time I said to Ma why don't the cook make us some pies & cakes & doughnuts I am so hungry. I then woke up May 23–1927

A beautiful blonde baby girl was christened Elizabeth Bonduel McCourt on October 7, 1854, in Oshkosh, Wisconsin. She was the child of Peter and Elizabeth McCourt, devout Irish Catholic immigrants. The McCourt family by 1870 numbered eight children and financially was moderately comfort-able from their real estate investments and a clothing store that thrived in the booming Wisconsin lumber region dominated by capitalists such as Frederick Weyerhauser. However, fires that swept through the town and the depletion of the lumber supply kept the McCourt finances in a precarious position: Peter McCourt's worth fluctuated from $75,000 to zero in 1875, the year of a major conflagration.[7] A nationwide economic depression forced the family to move to a modest cottage. "Elizabeth, however, wasn't greatly depressed by her father's business worries. Certainly her own capital assets were not depreciating as she entered adolescence. In her mid-teens she was already called . . . the 'belle of Oshkosh.'"[8]

Elizabeth, called "Lizzie" by her family, was approximately five foot three inches tall. "Her figure was already a challenge to the local forces of morality, plump in the places a nineteenth-century female wanted to be plump and pretended to be if she wasn't."[9] Noted for her striking blue eyes and friendly manner, Lizzie began to attract the admiring comments of men and the disapproving envy of women. One McCourt daughter had already been married off to a prosperous man, but the presence of the unmarried twenty-two-year-old Lizzie, regardless of her beauty, was conspicuous. "Elizabeth had made up her mind to this much: when she fell in love, the man must be something, or at least have excellent promise."[10] The social prospects of gentlemanly Harvey Doe, the son of Oshkosh's former mayor, represented promise on a modest scale to the McCourts. Despite the fact that the Does were a respectable Protestant family and the McCourts were Irish Catholic, Harvey knew of Lizzie as the prettiest girl in town. It is unclear if it was the audacious Miss McCourt or the admiring young Mr. Doe who initiated a more personal acquaintance. In spite of his mother's objections to immigrant papists, Harvey Doe married Elizabeth McCourt in a modest Catholic ceremony on June 27, 1877. The newlyweds immediately headed west toward Central City, Colorado, where Harvey's father owned a gold mine called the Fourth of July that his son could work. The West operated for the Does, as it did for many other families, as a safety valve to release tensions: the mother's dismay over her son's marriage to a rumored fast girl, the son's desire to escape his domineering mother. The McCourt family was also supportive of this venture, for the West represented opportunity to those who had the courage, stamina, and luck to pursue mining. For the beaming Lizzie Doe, the West symbolized escape from gossiping women to a freer masculine place where she would be appreciated. She would meet her destiny in the Rocky Mountains.

> *June 9–1904 I dreamed I went to the Episcopal alter & knelt down with Harvey Doe & was married to him by their minister & I said that Pa would be so happy & told Ma that I was now fixed up in our church . . . & Tabor was there all seemed happiness how funny to marry Harvey again*

The honeymooning Does spent two weeks at a nice hotel in the thriving city of Denver, population nearly thirty thousand. The bustle and energy must have been stimulating for a girl from Oshkosh. Harvey and Lizzie were headed for even wilder territory beyond Denver, where Harvey's father had preceded them to finalize plans for working the family gold mine. Like most mining towns, Central City lacked women, so someone as striking as Mrs. Doe was immediately noticed by the miners. She was a married woman, but her flashy figure and friendly openness were contradictory to notions of ladylike behavior. Soon Mrs. Doe was given the nickname "Baby" by the miners who called her Baby Doe. It is unclear whether this name was based on her diminutive figure and doelike eyes or was a variation of the salacious term "babe" with its sexual innuendo. It is also unclear whether Mrs. Doe resented this familiarity or relished the rough tribute to her beauty and gameness. Perhaps this suggestive term expressed the miners' relief that here was a woman with spunk who could do physical work—and would have to—for it was soon apparent that Harvey Doe's upbringing as a gentleman's son who could sing and play the piano beautifully had not prepared him for mining labor. Harvey Doe, Jr., believed he had inherited a gold mine but soon discovered he would first have to dig the shaft. The elder Doe had promised that any profits his son made as a result of working the Fourth of July would become partly Harvey's, and if the mine proved prosperous within two years it would be deeded to the young couple.

This seemingly wonderful opportunity was undercut by the fact that Lizzie and Harvey Doe had arrived in the Rockies twenty years too late: the easily accessible placer gold of the 1858–1859 Pikes Peak boom years was long gone and the day of the lone prospector was past. Most of the successful mines were now owned by large corporations that could supply the capital needed to hire Cornish workers. The Does' mine would require a two-hundred-foot-long tunnel to reach the lower-grade ore typical of the end of a boom, and to make matters worse, gold was being challenged by a rival ore, silver, that was making people in upstart towns such as Leadville very rich.

While Harvey hired miners, Lizzie moved their possessions from a costly hotel room into a more modest Central City cottage. She was either worried, ambitious, or bored enough to don men's clothing and help supervise the workers. This gender anomaly was noted in the local *Town Talk* newspaper: "The young lady manages one half of the property while her liege lord manages the other. . . . This is the first instance where a lady, and such she is, has managed a mining property." The ore the Does had assayed, however, was poor-grade quality and the funds that Harvey's father had provided to hire workers were soon depleted. To Lizzie's dismay, Harvey

became a day laborer, a bottom-tier mucker, at a mine in the nearby town of
Black Hawk. The Does' next move to a single rented room above a store
there must have reminded Lizzie of the descent made by her own parents
as their fortunes waned. Baby Doe again was not accepted among the few
genteel women of Black Hawk, so she and Harvey became a threesome with
a prosperous drygoods merchant named Jake Sandelowsky. It is unclear
whether Baby Doe gradually pursued a warmer acquaintance with Jake
Sands, as the Polish Jew called himself, or he pursued her. The scrapbooks
that Lizzie began to accumulate during this period show that their friendship contained elements of at least a fantasy romance. She developed a
code in an attempt to obscure his name and near a photograph of Jake were
clippings from poems titled "The First Meeting" and "Possession.[11]

Harvey Doe went back to Wisconsin, just as Lizzie discovered she was
pregnant in late 1878. His motives are unclear. Did Harvey leave in
response to his mother's requests that he come home, or because of a quarrel in which the child's paternity was an issue? Or had Harvey already
deserted his wife for so long that the paternity of the baby was unquestion-
able—and therefore grounds for permanent desertion?

> *June 9–1921—I had strong Vision to-day I saw a beautiful little white fat Baby
> with beautiful round big eyes looking up into my eyes the Baby was close up to my
> face on my left breast up on my heart close to my face the Baby was all in rich
> white with a fluffy white baby cap on & white cloak & I saw the Vision for a long
> time & I said "O you lovely dear little Baby" I love you it kept looking up at me
> all the time for a long time before Vision passed*

Baby Doe gave birth to a stillborn son on July 13, 1879, to whom she dedicated a poignant—and mysterious—page in her scrapbook. The Doe marriage also was dead. Baby Doe was increasingly seen in the company of Jake
Sands in the Shoo Fly, a bar where at least the sporting girls were congenial
to Baby Doe. The Doe and McCourt in-laws joined for social and religious
reasons in a rare cooperative effort to avoid a divorce—or at least a scandalous one. When Baby Doe pursued Harvey into a parlor house, giving her
cause for divorce due to adultery, Harvey pleaded in a letter to his parents
for help, claiming he had entered the place simply to pursue a business-
man: "I went into that parlor house thinking I might get some money to
help us along in the world. . . . Even my own father has worked against me
and wherever he could hinder me from making money he has done so. I
hope and sincerely pray my dear parents you will not blame me and do try

and get Babe to come back to me and for she is all I have got in this world."[12] The Does may have helped, for perhaps as a result of a modest property settlement made by Harvey to Lizzie, the divorce decree granted to Mrs. Harvey Doe in Denver on March 19, 1880, shows the grounds were modified from the initial charge of adultery to the less inflammatory one of nonsupport. Harvey drifted around various Colorado mining camps for the next four years until his father's death in 1884. Upon receipt of his inheritance, the feckless Harvey Doe moved back to Oshkosh to be near his mother, held jobs such as night watchman and janitor, and eventually remarried.

TWO LEGENDS MEET

Oct 13–1921—Dream of Beautiful Tabor. . . . Tabor came in & up the steps to where Silver and I stood he was magnificent looking tall straight big & so happy & well he had on a high black new silk hat & rich new over-coat black Velvet coller collor & his hair black & moustach black & perfect his face white & so handsome. . . . Then he said to me "Cant I see you tonight" "O Yes O Yes". . . .

The exact moment when divorcée Baby Doe met Silver King Horace Tabor is unclear, but for several years prior to their encounter they inhabited the same elevated space as legends, she for her beauty and he for his wealth. Even before he became rich, H.A.W. (Horace Austin Warner) Tabor had long been considered a fortunate man because he had a hardworking albeit plain wife. For twenty years Augusta Pierce Tabor did everything a woman could in the harsh mining camps, from selling home-baked pies to miners to running a post office and boardinghouse, while Horace occasionally prospected, grubstaked other miners, and ran for local political office. Horace Tabor's luck actually began when he first courted young Augusta. His parents were poor Vermont farmers, and Horace worked as a stonecutter for a quarry owner until he married the boss's daughter, Augusta Pierce, on January 31, 1857. (Elizabeth McCourt at that time was not quite three years old.) A brief attempt at farming in Kansas Territory, subsidized by the Free Soil movement, tested Augusta's mettle as a frontier housekeeper and convinced Horace that the way to get rich was not from tilling the earth but from mining it. In the summer of 1859 the Tabors moved their possessions and infant son, Maxcy, from politically tumultuous Bleeding Kansas to the promising Colorado goldfields. Augusta's home was now a tent in a series of mining camps and Horace's back was briefly bent to the shovel. Soon they ran a supply store near Oro City and occasionally gave a penniless miner urgently needed goods in exchange for a share of his unproved claim, a practice called grubstaking.

There were many such down-and-out characters in that area because sluicing for gold was made difficult by the dark heavy ore that infiltrated it. This ore turned out to be silver-bearing—and there was plenty of it. The area underwent a second boom, the town was renamed Leadville in honor of its surrounding lead carbonate, and affable Horace Tabor was elected mayor. In early 1878 two miners whom Tabor had grubstaked for a one-third share in their claim discovered a fabulously rich lode of silver at their Little Pittsburg mine. Horace Tabor finally struck it rich, almost twenty years after coming to Colorado: his grubstake of $65 worth of groceries to the miners netted him $500,000 by autumn.[13]

Amid all the excitement Tabor perhaps took his helpmate Augusta for granted. Her value was obvious to observers: "the difference between Tabor's eventual success and the failure of most of his fellow gold-hunters was, in one word, Augusta; his mainstay was her strength of character and her determination to do her share. . . . She saved him for the luck that awaited him." Now that he was a wealthy man, Horace's occasional (and prophetic) bad mining investments were overshadowed by more uncanny luck. The underrated Matchless mine up on barren Fryer's Hill repaid Tabor's $157,000 investment of capital and labor with $11 million in profits. Tabor sold portions of his claims to absentee capitalists, and when the mines were incorporated to offer public stock, his shares gained six times their value. Horace quickly earned the title of Silver King, but Augusta refused to play the role of queen. Her New England Protestant upbringing that valued hard work over luck, her experience with the cruel vicissitudes of mining, and her intimate knowledge of Horace's lack of financial acumen made her unable to join in his ostentatious displays of newfound millions. Augusta, in the hard lean years of the marriage described as "vinegary, efficient, managerial," at age forty-five was already considered old and unattractive. "Horace discovered that the strait-laced, God-fearing hardworking woman—her face becoming more severe every year, especially after she started wearing pince-nez glasses which made her look like a retired missionary—was not quite what he needed to enhance the life of the luckiest man in the West." In contrast, wealth considerably enhanced the stature of forty-eight-year-old Horace. His contemporary, *Denver Tribune* columnist Eugene Field, described Tabor thus:

"Stoop-shouldered; ambling gait; awkward with hands; black hair, inclined to baldness; large head; rugged features; big black mustache which spreads at ends; dresses in black; magnificent cuff buttons of diamonds and onyx; no public speaker; generous and charitable; carried his hands in his pockets; worth 8 million dollars."[14]

It seemed inevitable that the prettiest woman in the mining West would eventually meet the richest man. Young Mrs. Harvey Doe first visited Leadville at the urging of Jake Sands in December 1879, during the period of her marital estrangement. Jake was so certain of Leadville's promise that he was considering opening another branch of his store there and suggested that she move, too. Leadville was now the second-largest city in Colorado, despite its remote location and daunting altitude at ten thousand feet. "It boasted 120 saloons, 59 boardinghouses, 3 daily newspapers, 2 weekly newspapers, 118 gambling houses and private card rooms, 36 houses of prostitution, and 147 lawyers."[15] Tabor's name was everywhere. He sponsored the boisterous Tabor Light Cavalry, a group of sixty highly costumed men who regularly drilled and marched—mostly to the bar in their armory. The lavish 880-seat Tabor Opera House had just opened, for Leadville aspired to be more than an uncouth former mining camp. The famed Oscar Wilde lectured there, on the topic of aesthetic theory, to a surprisingly polite audience and earned a tour of a Tabor mine; ex-president Ulysses S. Grant was rumored to be Tabor's guest in the near future. For prosperous mine owners and investors, Leadville was heaven, but to most of the mine workers it must have seemed closer to hell. The local *Chronicle* painted this portrait: "The theaters close at three in the morning. The dance houses and liquoring shops are never shut. . . . A party of carousers is reeling through the streets. . . . A sick man is groaning in the agonies of death. Carbonate Hill with her scores of brightly blazing fires is Argus-eyed."[16]

Baby Doe would have already heard of Horace Tabor, for his power and money permeated beyond Leadville to Denver, where in his new role as lieutenant governor he sometimes jovially presided over the state senate. It was rumored that, because of his financial stature in the Republican Party, Tabor was being groomed for the governorship, the U.S. senate, even the presidency. Tabor was dubbed the Croesus of the Rockies, famous for his wealth rather than his wisdom. But the more showy Horace became, the more his wife, Augusta, felt ill at ease.[17] She traveled alone back to Maine for an extended family visit, showing that her loyalties still lay with the East—and giving Horace more opportunity for unfettered carousing. As the Tabor marriage lost its ballast, Horace's eye began to wander toward the sporting girls in the saloons he patronized. His female companions allegedly included a lady juggling performer from Leadville and a parlor house woman he met in Chicago.

Soon Horace's eye landed irretrievably upon Baby Doe. It is unclear whether this fateful meeting occurred in late 1879, when she made her first visit to Leadville before her divorce was finalized, or in 1880 after she had moved there, probably in the company of Jake Sandelowsky, as a divorcée. Tabor would have been familiar with the Baby Doe story, for his right-hand man, William Bush, had been the manager at a Central City hotel when the Belle of Oshkosh first arrived. It is also unclear whether Horace Tabor, after resting his gaze on Baby Doe in a restaurant, was the one who asked for an introduction from Bush—or whether the former Mrs. Doe had long ago set her sights on millionaire Tabor and artfully put herself within reach of his well-known appetites. When fifty-year-old restless wealth met twenty-six-year-old ambitious beauty, passion overthrew convention. "They knew without words that a balance had been struck, a compact made. Whither it would lead them neither knew. But Baby Doe walked among the stars and the lieutenant governor yanked down the moon and lighted his cigar in its burning face."[18] In an epic battle, covered in detail by major newspapers throughout the nation for next two years, passion and convention collided, shattering several reputations.

THE "OTHER WOMAN" FROM LUSTY LEADVILLE

Tuesday Dec 8–1914 I dreamed that Tabor darling was driving me we were in a buggy & . . . we were driving toward the west Tabor & I when we came to a bridge we did not go over the bridge but along by the side of it & work was being done down on the bridge near the bottom of the creek & a lot of red dirt was there & Tabor drove the horse to see what it was & the horse's front feet were off the ground over the creek & in an instant we would have been killed but Tabor drove him back on the earth again & we were saved as if by a mirical & then we drove along west but I was angry at Tabor to think he would run such a chance of being killed but all was well & we drove alone, he & I—

Horace Tabor was indeed running a chance with Baby Doe and he had much to lose: he now owned two fine homes, one in Leadville, the other a mansion in more genteel Denver. This made marital deceit easier, because

Augusta for the most part resided in Denver, where Horace was cementing his reputation by building the Tabor block, which included the tallest building in the bold city destined to become the state capital. He lavished a buggy on Augusta that was identical to the one used by the U.S. president, but she continued to resist his ostentatiousness by making her bed in the servants' area of their mansion, out of her husband's reach. Baby Doe, on the other hand, usually occupied an elaborate hotel suite in Leadville. Thus, while Horace's wife resided in the increasingly civilized city, the "other woman" was ordinarily in "Lusty Leadville" where Tabor practically owned the town. Some discretion was necessary, however, for Leadville was also sometimes the residence of Tabor's son, Maxcy, who was only four years older than Baby Doe. For a precarious period of time, Horace kept his affair private by keeping the sites of his relationships far apart. His comrades and male journalists accepted the sexual peccadilloes of a man who could maintain both a wife and a mistress as symbols of his virile power. They shared rumors that Tabor had engaged in a drunken orgy up in Leadville while both Augusta and Baby Doe were safely—and separately—ensconced in Denver. Even proper ladies begrudgingly acknowledged men's sexual wanderings, for their female beneficent organizations of the era considered prostitutes to be women driven by destitution into their nasty business fueled by men's moral weakness.

Leadville was growing uncomfortable for Horace Tabor, however, because miners demanding better wages from the Silver King were testing his power. There were torchlight marches, a mysterious fire, and strikes by the workers at Tabor's Chrysolite mine in support of a $4 wage for an eight-hour day. He responded by organizing a Committee for Safety to augment his Light Cavalry. Just when the labor dispute deteriorated to threats of worker riots and retaliatory vigilante lynchings, Colorado Governor Pitkin declared martial law and put Tabor's militia under new, disinterested leadership. The subsequent negotiations retained the old wage of $2.75 for a ten-hour day. But Tabor's image as a lucky good-fellow Midas changed to that of hardened strikebreaker. While absentee shareholders and capitalists admired Tabor's use of force, his rash actions alienated him from the very laborers whose support he would need for political advancement and, among more urbane Denverites, called his judgment into question. Adding to their unease was the fact that Tabor increasingly housed his paramour in Denver's plush Windsor Hotel, where the veil Baby Doe donned to avoid the gazes of gossips only made her more mysterious. "Denver, now called

Silver King Horace A. W. Tabor. Cour-
tesy Colorado Historical Society, Tabor
Photo Collection. Tabor, Horace. All
Rights Reserved.

Augusta Pierce Tabor, Horace Tabor's
first wife. Courtesy Colorado Historical Society, Tabor Photo Collection.
Tabor, Augusta. All Rights Reserved.

'Queen of the Plains,' was developing a society all its own. The rules of eti-
quette were strict; the moral reformers were strong."[19]

The uneasy relationship between this Queen of the Plains and the generous, albeit philandering, Silver King continued throughout 1881, the
year in which he announced he would build the Tabor Grand Opera House
fit for a capital city. Horace dedicated $1 million to creating a five-story edi-
fice that would overshadow what he called the "chicken coop" opera houses
of London, Vienna, or Paris. He sent to Brussels for carpet, France for
tapestries, the Honduras for mahogany. He commissioned a hand-painted
stage curtain, puzzling for its somber depiction of Roman ruins and marble
columns overrun by a forest. At the bottom was quoted a pensive couplet by
British poet Charles Kingsley:

So fleet the works of men, back to the earth again,
Ancient and holy things fade like a dream.

Elizabeth Bonduel McCourt, known as "Baby Doe." Courtesy Colorado Historical Society, Tabor Photo Collection. Tabor, Baby Doe. 10025775.tif. All Rights Reserved.

Had Tabor, who had received a volume of verse from Kingsley himself during a Colorado visit, chosen these lines to acknowledge the ephemeral nature of his own silver kingdom? Or was Tabor declaring that he intended his opera house to overshadow even the once grand Roman empire? After all, it was rumored that Tabor ordered a portrait of William Shakespeare removed from his opera house, stating, "What the hell did he ever do for Denver?" and replaced it with one of himself.[20]

Many whispered that Baby Doe had a role in the grandiose building construction as Tabor's planning confidante. The gala opening night at Denver's Tabor Grand Opera House was on September 5, 1881, the performance an appropriately light opera. (Perhaps Tabor recalled that after a production of Shakespeare's *Othello* at his Leadville opera house, a man from the audience had gone home and slit the throat of his wife.) In honor of the event, the citizens of Denver presented Horace Tabor with a gold watch fob. Its links depicted a bucket of ore, the Leadville store, the Denver Tabor block, and finally the Tabor Grand Opera House that symbolized his ascent. Horace, in turn, presented his lavish opera house to the civic leaders of Denver who had been abuzz all evening over the colossal gas-lit chandelier and the enormous silver "Tabor" nameplate ornamenting Box A. They also whispered over the fact that the box was glaringly empty. Had Augusta Tabor refused to attend this celebration of excessive wealth—or had she not been invited? Some glanced toward an unescorted, lavishly dressed beautiful woman seated in the area below the empty box. The curtain rose on the now public drama of the Tabors' marital disruption.

It is unclear which of the lovers—or if both—decided that Baby Doe should advance from her role of mistress to become "the second Mrs. Tabor." Much of the lovers' correspondence that Lizzie so painstakingly preserved was likely destroyed by powerful Coloradans with a distaste for the explicit and with access to the Tabor papers before they became public.[21] By upping the ante in the game of love, experienced poker player Horace Tabor and his Baby Doe now gambled for huge stakes in their quest for open happiness and legitimacy. Perhaps Horace misjudged the strength of his hand: "Tabor was too bluff and forthright, and perhaps too assured of the efficacy of his wealth, to lead a double life."[22] A poem Lizzie pasted in her ongoing scrapbook alluded to a more ominous denouement:

> Stolen Love
> Oh sweetest is the stolen love,
> The apples shaken from the bough
> Unseen, unseen, though eyes are keen,
> And such a love was ours but now. . . .[23]

In 1882 Augusta Tabor in her role as the wronged wife went public and sued Horace for financial support. It is unclear whether this was the act of a desperate wife who had been cut off by her estranged husband or of a wife infuriated by Horace's offer (via emissary Billy Bush) of a financial settlement in exchange for a quiet divorce that would not endanger Tabor's political future. Augusta sued for $50,000 in annual maintenance and claimed that she had been compelled to take in boarders because her husband no longer supported her. Horace was able to have the embarrassing suit quashed, but the damage was done. "The fact that the husband had left the home could be tolerated, but the charge of non support went beyond the bounds of decency." In a rash attempt to end the scandal, Horace single-handedly obtained a divorce decree in La Plata County, where he held properties and clout, but did not have the unknowing Augusta served with papers. It is unclear whether this secret March 1882 "Durango divorce" was the idea of Baby Doe or an act of arrogance on the part of Horace Tabor. Tabor's male legislative colleagues felt compelled to warn him at the end of 1882 that "his repeated violations of the seventh commandment were against him in the senatorial struggle."[24] This judgment by his male peers was ominous, for Horace dearly wanted the six-year U.S. Senate term that would be awarded by these powerful men in early 1883. His hopes for the Colorado governorship had weakened as a result of his actions during the Leadville miners' strike, which cost him the support of working men. Women concerned with the moral uplifting of the West found Tabor despicable, and his political enemies used his association with Baby Doe to tar him with the epithet "Mormon." At this point in history, U.S. senators were elected solely by the male legislature, where Tabor still wielded power, but as the election neared, even his legislative cronies signaled that unmitigated immorality could not be tolerated.

The quiet divorce Horace Tabor had planned was not in the cards. Instead, he would be irreparably and publicly damaged by indignant Augusta, who on January 2, 1883, sued for divorce on the grounds of desertion and was awarded $250,000 in property. Augusta was compiling her own scrapbook, and she pasted in it a newspaper article that lauded her ladylike restraint. It alluded to Augusta's response to the invalid Durango divorce that Horace had tried to finesse: "If the truth were known, it would be enough to ruin him forever. She loves him and that settles it. She will not say a word." It is unclear whether Augusta's motive was her ongoing love for Horace, her disdainful dismissal of Horace's botched machinations, or her abhorrence of additional scandal that would hurt their son, Maxcy. But Augusta's final words during the Denver divorce proceedings delivered the death blow to Tabor's reputation. She asked the judge what her name would be after the divorce decree, and he assured her she could retain the name Tabor. She responded, "I will keep it until I die. It was good enough for me to take. It is good enough for me to keep." She then requested in tears, "Judge, I wish you would put in the record, 'Not willingly asked for.'"[25]

This plea won enormous sympathy for Augusta, rendered Horace politically impotent, and doomed Baby Doe to social exile. The Tabor divorce scandal and love triangle became national news and the topic of a *Washington Evening Star* editorial: "Denver is morally rotten. There is a low tone to Denver society. Most of the bonanza kings are shockingly open in their liaisons. . . . O, ye wicked men and women of Denver!"[26] In response, the "wicked men of Denver" serving in the Colorado legislature punished Tabor by denying him the full six-year U.S. Senate term. They instead repaid his civic largesse—the Tabor block, the Grand Opera House, the post office site—on poor terms by granting him a one-month U.S. Senate term that had been vacated when its holder joined the cabinet of President Chester A. Arthur. An indignant Tabor chastised the legislature: "You have seen fit to favor me with an election to the short term—the baby-term—which is for only thirty days. It is not always that one who goes in for the big prize is put off with one seventy-second part of it as I have been."[27] His old cronies must have thought it was a poor bargain Tabor had made, reaping the baby term, all for the love of Baby Doe.

THE SHOCKING SECOND MRS. TABOR

Horace Tabor's senatorial term was forgettable and ineffective because of its brevity, but the Washington wedding he planned with Lizzie was spectacular and covered by major national newspapers. It contained the classic nuptial elements in hyperbolic scale: the beautiful bride, the esteemed guests, the lavish reception, the ugly scene. The Washington elite received invitations inscribed in silver for the March 1, 1883, wedding that promised to be the social event of the year. Most of the Oshkosh McCourts attended, dressed in black mourning in recognition of the recent death of Lizzie's brother. But the bride was resplendent in a $7,500 white gown that columnists described in detail, from its rich brocade to its daring low neckline. The late evening ceremony in Washington's Willard Hotel, conducted by Catholic priest P. L. Chapelle, was followed by an elegant reception in a flower-draped room reminiscent of a fairy bower. The *Washington Post* gushed: "The wedding cake rested upon a table devoted to its sole support, and decorated with appropriate and beautiful blossoms. Above this was a canopy of flowers with trailing foliage."[28] The paper noted that guest President Chester A. Arthur asked the glowing bride if he might have a single rose from her bouquet and that she stood on tiptoe to place the flower in his buttonhole. Horace Tabor gave Lizzie a necklace worth $75,000, anchored by what came to be known as the Isabella diamond because it was said to have been pawned by the Spanish queen to fund the Columbian expedition to the New World. When the gala event broke up after midnight, fifty-two-year-old Tabor was seen trailing the ropes of greenery into the bedroom suite of his young bride.

Divine God Saviour our All Blessed me O how He Blessed me this night I saw &
watched the whole celing of my cabin on Matchless Mine growing green folage all
lacey & in long streamers of the most dainty long vines coming growing out of
cealing and hanging almost to the floor the folage was so beautiful I can not
describe the granure. . . . —November 16 or 17 1932

Shortly after the ceremony, however, someone informed Father Chapelle
that the "Miss McCourt" he had joined in marriage to Horace Tabor was in
actuality a divorcée—and a scandalous one at that. The irate priest first
threatened to annul the marriage; instead, he returned the marriage license
to the clerk's office unsigned and the wedding was never recorded in the official records of the diocese.[29] Regardless, Horace and Lizzie conceived of their
love as self-consecrating, judging by his letter to her as they planned their
Washington wedding: "It seems almost as if it is too much happiness for mor-
tals but it belongs to us. We give ourselves to one another and whose business
is it. We do not rob anybody of anything that belongs to them."[30] Then
reporters covering the highly public wedding dug up evidence of an earlier
secret marriage, which preceded Horace's official divorce from Augusta by
three months. In the fall of 1882 Horace and Baby Doe had arranged a quiet
civil marriage in St. Louis, Missouri, where Tabor was a chum of a justice of
the peace. It is unclear whether this ceremony was merely an impulsive sign
of enthusiastic love, an anticipation that no Catholic priest would marry two
divorced persons, or a hasty response to concerns that Lizzie might be pregnant.[31] Tabor was again labeled a bigamist and Mormon. The *New York Tribune*
remarked: "There is nothing in Daudet so picturesquely vulgar as this gorgeous hotel wedding of a pair who had been married for months already,
but were determined to have the eclat of being married over again in a senatorial capacity." Even the *Rocky Mountain News* chimed in: "Mormonism
and infidelity go hand in hand on the Republican ticket."[32]

Tabor had again rubbed the noses of his colleagues in his immoral private
affairs through the public spectacle of his wedding and the subsequent revelation of the duplicitous secret ceremony. The social and political costs were
dear. None of the Washington dignitaries' wives had attended the nuptials;
Colorado ex-senator Henry Teller's wife had torn the invitation in two before
returning it to the sender. Mr. Teller recounted in a letter: "I humiliated
myself to attend his wedding because he was a senator from Colorado (but
Mrs. Teller would not). . . . Tabor is an honest man in money affairs and I
believe he is truthful, but he has made a great fool of himself with reference

to that woman, and he ought now to retire and attend to his private affairs."[33] Despite having his "private affairs" front-page news, Tabor was anything but retiring. The ebullient groom escorted his new McCourt in-laws to a Washington play. Ironically, he selected a play about a man who also overreached himself—*Faust.*

While Horace may have wounded his political future, he retained clout as a millionaire, and Lizzie surely anticipated that her social status would rise as the new Mrs. H.A.W. Tabor. No longer was she the veiled woman, Baby Doe. Upon her return to Denver with her new husband in the spring of 1883, she was officially unveiled to society in an elaborate banquet Horace hosted for two hundred people. Horace had the best suite in the Windsor Hotel remodeled as their temporary residence while he searched for a Denver mansion suited for future entertaining. The Tabors then made their first public appearance at Horace's opera house: "Immediately every lorgnette in the house was focused on the special Tabor box, and there she was—the siren, the hussy, the creature who had done poor Augusta wrong."[34] For the entire evening the new Mrs. Tabor upstaged the unfortunate actor, Lawrence Barrett.

While the cream of Denver's social elite felt free to stare at the gorgeous Baby Doe, however, they did not intend to admit her into their circle. In gossiping about her, they still used the name Baby Doe to reinscribe her tawdry history. Despite the young Mrs. Tabor's claim in an interview that the papers covering her desk were invitations she had declined in order to avoid jealousies among the established families known as the "Denver Thirty-Six," she was a social outcast. "Men were willing to do business with Horace, but the women generally supported Augusta against the threat to morality and sanctity of marriage."[35] During this uneasy time, the second Mrs. Tabor did receive a calling card that she preserved in her scrapbook; it bore Augusta's name. It is unclear whether the first Mrs. Tabor called at the Windsor Hotel in order to finally meet her nemesis face-to-face or if Augusta paid a social visit to break the ice surrounding the second Mrs. Tabor. Perhaps Augusta needed upstart Baby Doe as a conduit, however distasteful, to Horace in her ongoing effort to obtain a box of her own at the Tabor Opera House. Sadly, Augusta's own social acceptance shrank when she became tainted as a divorcée—much like the ex–Mrs. Harvey Doe.

Even the wife of Tabor's own manager, William Bush, would not entertain Baby Doe. It is unclear whether it was this affront by Horace's longtime friend, or pressure from Baby Doe to insinuate her brother Peter McCourt into Bush's powerful position, or Tabor's discovery of financial malfeasance by Bush that instigated a well-publicized series of lawsuits. First, Tabor sued Bush for embezzlement, then Bush countersued for almost $100,000 in unpaid wages he claimed were due for "personal" services rendered Horace in pursuit of the divorce from Augusta. In the ensuing trial that was covered even by the *New York Times*, Bush's testimony detailed the secret strategies he undertook while attempting to obtain an expedient divorce for Horace, including his efforts at soliciting outrageous charges of adultery against Augusta. Bush's attorneys even brought Augusta into the courtroom to recount the irregular procedures, and her withering stare caused Horace to turn his chair toward the wall. Her testimony was not permitted and Bush's suit was unsuccessful, but the avenue of a sympathetic and scandal-hungry press remained open for Augusta. In a rare interview granted to the *Denver Republican*, she observed of Baby Doe: "She is a blonde, I understand, and paints [uses cosmetics to paint her face]. Mr. Tabor has changed a great deal. He used to detest women of that kind." Augusta proclaimed that Baby Doe was only after Tabor's money and would leave him if it ran out: "She don't want an old man."[36]

Even though Tabor eventually won a $20,000 settlement from Bush, it was Augusta who again triumphed in the court of public opinion. People no longer saw her as an aging woman unable to keep her man; she was instead an aged and esteemed woman discarded by a cad. Tabor-observer Eugene Field, now editor of the *Denver Tribune*, proclaimed: "Society in Denver gave its verdict on his course when it recognized the kindly old lady whom, in his gulch ignorance, he put aside. He is a social and political outcast in all senses of the word."[37] Although the ongoing scandals extinguished Horace's political future, his money was still welcomed by the Republican Party. He was made chairman of the Republican State Central Committee, and occasionally his name was briefly mentioned for state office, and even the presidency, only to disappear inevitably. Horace Tabor would never hold elective office again.

The Tabors, excluded from Denver's polite society, were still welcome in mining towns they visited. They also found solace in their extended—and extensive—family circle. Augusta, in her newspaper interview, had acerbically noted that over a dozen McCourt Irish kin were now living off Horace's largesse. In 1884 the Tabor estate, an Italianate mansion whose three-acre grounds housed over one hundred peacocks, was completed as their retreat. However, it was sadly evident that Denver's social leaders would not be making housewarming calls despite their curiosity about a mansion containing no less than five portraits of its mistress. Famous visiting dramatists who were more open-minded and urbane did enter the Tabor home, including Sarah Bernhardt, Edwin Booth, and Lillie Langtry. While Denverites would acknowledge Baby Doe when she appeared among them by staring at her series of carriages, each with its matching livery for her coachmen, they shunned her socially. Lizzie Tabor occasionally fought back at Denver, which proved to be determinedly chillier than Leadville. When a neighbor criticized the naked statues of Psyche, Nimrod, and Diana in the Tabors' yard, purchased from Paris, Lizzie ordered her dressmaker to drape them in chiffon and satin costumes in a mock display of modesty.

December Friday—22–1916 I was blessed by our Divine Saviour with a wonderful dream & two others Our darlings Tabor and Silver were with me in the garden of our old home on Sherman & the trees had big white fluffy feather-like flowers on them I said get us a few of the flowers Papa. . . .

The crown jewel of the Tabor family circle, baby daughter Lily (Elizabeth Bonduel Lily Tabor), was born on July 13, 1884. Horace had gold medallions struck off declaring "Baby Tabor" and sent them to Denver's finest one hundred families. Newspapers described baby Lily's christening wardrobe in great detail, from the $15,000 lace gown to her miniature jewels and diamond-studded diaper pins. But Lily's christening was held in Oshkosh, because of an ongoing feud between Horace Tabor and Denver's powerful bishop Joseph Machebeuf who, a longtime friend of Augusta's, had refused Horace rental of a pew at St. Mary's Cathedral. This rebuff of the Tabors and their baby heiress opened the door for a more tolerant Catholic priest, Jesuit John Guida, who would become Lizzie's trusted spiritual advisor. He entered her life through a note acknowledging receipt of the Baby Tabor medallion (something the Denver elite ignored) and offering a gift and a gentle admonishment. He wrote on the card attached to a religious silver medallion, "Here is a somewhat better badge of consecration for the baby. . . . It is also a silver medal, blessed by the Holy Father in Rome."[38]

Baby Lily accompanied the Tabors everywhere, including their opera house box, where her cries often competed with those of chagrined performers. A sketch of toddler Lily by famed illustrator Thomas Nast graced the cover of *Harper's Bazar.* Nast was enchanted during his visit to Denver by the remarkable child, who he found "always posing herself without assistance." The magazine sold out in Denver, for the beautiful daughter was as

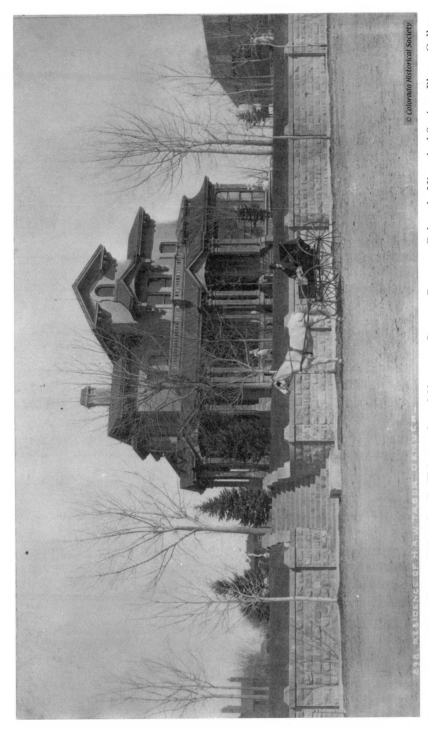

Denver home of the Horace Tabor family, Thirteenth and Sherman Streets. Courtesy Colorado Historical Society, Photo Collection. Denver Residences. 10026022.tif.

Montage of images of daughter Lily, including cover of *Harper's Bazar*, from Lizzie Tabor's Scrapbook. Courtesy Colorado Historical Society, Tabor Collection, FF 1438. 10026930.tif. All Rights Reserved.

much an object of attention as Baby Doe, who hoped her charming child would eventually legitimize Horace's second family. In late 1888 Lizzie bore another stillborn son, dashing their hopes of a male heir to the silver empire. Then on December 17, 1889, a second daughter was born and christened with the outrageous name Rose Mary Silver Dollar Echo Tabor. This name emerged when orator William Jennings Bryan observed, "Why Senator, that baby's laughter has the ring of a silver dollar!"[39] The mineral had transformed Horace Tabor into the Silver King, and this daring name for his daughter indicated his ongoing—some would say blind—confidence in the ore that had made him rich. By 1896 this allegiance to silver would make Horace Tabor a pauper.

Prior to 1873 silver and gold had shared equal status as monetary standards for U.S. currency; paper dollars could be redeemed in either valuable metal. Then silver was demonetized, leaving gold as the sole currency standard. However, powerful western silver proponents in Congress passed legislation requiring the U.S. Treasury to annually purchase huge amounts of the metal, which artificially supported its price. The debate between eastern gold-standard proponents and western rural silver champions made a return to the silver standard a political issue for the next two decades. This provided time for wise silver-mine investors to divest—but Horace Tabor held on. He proudly hosted prosilver presidential candidate Benjamin Harrison's visit to Leadville during the 1888 campaign and basked in the little man's speech honoring the mining town as "the highest evidence of American pluck to be found in the United States."[40] However, others found silver to be antiquated: "Obviously the silver magnates of Tabor's naive stripe, for all their economic significance during the eighties, were destined for a wipeout. They were 'lucky,' but Wall Street was 'smart.'" Even as the value of silver plummeted internationally with the election of Harrison's successor, Grover Cleveland, and the full force of the economic depression hit, Horace stayed true to silver. He proclaimed, "I always say to Mrs. Tabor, 'Hang onto the Matchless,'" a mine he repeatedly mortgaged but always reclaimed because of its seemingly endless veins of ore.[41] While many of the wealthy—including the astute Augusta Tabor—weathered the 1893 depression through diversified investments, Horace had been speculating unwisely for years, squandering $12 million on unprofitable prospects such as a mahogany "forest" enmeshed in a jungle, a mothballed yacht, and unseen Mexican gold mines. The legendary Tabor luck ran out: "One risky investment followed another, the odds steadily becoming longer and the plunging greater."[42] As early as 1883 a national newspaper had predicted Tabor's fall because of poor business deals, but his lavish lifestyle belied the claim. Horace had mortgaged his properties to the hilt, however, so that when the Tabor house of cards began to tumble down, the end was stunningly rapid.

The beloved Tabor Opera House was forfeited to the bank, then Horace was assaulted by twenty-one lawsuits for unpaid loans. The Tabors continued to live in their mansion even after the servants, carriages, electricity, and water were gone, pretending to the children that they were "camping" when their furniture was auctioned off. They then moved to a rented house, and Baby Doe kept detailed notes of precious personal items they pawned, including the bejeweled diaper pins. Baby Doe's appeals to her brother Peter McCourt, whom Tabor had bankrolled a decade before, were rebuffed, which led to their estrangement. Horace's son, Maxcy, minimally aided his father with some money he inherited from his mother's estate totaling $500,000 in 1895. All but one of Tabor's former cronies ignored his requests for "loans," which he saw as traitorous signs of their lack of faith in the silver with which he proposed to repay them. Baby Doe saw these rebuffs of the man who had once helped Denver grow into a genuine city as an extension of the snobbery she had long borne. "The granite features of the Old Guard reflected nothing but grim satisfaction at the final exclusion of the interlopers, at the almost Biblical comeuppance the Tabors had suffered for breaking at least one of the Commandments and flaunting their wealth with such vulgar exuberance."[43] In reality, many of those who might have helped Tabor were themselves strapped by the 1893 depression: twelve Denver banks were forced to close in one week. The once lucky Silver King, who had so recently been president of the Chamber of Commerce, was dethroned piecemeal: worth $9 million just a decade before, by 1896 he was ruined. Denver anticipated the flight of Baby Doe, his gold-digging consort.

I dreamed of being with my Tabor he ~~asked~~ told me to give him my blue & diamond ring (sapphires) to show the man we owed he came back & was sitting on great long white marble steps so many & all accrost a great white marble building like a public building he said the man has kept your ring he had the right if he was bad enough to I'll get you another. I said O how dare you say that to me no ring but that one I was terribly mad at Tabor. . . . —December 1, 1917

But Baby Doe stuck with her aging husband during the difficult 1890s. His letters back home to her from one of his trips to mine holdings in Mexico show his passionate affection for his wife and their daughters. He fondly referred to Lily as "Cupid" and Silver was nicknamed "Honeymaid." He wrote at the bottom of a letter in 1893: "Dear Babe, I do love you so dearly." Tabor exuded his typical optimism from Mexico: "This mine will give us money enough to enable us to disperse charity with a liberal hand as long as we may or can live and leave our children with lots of money."[44] While Horace was gone, he gave Lizzie power of attorney and she negotiated with creditors. When he returned from Mexico without funds, Horace resorted

Things put in Safe
at Jesuits
Dec 31 - 1899" House   19

Papa's Watch Fob given him when he
Built Opera House by citizens of Denver
Honeymaids Silver Beeds given by her Page
Lilys gold chain diamond + gold military
badge gold + diamond heart all on chain.
gold Another plain gold military badge
1 gold diaper pin
1 " + diamond diaper pin
1 paper of fine seed perls given by Pete
1 choice Yellow Topas given by uncle Andrew
to Lily
1 Silver dollar with Silvers picture
inside of it - for Silver given by
Boyd Skelton
2 choice pieces of blue turquois given
to mamma from Papa
3 Settings for Isabel diamond all gold
2 gold Sets of Studs with chains Each
Set has 3 diamonds in them
1 Diamond Christning ring Stone
cost 100.00 dollars done up in
Pink paper
Lilys gold Beeds given her by Mr Page
1 small moss aget
1 head of Christ Cameo
1 white head of a woman pink
flowers in her hair

Lizzie's list of "Things put in safe" following Horace Tabor's death in 1899. Written on the second page of the list is "add 1 heart Pin fooled them," probably referring to creditors. Courtesy Colorado Historical Society, Tabor Collection, FF 920. 10036655.tif. All Rights Reserved.

to pick-and-shovel manual labor in one last gold mine he owned near Boulder. But when that venture failed, sixty-five-year-old Horace returned to Leadville to work as a day laborer, removing slag from mines with a wheelbarrow. The man who had used force to keep miners' salaries at $2.75 a day during his reign as Silver King now tried to support his family on just such a wage. While Horace worked up in Leadville, several of Tabor's former associates approached Baby Doe in hopes she would desert the old man for their riches, but she rebuffed their advances.

When Tabor could no longer endure wheelbarrow work, he returned to Denver and in 1898 was nominated by U.S. senator Ed Wolcott for the job of city postmaster. The annual salary of $3,500 (an amount Horace had habitually bet on poker in a single night when he was a millionaire) allowed the Tabors to move to a small suite in their beloved Windsor Hotel and to keep food on the table. Baby Doe, who paid attention to portents, may have seen this return to the role of postmaster, which Horace had once held up in Oro City, as the start of renewed luck. Tabor did his job honorably; the man once notorious for spending days in a saloon now ate a sack lunch at his desk. But after fifteen months on the job he suddenly fell ill with appendicitis, which worsened into peritonitis and coma. During the deathbed vigil of several days, Horace's last words to Lizzie were, "Hang on to the Matchless. It will make millions again."[45] She called in a priest to baptize Horace into the Catholic Church, and on April 10, 1899, he died.

Those who turned away from millionaire Tabor in moral judgment and avoided impoverished Tabor with satisfied contempt now honored him ostentatiously in death. Flags flew at half-mast, his casket lay in the state capitol building for thousands to observe, his widow and children received flower and telegraph tributes. The Leadville paper observed: "What Tabor did must be long remembered and will be retold whenever the story of the upbuilding of Colorado is recounted."[46] At Sacred Heart, the modest Denver Catholic church that had accepted the Tabors, one of the four priests officiating at Horace's funeral observed, "But the whips and scourges of adversity came upon him, and those once his friends turned their backs on him. He did not despair but bared his arms and went to work once more. Here, young men and old, is a lesson in perseverance." Some may have scoffed at the idea of Horace Tabor personifying virtue, for they attributed his financial ruin to moral baseness and limited mental abilities. But others who remembered Tabor in a better light suggested that his lavish generosity bordering on naivete was the probable cause of his failed investments. Impressed by the Tabor couple's six years of hard work to support their family after bankruptcy, some even admitted, "About one investment he had been right: his second wife. She had not deserted him in his time of trouble, as everybody in Denver predicted. She was still his beautiful Baby Doe."[47]

THE SHUNNED WIDOW AND MOTHER

While Horace Tabor achieved heroic stature upon his death, Baby Doe, veiled this time in the traditional widow's black, was still shunned. In private she received offers of "help" from several men; in public she remained a lovely pariah who was again unattached and therefore potentially danger- ous. "Prettiest widow in Colorado, everyone (jealous women excepted) said." Baby Doe, who had spent the first half of her life as a beloved daugh- ter and girlish wife enjoying luxuries few would ever equal, now began the second half as a forty-four-year-old widow with two young daughters and a deathbed edict from Horace to hold onto the Matchless mine as her key to future wealth. "Those words would echo through the rest of his widow's long life, which was as bizarre in its obedience to Tabor's last words as the destiny which raised Tabor from a storekeeper to one of the richest men in America within a year."[48] Baby Doe Tabor and her daughters remained in Denver for two years while she unsuccessfully entreated businessmen to invest in getting the Matchless up to full operation again. In reality the Matchless had been unproductive for years, and its lower depths were flooded because its pumps had been stopped when the silver crisis occurred. Horace had leased it out several times in his effort to retain this last sentimental piece of speculative property, but no one could get the Matchless to pay.

Then in 1901 the Matchless was put up in a sheriff's sale and secured by Lizzie's remaining loyal Midwestern sister Claudia McCourt, although in subsequent decades its ownership would be repeatedly contested. Deter- mined to return the Matchless and the Tabor name to their former glory, Baby Doe decided to move her family up to Leadville where she could work the mine herself until she raised sufficient capital. She became so worried about claim jumpers that she eventually moved into a deserted miner's shack on the property. "All told, it was no larger than a medium- sized room. Two windows had been cut into the flimsy weatherboards, but these had been nailed up, for there was more than enough air that whined through the loose flooring and unplastered walls."[49] Up in harsh Leadville, the contrasting characters of the two Tabor daughters emerged: older Lily could recall her family's former luxuries and chafed at the rugged life whereas Silver considered working in the mine and riding a burro into town a great adventure. Some said that the quiet, dour Lily reminded them more of Augusta than of Baby Doe and that the gossip that shadowed the Tabors affected her. "She hated her mother for having passed on that legacy of shame and disrepute."[50] Lily corresponded with her McCourt relatives back in the Midwest, and in 1902 her Denver uncle Peter McCourt helped Lily move to her Aunt Claudia's in Wisconsin, leaving the poverty of Leadville behind. It is unclear whether Lily ever visited her mother again.

> I had the most horrible dream I was in a house of several rooms & Ma my mother, Pete & Claud had taken my children away from me & made the children not care for me any more & that set me wild. . . . I thought I would die of grief & anger & told Mother I would kill her & kill Pete & Claud for robbing me of my children Mother & them all looked at me calm & difiant it was a terrible dream then Silver came she sat on the floor & all her hair was the color of the goldfish & her eyes looked strange the whites of her eyes were yellow she looked terrible & talked with some man, my heart was broken. . . . —June 4, 1917

Deserted by her eldest daughter, Baby Doe increasingly sought solace in her Catholic faith and in her remaining child, the shining Silver Dollar. Mrs. Tabor spent many hours praying in Leadville's Church of the Annunciation and pored over a book, Butler's *The Lives of the Saints*, to find inspiration. She indulged Silver's passion for writing fantastical stories and gloried in her younger daughter's warm spirit, so reminiscent of Horace's, which drew people to her. During those winters in which it was financially possible, Lizzie and Silver rented rooms in Denver where Silver could explore her interests in spiritualism while her mother continued to seek investors for the Matchless. "There is a legend in Denver and Leadville that Baby Doe never went to Tabor's friends for a penny for herself, but she would go to extremes to obtain money in a crisis that might threaten the loss of the Matchless."[51] To keep the Matchless running, Baby Doe had reluctantly sold her beloved Isabella diamond necklace, but mother and daughter were determined to retain the gold watch fob Denverites had presented to Horace at the pinnacle of his glory and a diamond engagement ring surrounded by sapphires.

A glimmer of hope for the return to glory occurred when nineteen-year-old Silver wrote song lyrics commemorating President Theodore Roosevelt's 1908 Colorado bear-hunting trip, lyrics that were put to music and published at her mother's expense. The pinnacle of joy occurred in 1910 when Silver pushed her way through a crowd surrounding the ex-president and handed

Silver Dollar Tabor presents a copy of the song she wrote to ex-president Theodore Roosevelt, 1910. Courtesy Colorado Historical Society, Tabor Photo Collection. Tabor, Silver Dollar. 10026917.tif. All Rights Reserved.

him her song. In the next day's newspaper there was a photograph of Silver presenting Roosevelt with the music she had dedicated "to my beloved father H.A.W. Tabor." While her mother took pride in Silver's imagination and passion, to others it seemed that this flamboyant daughter so like Baby Doe demonstrated the Tabor exhibitionism that could only lead to tragedy. "Born for trouble, people said knowingly." In fact, Baby Doe was the last to know that her daughter was engaged in an affair with a Leadville stable owner. When Silver came home disheveled and drunk, her distraught mother planned a strategy to remove her daughter from harm's way. Having poured all of her funds into the Matchless, Lizzie compelled Silver to write to her uncle Peter McCourt for money, so that her second daughter could move away to Denver in 1911. Although Baby Doe tried several times to reunite with the prodigal Silver, and Silver's frequent pleading letters from afar would haunt her mother, "that day a quarter century of solitary life began."[52]

Freed from home, Silver sought fame in the world of arts and letters. She became a reporter for the *Denver Times* and dutifully sent home five dollars a week to Leadville. Because she was a woman journalist, during her brief career Silver was assigned to cover the very society ladies who had snubbed her mother. The chronology and locales of Silver's various pursuits are unclear, but the trajectory was relentlessly downward. Silver tried publishing a short-lived newspaper named the *Silver Dollar Weekly*, then wrote and illustrated a novel called *Star of Blood*, which her mother got printed by a Denver publisher who perhaps hoped the Tabor name would sell books. *Star of Blood* was a sensationalist story of an ill-fated heroine named Artie Dallas who ended up in a pauper's grave after a seamy death "in a notorious resort in the underworld. . . . never again would she be found drunk in the Market street gutters; never again would Artie suffer."[53] Silver was gaining experience in just such a world: she had been arrested for stealing an actress's ring at a drunken party, and although she was cleared of the charges, the accusations printed in the newspapers made Denver an uncomfortable locale for yet another errant Tabor. The increasingly religious Baby Doe was furious over Silver's misadventures with men and during her rare trips down into Denver was horrified to witness Silver's nightlife. Silver rebelled against this scrutiny, even threatening suicide in 1914: "My head is covered with self-inflicted bruises and my heart is weak and my lungs congested, for I am a frail girl, a nervous wreck from the life I live."[54] Baby Doe also suffered horrors that pierced a mother's heart.

> . . . I had a Vision O so plain and strong I was walking on the street and my Silver came quickly to me with her dear arms & hands lovingly stretched out to me so close to me she smiled and she was dressed all in black her hat was black and small and sat down over her right eye but O my God she looked like a corpse that had been buried she looked like a living corpse a deathly grey like a dead corpse smiling her dear eyes were sunken & O my poor heart ached in agony and she was all like a battery of electricity, no light, only like electricity & I was so frightened she came so suddenly to me in that way and then she Vanished as all visions do and to day I have suffered agony for her my poor darling pet my Honeymaid [on back:] Vision of my darling child Silver October 29–1914 Dear God cast the devil into everlasting hell, and come to us now and bring this sin and this world to an End O God in Thy dear Mercy Come quickly

It is unclear whether Silver moved away from Colorado to escape her mother, Denver gossipers, or both. She chose Chicago, where she again attempted to break into publishing and found that even far away from Colorado, as a legendary Tabor, she was herself the subject of an interview, in which she observed: "Money is the god of Chicago. Manhood and womanhood and character are all that count in the mountains." Although Silver described herself in the interview as a free spirit akin to nature, she eventually became a kept woman in Chicago's underworld after having tried to make a living by acting, dancing in films, and then performing in burlesque shows. She wrote letters back to her mother in Leadville begging for money and informing her that envelopes should be addressed to "Mrs." Murphy, then "Mrs." Taylor, then "Mrs." Ruth Norman as she formed successive short-term relationships. During these tarnished years Silver may have briefly reconciled with her mother, joining her to visit Lily in Milwaukee, but it is unclear. Devout mother and drifting daughter discussed the idea of redemption through convent life, even though it would mean silence between them if Silver took vows. But on September 18, 1925, at the age of thirty-five, Silver Dollar Tabor died from being scalded under suspicious circumstances. It took the Chicago, New York, and Denver papers a few days to discover the true identity of the "Ruth Norman," which the coroner ascertained from a McCourt aunt who came to identify the body. Then the headlines were unrelenting: "Tabor's Daughter Dies Mysteriously. Found Unconscious in Chicago after Cries for Help." "Drink and Dope Blamed for Death of Once Wealthy Daughter of Senator."[55]

The diminutive Baby Doe Tabor was allowed to enter the Denver Public Library after closing hours in order to read these newspapers, sensing that while she read, the librarians observed her and awaited a reaction. It was unclear if she had received a telegram regarding Silver's death or, learning of the sordid story from some kindly Denver person, desperately sought the newspapers for more information. When she was done reading Mrs. Tabor rose and announced that the dead woman was not her daughter. She declared that Silver was alive and secluded in a convent. The motive is unclear for Baby Doe's allegiance to this image of her daughter as a living saint and her public denial that her daughter was the deceased sinner. Some said Baby Doe concocted the convent story in order to deflect further shame from the Tabor name: "She simply could not acknowledge to herself—or if, secretly, to herself, not the rest of the world—that her beloved younger daughter's life had ended in such tragic squalor."[56] Others claimed Mrs. Tabor lived in a fantasy world where her wish for Silver's safety in a convent became her reality. "It was just as plausible to the mother that Silver had taken the veil as it was that she was worth millions of dollars because she lived in a shack beside the Matchless." In contrast, daughter Lily and her uncle Peter McCourt publicly claimed that the dead girl was Silver, the

Tabor reprobate. The *Chicago Tribune* interviewed Lily Tabor, now Mrs. John Last of Milwaukee, who acknowledged Silver's death—while at the same time distancing herself from the Tabor stigma. Lily said, "I didn't want to be reminded of my sister, nor of my mother. I wanted a quiet, decent, sheltered life. They didn't. We were just different."[57] Again Peter McCourt came to the rescue, providing funds for Silver's modest burial in Chicago, although no family member attended her funeral. His act seemed to some a sign of family loyalty, but Baby Doe saw his identification and burial of this girl he claimed was Silver as the ultimate betrayal.

THE MADWOMAN IN THE CABIN

Permanently estranged from her brother Peter, publicly chastised by her only living child, widow of a penniless man, mother of a daughter buried in a pauper's grave, Baby Doe Tabor had ample reason to retire to her cabin at the Matchless mine in Leadville. The former boomtown was becoming a ghost town with a mere four thousand souls, many of whom retreated during the harsh winters, and the widow Tabor fit in as another ghost of past glory days. In Leadville, "The people paid no more attention to Baby Doe than if she did not exist."[58] Several storekeepers allowed her to charge her modest bills to "the Matchless mine account," knowing they would never be repaid. Baby Doe, however, loathed charity and often warded off strangers by waving a shotgun from her cabin door. She tried to avoid scrutiny by venturing into town during the night to retrieve whatever few letters might be at the post office. Her half-masculine, half-feminine dress became legendary. When she appeared in Denver, she was a sad specter of Baby Doe to old-timers, a spectacle to the young: "People turned to stare at her when she clattered down the street in her men's work boots, even those who didn't know she was the once-famous Baby Doe. Invariably she wore a long black skirt turning green with age, a man's khaki shirt and coarse black cotton stockings. Over this she wore an ancient black cape, with a well-worn woman's motoring cap on her graying blond hair. The cap was equipped with a veil which she drew over her face when she sensed that people were staring at her. In place of the supposed jewels of Queen Isabella and the $90,000 diamond necklace, she now wore an ebony cross strung around her neck on a piece of twine." The woman whose low-cut gowns were once considered so risqué in pioneer Denver was now an embarrassment to the modern city in her widow's rags. She dressed like a madwoman—married to the past, the

Elderly Mrs. Tabor in downtown Denver. She wears miners' boots, a crucifix hangs near her scarf, and she carries a bundle on her left side. Courtesy Denver Public Library Western History Collection, Z-232.

church, and the Matchless mine. Yet those in whom she confided said she was happy, having made her peace with God. Others claimed that, when she stayed in hotels, she conversed in a most unpeaceful manner with a spirit world late into the night, keeping lodgers awake. Baby Doe "would haunt the financial district, a 'bedraggled fey figure' as one local historian described her, a curiously dogged survivor of a time up-and-coming men would prefer to forget, but a very lively and sharp-tongued ghost." Her grand, torturing obsession was the Matchless mine: working it, keeping it safe, dreaming of its hidden riches: "the Matchless was a holy cause, a dedication to the memory of Horace Tabor."[59] Other monuments to Horace had been razed, the Tabor Opera House in Denver was now a movie theater, but the Matchless survived under the solitary attention of caretaker Baby Doe. She had otherworldly visions about it and guarded it through the winters, even though it meant she sometimes crawled through the snow and lined her clothes with newspapers to keep alive.

*Holy Thursday—April 19, 1925—I dreamed of being with Tabor, Lily, Silver
and seeing rich ore in No. 6 shaft*

In 1932, as she neared eighty, Baby Doe's solitude was interrupted by
"that book and that show," which retold the Tabor saga in particularly sordid detail. Advisors suggested that Baby Doe sue the filmmakers for slander
in order to reap a virtual gold mine, but pride forbade her from going to
court and resurrecting hurts of the past. Although Mrs. Tabor refused any
association with the film *Silver Dollar* and never viewed it, the movie revived
interest in the lone survivor of the silver era, and Coloradans made pilgrimages up to the Matchless to meet Baby Doe, where she reportedly
greeted them cordially. By 1934 Baby Doe had returned to obscure poverty,
but her pride remained: she would return parcels of food left on her
doorstep and only asked for rides back to her cabin in severe snowstorms.
She still had one old Leadville friend, newspaper editor Henry Butler, who
could also remember the past grand days. He wrote: "I wonder how it can
be possible for one who once had so much to now have so little and want to
live. Then I realize that she lives not in the same world as I, but in a world
of her own creation—a world carried over from the past, peopled with the
memories of those who have passed on."[60]

She also made one new friend, a young woman named Sue Bonnie, who
listened avidly as Baby Doe Tabor retold her story. Bonnie joined Mrs.
Tabor in using a ouija board to contact the spirit world from the Matchless
cabin, where the wall calendars were covered with her scribbled notations
of otherworldly visitations. It was neighbor Sue Bonnie who noticed that no
smoke was coming from the Tabor cabin after a three-day blizzard in 1935.
She worried about Baby Doe, as did those in Leadville who had seen "her
small, bent figure trudging over the snow-covered road from Fryer's Hill
wearing an old overshoe on one foot and the other wrapped in burlap."[61]
When the storm broke, on March 7, Bonnie and a male helper dug their
way to Mrs. Tabor's cabin and found her lying on the floor, frozen to death
although there was firewood left. Her face was serene.

News of the death of Baby Doe Tabor sped around the world, and full
pictorial versions of the family's rise and tragic fall disseminated the legend
to yet another generation. After nearly thirty-six years of "penance," Baby
Doe was treated sympathetically in most accounts as a faithful widow who
outlived her critics and proved them wrong. Daughter Lily Tabor Last, con-
tacted in Milwaukee about her mother's death, denied that she was the

daughter of Horace and Baby Doe Tabor. Lily insisted she was the daughter of Horace's elder brother, the more respectable John. Thus Baby Doe, who ten years earlier had denied her wayward daughter Silver in death, was now denied by her lone surviving child. Two of Lizzie Tabor's brothers arranged for a modest burial. Several years later, Denver citizens paid to have Horace Tabor disinterred and buried by her side in Denver's Mount Olivet cemetery under a large marker that enclosed both graves. The lavish tombstone said of Horace, "Chance suddenly brought him considerable wealth and reputation. A few years later another throw of the dice as quickly returned him to his former obscurity." Outliving Horace for over three decades and preserving his name from obscurity was the beloved wife he called his Babe, his Lizzie. Inscribed on the headstone for all eternity, however, was the name of the legend: Elizabeth Baby Doe.

CHAPTER 2

Obsessed with Baby Doe

The Legend Expands

I dreamed I was standing down in a deep long (oblong) square Grave in a white night dress, in a large beautiful grave yard, trees & and the loveliest green sod the grass was so fresh & such a bright beautiful green. . . . I stood in the grave looking around for a long time and feeling with my fingers the short grass & admiring it and pulling my fingers thru it. The Sun was shining brightly & all was quiet & calm & I was happy. I stood in grave & I was holding my clothes under my left arm. I said I must take off my night dress & put on my clothes before any comes. . . . —May 31, 1921

Baby Doe Tabor was even more sensational in death than she had been in life. "'Baby Doe' Tabor Found Dead / Aged Recluse Freezes in Old Shack at Mine," declared a banner headline in the *Denver Post* on March 8, 1935. The news story spread throughout the country, even though people routinely died in high-altitude mining regions during the winter, and once their fires went out, the bodies froze. Such a fate had happened to Mrs. Tabor's night watchman only a few years earlier. But this frozen body was that of Baby Doe and it was big news. The grisly manner of her death, followed by postmortem discoveries of her rich personal treasures, gave new energy to the Tabor legend. Photos of the once beautiful Baby Doe were published next to ones of the shabbily dressed elderly Mrs. Tabor glaring at a cameraman during one of her rare trips to Denver. Now that the feisty Mrs. Tabor was deceased, commodification of Baby Doe ran rampant, expanding to serve the needs and anxieties of Americans, and changing as their appetites changed. As Richard Slotkin observes: "the process of mythogenesis in a culture is one of continuous activity rather than dramatic stops and starts."[1] Immediately following Baby Doe's death, the film *Silver*

Dollar that so wounded her in 1932 came out of Hollywood storage to be consumed by eager Denver audiences yet again. But the tone of national and international news coverage of Baby Doe's death indicated a sea change: the woman formerly labeled a marriage-wrecking wanton was now reconstructed, "re-membered," as a determined pioneer widow who held fast for over three decades to the Matchless mine. One headline proclaimed, "Aged Woman Faithful to the Last to Dying Command of Husband to 'Hold onto Mine' Lived as Hermit for Years."[2]

REVISIONS OF BABY DOE

Several factors contributed to this upgraded revision of Baby Doe. First, by the very act of surviving until age eighty she outlived the outraged supporters of the much older Augusta Tabor. Those critics were now depicted as old-fashioned Victorians in their attitudes toward the timelessly alluring Baby Doe: "She had done nothing but be too enchantingly beautiful in an age when woman's place was fixed by tradition."[3] Second, Baby Doe had performed public penance for decades, symbolized by the large omnipresent crucifix around her neck. A reporter recalled once following her into a church and watching as she prayed, "apparently making her peace with her God . . . asking forgiveness for violating the rules of a church which rebels against divorce."[4] Such evidence of a former sinner's "conversion" rebalanced the moral scales. Third, in 1935 the nation was in the midst of the Great Depression, and for financially strapped Americans the Tabors embodied the grand past era of mining kings. Photographs of the Tabors' mansion and jewels allowed many to enjoy this wealth vicariously, while tales of their subsequent plunge into poverty found empathetic audiences during the depression. Finally, the sheer magnitude of Baby Doe's decades-long "lonely vigil" at the Matchless mine assuaged even the harshest critics and led to a tipping point in the legend, in which Baby Doe was now converted from whore to heroine. The *Denver Post,* so critical when Horace Tabor cast aside hard-working Augusta in the1880s, now praised his steady Baby Doe: "Society, which had been quick to condemn her as a frivolous coquette when she divorced her first husband and married Tabor, had learned in thirty-six years to wonder at and then admire the quality of the courage that held her to the old mine and its stark poverty."[5]

Graphic descriptions of her wintery death accompanied the headline "Blasts Open Icy Grave for Baby Doe / Iron-Hard Soil Will Receive Silver

Queen / Naked Hills Where Beauty of Long Ago Wore Out Life Now Tomb."
This chilling news initiated a skirmish for Mrs. Tabor's bodily remains. A New
York man telegraphed the *Denver Post*: "The people will want to make good
the promise to Baby Doe that Tabor made but could not keep. They will want
suitably to award her for her unfailing loyalty to an ideal. Permit me to join in
the public contribution to a fund to provide a silver casket for her remains
and internment."[6] The Leadville grave digger had almost completed dyna-
miting a hole in the frozen earth for Baby Doe's body when prominent Denver citizens offered to help pay for a funeral and burial in their city.
Predictably, the metropolis that socially had never accepted Baby Doe while
alive won custody of her body from the faded mining town that had harbored
her for thirty years. Up in Leadville, Mrs. Tabor's favorite priest from the
Church of the Annunciation performed mass, and dozens of old residents
filed by the casket for one last view of the eccentric widow. Then the casket
was put on a train to Denver, where only four young people met it at the sta-
tion, a sign that sophisticated city people were more intrigued by the legend
of Baby Doe than by her earthly remains.

In fact, the actual burial of Baby Doe Tabor was delayed for over two
weeks after her death because authorities waited for word from her only
surviving daughter, Lily (Mrs. John) Last of Milwaukee. Lily Last's denial
that Baby Doe was her deceased mother increased public sympathy. It was
Lizzie's brothers Philip and Willard McCourt who arranged for her tiny
funeral. When asked about Baby Doe's similar denial-in-death of her
daughter Silver Dollar a decade earlier, Philip McCourt both defended his
sister's sanity and shared his insight about her as a mother: "Do they laugh
at her because she insisted Silver Dollar was not dead? Only two years ago I
spoke to her about it. She said, 'Phil, I do not know she is dead. They tell
me she died in a fire in Chicago. But they were not sure at first. I did not see
the body they said was my little girl. How can I be sure she is dead? And if I
am not sure of that, I must believe she is alive.' Did that sound like the
speech of an insane woman?"[7]

While the battle over Baby Doe's body ended quickly, the war over her
reputation and her sanity continued. Leadville residents got a taste of the
intense uninvited curiosity that had dogged Baby Doe Tabor all her life.
Reporters roamed Leadville's streets trying to find citizens who would talk
about her, but they faced a protective wall of small-town privacy. One old-
time resident, Mr. Zaitz, who finally agreed to talk "only under the pressure of questions" disputed the charges that Mrs. Tabor was eccentric or

insane, saying, "I have seen her draw up legal contacts within the last few years that could not have been improved upon by a lawyer. She wasn't crazy but only about one thing—the Matchless mine. You couldn't talk to her and believe that she was crazy."[8] But the idea of a madwoman freezing to death for long-ago sins was a more appealing denouement for the growing legend. As Elizabeth Janeway observes: "myth has its own, furious, inherent reason-to-be because it is tied to desire. Prove it false a hundred times, and it will still endure because it is true as an expression of feeling."[9]

I saw Visions of 2 men in black slough [slouch?] hats awful in the dark peaking and sneeking around No 6 Engine house & after I went to bed at night saw another on trussel—August 12, 1925

Now that Baby Doe was deceased, photographers entered the Matchless mine cabin that she had defended from interlopers with her shotgun while awake and with her faith while dreaming. Newspaper pictures showed the interior of the cabin overrun with religious objects and boxes of jumbled papers. A headline above a photo of her chair near a picture of the beloved Virgin Mary shamelessly proclaimed, "This Was Throne of Silver Queen After the Tides of Fortune Turned."[10] Reporters also got their first glimpse of Lizzie's Dreamworld by reading the scraps of papers, the notations about spirits on her calendar, and the loose diary notes scattered about the cabin. Accounts of her tea-leaf readings and spirit visions, which one journalist called her "weird diary," confirmed for readers that Baby Doe was a delusional madwoman. Diary entries from her last days, published in the newspaper, portrayed the heart-breaking determination of old Mrs. Tabor:

Went down to Leadville from Matchless mine. Snow so terrible I had to go down on my hands and knees and creep from my cabin door to Seventh st. Mr. Zaitz [a Leadville grocery man] drove me back to our get-off place and he helped pull me to cabin, I falling deep down through snow every minute. God bless him.[11]

DISMEMBERING BABY DOE

Briefly after Baby Doe's death, over two thousand Tabor family papers and countless personal items were discovered in seventeen trunks held at a Denver warehouse, where she had paid for storage at great personal sacrifice. Several bundled sacks of "Dreams and Visions," plus trunks full of mementoes, emerged a few months later from the Leadville Catholic hospital

This Was Throne of Silver Queen
After the Tides of Fortune Turned

The distressing circumstances in which Baby Doe Tabor chose to live in carrying out the injunction of her husband to "Hold on to the Matchless" are vividly shown in this picture of the interior of her shack. Here is her chair, and her improvised shrine.

Interior of Matchless mine cabin shortly after Baby Doe's 1935 death, as shown in the *Denver Post*. Courtesy Colorado Historical Society, Tabor Collection, FF 1438, Ellis scrapbook page 116. All Rights Reserved.

whose nuns had befriended Mrs. Tabor. The Denver trunks were opened and hurriedly inventoried by the estate administrator assigned to this case, the secretary of the Colorado Historical Society (CHS), Edgar C. McMechen. Three weeks after Baby Doe's solitary death, newspaper readers were vicariously peering into her trunks. Included was a tasteful picture of Lizzie's fragile water-damaged scrapbooks "which historians believe to be the richest discovery ever made of historical documents, clippings and pictures pertaining to the west."[12]

> *I dreamed I gave my bundle to Ma to take care of for me while I went with a lot of folk somewhere when I returned Ma said she did not know where it was. . . . we found it in the feather bed sewed up in there where Ma had put it to hide it from me. Thank God it is only a dream I had that terrible feeling came on me in the dream—Good Friday, April 2, 1915*

The *Denver Post* gave most coverage, however, to discoveries from the trunks of personal items everyone assumed had long ago been lost in the Tabor bankruptcy. Lizzie had hidden away from creditors the gorgeous Washington, D.C., wedding dress, the expensive baby christening clothes, and items of silver. The beloved golden watch fob presented at the 1881 Tabor Opera House opening nestled within a bundle of rags that were braided into a tightly bound ball. McMechen said: "In the center was the fob, symbolic of the manner in which Baby Doe, after Tabor's death, had withdrawn from the world and hidden her grief within a protective shell of silence and reserve."[13] After learning that eastern collectors were interested in Baby Doe's possessions, one reporter suggested: "The very fact of her death increases the collectors' evaluation of her mementos. Perhaps in that squalid cabin near Leadville, where she was found dead a few weeks ago, there may be other items that will interest collectors." The item that generated greatest speculation was the shabby bag that Baby Doe was seen constantly lugging when she came into town. Reporters wondered if it held ore so valuable that she needed to guard it.[14]

Perhaps there were piles of silver lying beneath the madwoman's cabin floor, and that was why she guarded it with a gun. Thus began the piecemeal "dismembering" of Baby Doe by a public eager to own a relic of this legendary symbol of the mining-frontier West. A newspaper article of March 14, less than a week after Mrs. Tabor's body had been found, reported that numerous papers remained in the cabin. By March 27, insurance agents wrote to CHS board of directors president Ernest Morris in frustration over

their inability to keep vandals from the Matchless property. They noted, "The
room is in a very littered condition. . . . The old letters and papers which are
strewn around the floor might contain information of interest to someone,
but it would be quite a task to pick everything up. Personally we see nothing
of value in the room, altho [sic] someone might make a more careful investigation and find something of interest."[15] Evidently Morris did not follow up
on this report, because soon the *Denver Post* reported that nothing remained
of the contents of the cabin. Despite McMechen's charge to protect the
Matchless, by August 1935 the cabin itself had been entirely dismantled by
treasure hunters. McMechen, writing twenty years later about the deface-
ment of Baby Doe's home, was still furious: "Disregarding the administrator's
written warning, pasted upon the door, intruders broke into the cabin, tore
from walls and ceiling the cheap paper covering, ripped the shabby mat-
tress to shreds, tore boards from the floor and probed the earth beneath for
treasure or jewels that they thought might have been hidden there. In
death, as in life, her privacy was invaded and violated to satisfy morbid
curiosity and greed."[16]

A more orderly dismembering of Baby Doe was supervised by estate
administrator McMechen himself, via an auction aimed at satisfying creditors' claims against the deceased Mrs. Tabor. One of the claimants was one of
the brothers who had buried Lizzie, Willard McCourt, on whose behalf a
friend wrote to Leadville judge John Evans a month after the death, "Mr.
McCourt would like very much to be considered and to be allowed to dispose
of her effects," with potential recipients including an Oshkosh museum, the
Denver Public Library, and the Denver Museum. The letter continued: "He
objects vigorously to the publication of the letters, pictures, and effects of
Mrs. Tabor's in the newspapers and wants to have it stopped."[17] Nonetheless, on June 21, 1935, the *Denver Post* proclaimed, "Old Wedding Gown Will
Go under Hammer," reinscribing the image of Baby Doe as a "public
woman" rather than a sister mourned by her surviving brothers. The paper
printed photos of models wearing Baby Doe's clothes and holding her jewelry. Photographs found in the trunks showed the remarkable interiors of
the Tabor mansion—a mansion nice Denver citizens of the 1880s would not
deign to enter but which their grandchildren now vicariously visited. The
auction of Baby Doe's keepsakes reaped a disappointing $700. The sale was
also a considerable loss to history because fragments of Lizzie Tabor's writings were sold. Particularly poignant was the discovery, within one of Silver's
socks, of a diary entry from the troubled year 1915. The *Denver Rocky Mountain News* reported, "A tall, dark man who refused to give his name bought

the stocking and the piece of paper."[18] The same man purchased a diary page written in 1895 by Silver when she and her mother considered themselves spiritual soul mates. The price of these documents was one dollar.

> *after I went to bed Vision of the tallest man and woman . . . man was I think 7 or more feet tall in light brown shirt & pants he was strong very powerful—not fat—they were devil spirits—they came at my left side to harm me—I feared them & clung to my crucifix—many priests have blessed it after a few minutes the devils left—April 7, 1932*

Several foresighted Denver citizens quickly organized a Tabor Association to purchase many items that they then presented to the Colorado History Museum for future display. Luckily, most of the Tabor papers were not put on the public auction block. Before they were sealed, these newly discovered papers stimulated a twenty-part series in the *Rocky Mountain News* with its revised assessment of the second Mrs. Tabor: "Baby Doe Leaves Heritage of Fortitude, Will Live as Heroic Example." While an early part of the series vividly described the once scandalous Tabor love triangle, it managed to praise all three parties: Augusta for her hearty pioneer work ethic, Baby Doe for her "haughty beauty," and Horace for a "hardihood which caused not one woman, but two to struggle thru [*sic*] the bitterness of poverty." The once ostracized Tabors were even reconstituted as a model family: "But let us start at the beginning—if we who live today can capture the inspiration of the beginning of the great love of Horace Tabor and the beautiful Baby Doe and the great love they bore their children." The series claimed, "Tabor and Baby Doe did not break up each other's homes."[19]

The newspapers heavily illustrated their coverage of the Tabors with two photo arrangements that remain the visual bedrock of the legend today. One was a triptych of Horace looking darkly masculine, Baby Doe looking flirtatious with her head slightly tilted, and Augusta peering over her unflattering pince-nez glasses with the piercing stare of the older wife. The second depicted the Baby Doe penance saga in a nutshell: a soft cameo portrait of the smiling youthful beauty contrasted with a photo of the elderly Mrs. Tabor in rags. This juxtaposition of the Beauty and the Mad Crone cemented the moral of the newspaper series: "Once-Glamorous Beauty Soon Became Just Weary Wrinkled Woman Dressed in Shabby Garments Long Outmoded."[20] The intent of these photo arrangements may have been to laud the irresistible beauty of youthful Baby Doe (especially in contrast to the middle-aged Augusta) and then to show the cost of guarding the Matchless mine inscribed on her ravaged body. But both montages also

Postcard showing cameo of young Baby Doe juxtaposed with photo of the madwoman in front of her cabin. Courtesy Colorado Historical Society, Tabor Photo Collection. Tabor, Baby Doe. All Rights Reserved.

sent—and perpetuate—a message germane to women's anxieties in a culture that still counts beauty as the primary (and ephemeral) source of their power: when you lose your looks you may lose your husband to a younger woman, or if you are the younger woman, you still will inevitably lose to Cruel Time. One could argue that the Tabors themselves initiated the photographic fetishization of beauty in their family, for in 1887 they were delighted by the Thomas Nast illustration of "Baby Tabor" that first appeared on the cover of *Harper's Bazar* and was later reprinted throughout Europe. Lily Tabor was characterized as the most photographed child of her era, as the numerous poses Lizzie pasted into her scrapbooks confirms. Lizzie also preserved in her scrapbook a homage to her own beauty among manly men: a Colorado Cigar company advertisement from the 1880s for "Baby Doe Havanas," illustrated with love birds and Cupid.

Oct. 24–1915 dreamed of seeing Silver in a red dress with another girl in red I think also walking in loby of Hotel & two business old men following them for bad

While readers in 1935 found it acceptably titillating to see the Tabor name in large headlines day after day in the newspaper series, it was unthinkable for the names of still living Denver men to be printed in association with Baby Doe or her licentious daughter, Silver. Mrs. Tabor had named names of the men who either tried to defraud her or had trifled with Silver, the brief inventory of the papers revealed. Consequently, just eleven days after news of Baby Doe's death, the Tabor papers were sealed, despite pleas from the *Rocky Mountain News*. This history-changing action was in response to a phone call received by the CHS from the Leadville judge assigned to the Tabor estate, "giving definite instruction that no letters, papers or documents are to be exhibited by you or permitted to be inspected by any press reporters."[21] This sealing of the papers silenced Lizzie's authentic private voice and simultaneously fanned public curiosity about Baby Doe. When the floodwaters of curiosity encounter such a barrier, they naturally overflow downward to the lowest level. Because the Tabor legend fed on anxieties about female power, decidedly low variations on the Baby Doe story exploded upon the scene.

GIVING "VOICE" TO THE LEGEND: (UN) *TRUE STORY*

"Silver Queen: Baby Doe Tabor's Life Story as told to Sue Bonnie" appeared in the 1938 popular serial *True Story* and became the mother lode of the evolving legend. The magazine's hyperbolic teasers introduced the iconic

elements of the growing Baby Doe myth: "She lived one of the most amazing and dramatic lives ever to be the destiny of any American woman.
Abject poverty! Famous riches! The adulation of the crowds! Absolute loneliness! Sought after by great and small! An outcast scorned and laughed at!"
The purported author of this account, Sue Bonnie, began her tale by filing
a claim to her own authority. She was the young woman who lived in a cabin
nearby the elderly Mrs. Tabor, befriended her in her final days, and dug
through the snow to find the frozen body. In a cruel irony Bonnie opened
her tale by mentioning Mrs. Tabor's own writings, the very ones that were
currently unavailable because they were sealed away: "I can remember how
she used to smile and put her head on one side and say, as she pointed to
the packets of dreams and thoughts she had scribbled down, 'Songbird,
these are my real memoirs. Some day the world will know me for what I
am!'"[22] In five installments in *True Story* "Baby Doe" told the tale of her life,
often in dialogue with Harvey Doe, Horace, and others. The series was then
uncritically mined by authors of legend-building books about the Tabors
for the next sixty years.

The *True Story* account of Baby Doe's life "in her own words" was false. It
was not told to—or even written by—Sue Bonnie. It was in reality the creation of a popular historian, Caroline Bancroft, who had purchased the
right to use Sue Bonnie's name in order to fulfill the as-told-to format
required by *True Story*. Bancroft was a third-generation Coloradan whose
grandfather was one of the founders of the CHS and whose father had been
a mining acquaintance of Mrs. Tabor. An ambitious writer with a flair for
drama, Bancroft had proposed a novel about Baby Doe to Houghton Mifflin
in 1937, but the publishers replied that in their estimation there was not
enough material for a book. Her literary agent then arranged the *True Story*
deal, which earned Bancroft $500 for each installment, a princely sum dur-
ing the depression. Bancroft knew about the letters and diary that had been
found in the Tabor trunks, and she tried to obtain an advance from the *True
Story* editor in order to gain access to those papers. She wrote that her literary agent "is of the opinion that her letter and diary are still in the possession
of Edgar McMechen and have not been given to the Colorado Historical
Society. He thinks for me to see these some payment would be necessary."[23]
Bancroft received a $200 advance.

Bancroft's dilemma—whether to simply pick up nuggets of Tabor lore
that were easily available on the surface or to somehow gain access to closed
manuscripts in order to drill deeply for authenticity—set the tone of biogra-

phies about Baby Doe Tabor for decades to come. This choice between manuscripts or myth was Bancroft's Rubicon. Whether because of lack of money or time, or cooperation from McMechen, Bancroft did not read any Tabor papers. Instead, rather than dig for the pleading voice of Lizzie, she invented a voice for Baby Doe. Bancroft relied on newspapers and interviews with old-time Leadville folks who recited their versions of the Baby Doe story. The terse journal Bancroft kept during this period mentions buying a "treasure trove" of materials from Sue Bonnie. One historian suggests that the reclusive Mrs. Tabor had hoped Sue Bonnie would help her write her autobiography, but unfortunately Bonnie was not an accomplished writer. Bonnie left only a brief account of her visits with Mrs. Tabor that contained few new insights.[24] Undaunted by this detail, Bancroft, acting as ghostwriter and ventriloquist, constructed a faux voice for Baby Doe. Many years later Bancroft stood by her method: "I improve history when it seems logical. . . . My characters talk, dress up and get involved in things, because history has to have popular appeal. I put in the truth, and the folklore, too."[25] In spite of—or perhaps because of—its unverifiable sources, the legend of Baby Doe grew from Bancroft's untrue story, permeating subsequent histories in insidious veins. Even though Bancroft's biography was factually weak, the mythic elements of her story rang true, touching the eternal issues that drew people to the Tabor tale: seduction, adultery, riches, ruin, and redemption.

The fluid legend of Baby Doe, unencumbered by complexities such as historical documents, was rich in fictional potential. The first of several novelists to tackle it was Marian Castle of Denver. Castle's novel, *The Golden Fury*, was published in 1949 by William Morrow, favorably reviewed in the *New York Times*, became a best-seller, and was translated into six foreign languages. Set in a wonderfully detailed Leadville and other mining towns, the book employed the legendary Tabor wealth and social exclusion to foreshadow the fate of its heroine, Cara. Marian Castle, like her colleague and friend Caroline Bancroft, put at the center of her story a young woman whose golden-haired beauty was reminiscent of Baby Doe's and whose inner strength overwhelmed her inferior husbands. Wrongly accused of being a prostitute, pregnant, and deserted by her first husband, Cara attempts to make a life for herself in a different mining town but is still dogged by rumors: "The only way she knew how to fight was in the open. But you couldn't grasp and throttle a slimy whisper. It slid out of your hand, leaving you defiled and helpless."[26] When Cara strikes it rich and moves to

Denver, she is dubbed the "Golden Widow" by the elite "sacred Thirty-six," the same group who in real life excluded the Tabors. In a plot turn that Lizzie Tabor would have envied, Cara, despite having lost her wealth, has a satisfying relationship with her happily married daughter and leaves stodgy old Denver for a new start in the company of a wonderfully solid man.

In 1950 Caroline Bancroft published a pamphlet version of her 1938 *True Story* account, now titled *Silver Queen: The Fabulous Story of Baby Doe Tabor*. Immediately popular then and still in print today, the highly illustrated eighty-page "autobiography" in the voice of Baby Doe went through many editions, each endorsed in the fore matter by subsequent governors of Colorado. In her introduction Bancroft confessed that, when she was a child, she met Mrs. Tabor only once and therefore relied heavily on Sue Bonnie's accounts of her chats with Baby Doe. In a move of almost postmodern legerdemain, Bancroft wrote: "Neither her friend [Sue Bonnie] or I had any way of telling whether these many intimate memories of Baby Doe's were literally true."[27] Other than the introduction, Bancroft's text essentially followed the old 1938 tale and included no new research into Lizzie's own writings. This was because in 1950 Bancroft, despite her pioneer family connections and local popularity, still could not get access to the sealed Tabor papers. (Many years later, during a lecture, Bancroft boasted that she once bribed a CHS guard to allow her to spend a night in the building with the Tabor collection, a claim some current-day historians doubt.) The story of Caroline Bancroft, her pursuit of Mrs. Tabor's bundles of papers held by McMechen, and the compelling Baby Doe figure that emerged from Bancroft's avid imagination are legendary in themselves.

THE BATTLE OVER THE BUNDLE OF PAPERS

July 4, 1921—I dreamed I was walking on sidewalk with Mrs. R.J. Moran & her Attorney & Mr. Moran & they expected I would go with them down a west side street & then they intended to do me harm very serious harm—& when we reached corner I saw on my left & on East side O the biggest hill of snow going down for blocks long hard packed snow & very steep I quickly lay flat on my back holding on my bundle of papers & I slid so quickly like lightning down that great steep long hill out of sight from them. . . . I left them all (the devils) standing at the corner God fooled them & saved me

Caroline Bancroft was continuously thwarted in her quest for access to Lizzie's papers by Edgar McMechen, who took his 1935 charge as the Tabor estate administrator to his death. McMechen, promoted to curator of the CHS, kept the papers under his strict control, despite Bancroft's protests, until his retirement in 1953. He unexpectedly passed away a few months later, and the *Denver Post* reported, "Mr. McMechen who had long hoped to write the authentic Tabor story, died last summer on the threshold of his task."[28] Yet nothing remotely resembling a book manuscript was found among McMechen's papers. Was Edgar McMechen simply a colossal procrastinator, unable to complete a history of the Tabors that was to his liking —or were there other motives for his obsessive control of Baby Doe's literary remains? One clue from McMechen's personal papers is an unsigned newspaper column of 1942 that he presumably wrote while going through the belongings of Baby Doe as the estate administrator: "I never wrote this before, because I loved Elizabeth McCourt (Baby Doe) Tabor. She was very old. I was very young. It was not a romantic love, but the adoration of youth for a great woman who was also a great lady."[29]

McMechen must have been mortified when he began reading the jumbled "Dreams and Visions" writings of his idealized Mrs. Tabor, for they contained sexual codes, prominent names, and descriptions of excrement. They certainly did not fit his image of the "great lady" he felt honor bound to protect. He probably recalled the insolent newspaper headlines of 1935 that excerpted Mrs. Tabor's "weird diary," discovered while reporters rummaged through her cabin. I believe that for McMechen, protecting the papers became conflated with protecting "his" beloved Baby Doe. Present-day CHS archivists have shown me the notation "Burn" on some of the Tabor correspondence in what they believe is McMechen's handwriting. This has led them to suspect that the protective McMechen culled materials from the bundles of Tabor papers he kept in his possession in an attempt to preserve a modicum of honor for the pioneers. McMechen may have justified this destruction of documents as an "editing" task in keeping with the biographical custom of that time to elide the personal messiness of real life. This was the tack McMechen took in his only account of the Tabor history, a forty-page booklet published by CHS in 1951, a year after upstart Bancroft's *Silver Queen* pamphlet had appeared. In his booklet he avoided reference to Horace's ugly divorce from Augusta, instead attributing Tabor's demise to a smear campaign by his political enemies. This tasteful omission would have pleased Horace, for in 1889 Tabor had suggested to biographer Hubert Howe Bancroft (the wealthy California uncle of Caroline Bancroft) that any mention of his first wife or his son be avoided, although he conceded it probably was necessary "to include them in history." H. H. Bancroft's goal was "to steer clear of all these things," in his biography of Tabor, who paid a fee to be included in Bancroft's multivolume *Chronicles of the Builders*, published in 1892.[30]

I see the McMechen-Bancroft custody battle over the Tabor papers as a lovers' quarrel between a genteel man who loved the good name of pioneer Coloradans and an ambitious woman who loved a good story that could generate fame. McMechen and Bancroft were both former reporters—he for the flagship newspaper the *Denver Rocky Mountain News* and she for its rival, the *Denver Post*. Perhaps this is why each referred primarily to their own work on Baby Doe and rarely mentioned the other's. It was also a battle of the sexes—between a male whose education and state employment rendered him a "professional" historian and a female self-employed "popular" writer of history-inspired booklets such as *The Unsinkable Mrs. Brown* (based on S.S. *Titanic* survivor Mrs. J. J. Brown) and *Six Racy Madams of Colorado*. Bancroft at age forty-three eventually earned a masters degree. Her thesis about Central City, Colorado, demonstrated that she could be erudite, but it was the lively prose of her popular booklets that provided her income. Bancroft was unapologetic about her imaginative style of writing: "I cannot defend the exact dialogue in my books. I don't know that that person said that thing at the moment. But they jolly well better had because I had done so much research that I knew it was the kind of thing they would have said. I did what's known as popular history or fictionalized history, except it's almost no fiction."[31] By contrast, McMechen's powerful historical society position provided his livelihood, and as the Tabor estate administrator (though he had been officially discharged in 1936) he maintained lifelong control over the resources Bancroft craved. McMechen "held onto the papers" as doggedly as his beloved Baby Doe had held onto her little bundle and the Matchless mine.

Would Caroline Bancroft have written a better book if she had been given the opportunity and time to study the papers so carefully preserved by Lizzie Tabor? Bancroft clearly thought so, for her 1937 letter to the *True Story* editor warned that, without the opportunity to look at the Tabor papers, she would do "merely a straight re-hash of the story from her angle told to some fictitious person and compiled from what has already been written about her in books and newspapers."[32] Bancroft, denied access to Lizzie's authentic voice, simply invented one for Baby Doe, which enabled her to tell the Tabor story for the first time from the compelling perspective of the misunderstood woman, with whom she undoubtedly identified.

Today's historians have mixed opinions of Bancroft. They have discovered her handwritten "autographs" on historical documents for future researchers to find and suspect it was Bancroft who cut out and removed irreplaceable Tabor articles from the archives of the *Leadville Herald*. My analysis of Bancroft's motivations for becoming the ventriloquist of Baby Doe appears in the next chapter. McMechen, in his role of Gentleman Historian (who also wished to protect the reputations of other gentlemen associated with the infamous Baby Doe or Silver) probably feared what an outlier like Caroline Bancroft would do if she read Mrs. Tabor's accounts of Silver's liaisons (accounts that used words like "whore"). McMechen reflected the masculinist mores of his times. For example, when the manuscript collection was briefly made public after his death in 1953, the *Denver Post* teased, "The skeletons in some Colorado closets were rattling Monday as workers at the State Historical museum sorted through thousands of personal letters that belonged to Baby Doe Tabor. A number of the letters—including those from Silver Dollar, Baby Doe's daughter—will be 'restricted' material, the museum reported reassuringly. Silver Dollar was known in her girlhood here as a 'spirited' young woman, and her escapades involved various citizens, some of whom are still living. They need have not fear—Silver's letters will not be made public."[33] Almost twenty years after Baby Doe's death, the legendary sexuality of the Tabor women still threatened to disrupt polite society. The accepted double standard ruled: while Silver's exploits, alcoholism, and tawdry death were fodder for speculative newspaper articles, her willing male counterparts were reassured of anonymity under the restrictive cloak of "decency."

Serious historians' worst fears were indeed realized when the *Denver Post* in 1953 ran a new Tabor series based on the papers so briefly unveiled after McMechen's death. Headlines such as "Exclusive! Baby Doe's Memoirs Bared: Why She Died in Rags," accompanied the ubiquitous young-old photos. Young *Denver Post* staff reporter Eva Hodges wrote the series articles, which revealed that Baby Doe had devised a code to conceal private matters in her writings. Then Caroline Bancroft's first publication in 1955 utilizing the contested papers confirmed McMechen's protective instincts. Bancroft's "Baby Doe's Secret Love Code" appeared in the *Denver Post*'s Sunday *Empire* magazine. It was illustrated with a silhouette of a couple embracing, to signal its torrid tone. Rather than exploring the complex and deeply moving "Dreams and Visions," Bancroft took the easy—in both senses of the word—route and exploited the image of a salacious Baby Doe: "The clandestine affairs of Colorado's most intriguing beauty stand revealed, now that her mysterious scrapbook cipher has been solved."[34] After this brief public sensationalized exposure in the mid-1950s, the Tabor collection was again closed to the public, until 1967, when archivists had completed processing its fifty thousand items, which ranged from traditional correspondence to tiny scraps called "Dreams and Visions." The thirty-two-year-long gap between Mrs. Tabor's gift of her extraordinary papers to history and the ability of patient scholars to receive those precious papers was filled by at least nine books written about Baby Doe.

RECONSTRUCTING BABY DOE

I dreamed this 22 of December [1915] that I was with very Important men they or me at times were riding & look upon me as the Bell of all

While the legend of Baby Doe as sinner grew, in spurious biographies weak on primary source foundation, several museums created exhibits that remembered the Tabors as quasi-saints, from a fantasy frontier that the public eagerly embraced. The first to re-member Baby Doe with a 1935 exhibit was the Colorado History Museum. The display filled eleven museum cases with items rescued from auction by the Tabor Association. It was lavishly praised by Tabor estate administrator Edgar McMechen in the CHS's *Colorado Magazine.* He touched briefly upon Horace Tabor's political career but did not mention that Baby Doe was Horace's second wife. The loyal McMechen quickly turned to the true focal point of the exhibit, Baby Doe. He observed, "Dominating all, the spirit of an extraordinary woman seems to hover over the entire exhibit. No more intimate and touching story of a woman's ambitions, hopes and heart has ever been told by a collection of inanimate objects." McMechen explained that Baby Doe's scrapbooks were not on display because of their fragility, but he lovingly described her gown, hats, toilette items, and babies' shoes now open to the public's gaze. In his description of the "case of romance" that featured Baby Doe's $7,000 Washington wedding gown, McMechen did not mention the most unromantic divorce from Augusta that had preceded the nuptials. In fact, no picture of Augusta Tabor intruded upon the exhibit. A caption in the article described a portrait of "'Baby' *Tabor*," a term legitimizing the Tabors' marriage and a direct challenge to the popular moniker Baby Doe.[35]

A flattering portrait of a youthful Horace hung next to a brand new one of Baby Doe completed in 1935 by Waldo C. Love. An artist employed by the WPA, Love drew upon a nineteenth-century photograph of young Baby Doe to create a stunningly lush image for CHS that has become *the* Baby Doe Tabor for modern viewers. In the original photograph, a frame of foliage tastefully covers Lizzie's bust so that the eye is drawn to the famed Isabella diamond necklace. Love's portrait of Baby Doe extends nearly to her waist, revealing an ample bosom that overwhelms the jewels. Poor Augusta's portrait (a characteristically dour and unflattering one) was not placed in the museum until 1960. The Colorado History Museum has modified its Tabor exhibit several times, and Horace is now suspended uncomfortably between the portraits of his two wives. The centerpiece of the exhibit remains the wedding gown of Baby Doe. When curators contemplated putting the old gown away, the public protested, and so the dress that once caressed the skin of Baby Doe is on perpetual display.

By 1940 the Tabors' image was so reformed that the good citizens of Denver felt it appropriate to reunite Horace and his Baby Doe in a joint burial plot. An impressive marble monument was unveiled at the new Tabor grave site at Mt. Olivet Cemetery, Denver, on March 31, 1940. Three hundred people representing many pioneer organizations gathered to commemorate Horace Tabor and Baby Doe, the name Lizzie never used for herself. Horace's etched profile graced the tombstone, but the carver omitted a portrait of Baby Doe, the most recognizable woman in Colorado history. Perhaps he was plagued by indecision about whether to portray the young or old Mrs. Tabor—or by the realization that no cold stone could capture the warm vitality of Baby Doe. The newspapers, showing uncharacteristically good taste, only briefly mentioned the process by which what was hoped to be Horace's body was located in the old Calvary Cemetery prior to its removal to Mt. Olivet. Many grave markers had been removed from their original sites by vandals, so officials relied on the memory of a man, who as a young boy had been paid by Mrs. Tabor to regularly pray at her husband's grave, to indicate the spot in which he believed Horace was buried.

I dreamed to day I was in the theatre a man was sitting next me I had 2 quart bottles of champayne I had drunk so it was pale yellow & a lot of silver dollars change for a 20 dollars—June 3, 1915

Portrait of Baby Doe Tabor painted by Waldo C. Love in 1935.
It is featured on the Colorado History Museum millennium
mural and was the cover art for *Life* Magazine's May 11, 1959,
feature, "Pioneer Women—Good and Bad." Courtesy Colorado Historical Society, Tabor Collection. 10026516.tif. All
Rights Reserved.

Interest in the Tabor saga revived in 1951, when the 1932 film *Silver Dollar* was again taken out of Hollywood storage and screened at Denver's
Tabor Opera House to commemorate the building's seventieth anniversary.
Sadly, it was an opera house in memory only, for this monument Tabor had
constructed to his own civic largesse had been converted into a movie theater called the Paramount-Publix. The feature-length film starred Edward
G. Robinson as a rather swarthy "Yates Martin," and Aline MacMahon
played the role of first wife, "Sarah," who brought both the brains and the
capital to the marriage. "Lily," the veiled femme fatale, was portrayed by

Bebe Daniels. In the film she wears a dress cut nearly to the waist at the back when she first paces back and forth like a tigress awaiting her prey in front of Yates's opera house in "St. Charles," Colorado. She is the one who initiates the divorce idea and assures Yates, "Your wife won't make any trouble if you, er, make her comfortable enough."[36] When Yates later faces financial ruin, good-hearted ex-wife Sarah offers to help him, but he with great pride rejects her offer. The movie ends with the unexpected death of Yates, a man mourned by two faithful women. While the film bore the name of the Tabors' second daughter, it avoided treatment of her tawdry death, unlike the 1932 Karsner book upon which the movie was based. How many men would have squirmed uncomfortably in their seats if Silver's Denver liaisons had been dramatized? Caroline Bancroft's ubiquitous *Silver Queen* pamphlet was on sale in the theater lobby so that those unfamiliar with the lurid details of the Tabor legend could learn about it in Baby Doe's "own words."

In 1953 another museum dedicated to Baby Doe opened in Leadville. A nonprofit organization made up of Leadville citizens and supported by Caroline Bancroft completely rebuilt the demolished Matchless mine cabin on its original site as a museum that remains open to this day.[37] The *Denver Post* featured a picture of some jovial people from the crowd of ninety who made the pilgrimage to Leadville in a tour bus with the caption, "They're off to Dedicate Baby Doe's Cabin."[38] The group looked as if they were going to a festival rather than to the final hovel in which Mrs. Tabor lived, dreamed, and died. Indefatigable Caroline Bancroft, by now known as the "caretaker of the Tabor legend," signed copies of her pamphlet at the pseudo-cabin. In 1955 longtime resident Evelyn Furman purchased the aging Leadville Tabor Opera House with the intention of preserving it as a museum.

Today, the opera house remains in a precarious state of "arrested decay," while the Matchless mine museum staff present an ever-evolving version of the Baby Doe legend to new visitors. I took the Matchless mine tour in the summer of 1981. The high school student who guided us touched upon the total destruction of the original cabin so briefly that a casual listener could miss this fact. When Colorado writer Kristen Iverson attended a tour in the 1990s, she noted that the guide added his own imaginative twists to the Tabor legend, demonstrating that the mythic elements within the tale enable its adaptation to current tastes. The guide described the requisite tragic death of Bad Daughter Silver, then emphasized the little-known fact that Good Daughter Lily married her first cousin. He then, with authority, stated that Lily's marriage resulted in mentally deficient children who died unnaturally young. This claim has no documented veracity but serves up for

Beverly Sills in the title role of the opera
The Ballad of Baby Doe. Courtesy New York
City Opera Company.

a new generation of history buffs ever-greater punishment of Baby Doe as
the tainted mother who bred not one but two sinful daughters and was
cursed with abnormal grandchildren.

BABY DOE AS SINGING GOLD DIGGER

The version of the Tabor legend that national audiences know best is an
opera, *The Ballad of Baby Doe*, which debuted in Colorado's Central City
Opera House on July 7, 1956. Douglas Moore, whose musical score for the
opera *Giants in the Earth* had earned him the 1951 Pulitzer Prize, was over-
joyed when he was invited to turn his talents to Baby Doe. Moore composed
the opera for the Central City Opera as part of their centennial celebration
of the discovery of gold in Colorado, but he had been drawn to Baby Doe
long before. Moore wrote, "In 1935 I read in the morning paper of the
death of an old woman who was found frozen in a miner's shack outside
Leadville, Colorado. . . . This certainly seemed like opera material."[39] While
the dramatic potential of a love triangle combined with the meteoric rise
and fall of Horace Tabor may have thrilled the composer from the east
coast, "many older natives of the state were dismayed. It was disgraceful they
said, to make a hero of an adulterer."[40] However, *The Ballad of Baby Doe* was
so popular that the Central City Opera had to add three extra performances, for a total of nineteen, during its premiere.

The opera plot was based on Karsner's *Silver Dollar*, because of legal battles with Caroline Bancroft, who insisted that she even owned the rights to
the name Baby Doe. In the opera Baby Doe fulfills the role of sweetly
singing seductress. Horace, however, does not seem like the hero of an
opera; he is indecisive and financially naive. It is Horace's wives who propel
what Moore called "The dramatic treatment of Tabor's life, and the two
women who dominated it."[41] As Horace's end comes near, Augusta returns
to taunt him with foreknowledge of his daughter's sad fate, dramatized by a
drunken Silver Dollar staggering across the stage in the arms of two seamy
men. Nevertheless, Baby Doe remains faithful to Horace, proclaiming in
her closing widow's aria:

> *Always through the changing of*
> *Sun and shadow, time and space*
> *I will walk beside my love*
> *In a green and quiet place.*
> *Proof against the forms of fear*
> *No distress shall alter me*
> *I will walk beside my dear*
> *Clad in love's bright heraldry.*
> *Sound the battle's loud alarm*
> *Any foe I shall withstand*
> *In the circle of his arms*
> *I am safe in Beulah Land.*
> . . .
> *As our earthy eyes grow dim*
> *Still the old song will be sung.*
> *I shall change along with him*
> *So that both are ever young.*
> *Ever young.*

Moore's stage directions for this last aria indicate, "Baby Doe's mantle falls
back, she is a white-haired old woman. The rear stage becomes transparent
and the Matchless mine comes into view, a bright blue sky yearning above
it. Baby Doe moves toward it. As a white drift of snow begins to fall, Baby
Doe sits by the mineshaft, waiting."[42] The curtain falls as Baby Doe sings
"Ever young," her white hair the only indication that she will spend three
decades in isolation listening to and fighting a growing chorus of devils.

The news of "the death of an old woman" may have drawn Douglas
Moore to the story, but the legend of a perpetually desirable young Baby

Doe dominated his opera. Instead of inventing lyrics about some Beulah
Land, opera librettist John Latouche could have used excerpts from Lizzie
Tabor's last writings, which had been widely published in newspapers both
in 1935 and in 1953. Her ravings about evil spirits that invaded her cabin
and her poignant diary passages about crawling through heavy snow would
have made superb opera. Regrettably, the rich treasure of Lizzie Tabor's
own words, some touchingly poetic, that could have supplied Latouche with
an entire third act about her life—as the opera's title figure—were in 1956
still sealed away from view. Thus another generation of ventriloquists—this
time eastern males steeped in highly fictionalized materials about the
Tabors—put their words into Baby Doe's mouth. The opera should not
have been over until the mad lady sang:

> *Dawn of Sorrow*
> *I see the day breaking*
> *my tired hearts aching*
> *Snow is falling ore mound & forest*
> *Winds are wafting the flakes around us*
> *Our blood is congealing and freezing*
> *As the tinkle of burying bells come nearer*
> *Mocking the sying of the trees as they sound*
> *The death Knell*
> *Through the woodland*
> *They are bearing the shroud of pines for*
> *Our Lilys sad and living grave*
> *God help me I love her so—June 21, 1912*[43]

In 1958 the New York City Center Opera Company premiered *The Ballad
of Baby Doe* in the East, with young Beverly Sills in the title role. Sills, like her
New York audiences, was drawn to this steadfast heroine: "Baby became an
integral part of my operatic experience; it was difficult to shake her off even
after I left the opera house. If I have ever achieved definitive performances
during my career thus far, Baby Doe is one of them."[44] Musicologist Randie
Lee Blooding suggested why Baby Doe is so appealing: "Opera heroines
often kill themselves or accomplish nearly impossible feats in the name of
love. Baby Doe lived the last 35 years of her life quietly, remaining true to
her love for Horace and trying to live according to her ideals. Her feats may
have been more difficult than that of other heroines because she had years
to reflect on her decisions and countless chances to reverse the course of

her life. That she did not reconsider her choices makes her a character who seems larger-than-life and is perfect for the operatic stage."[45]

The Ballad of Baby Doe has become, second to Gershwin's *Porgy and Bess*, the most often produced American opera.[46] The opera celebrated its fortieth anniversary with renewed Central City performances and a new CD version of the New York recording. The fiftieth anniversary brought several original cast members back to Central City for a reunion. Something about the Tabor story continues to seduce audiences. *Opera News* reviewer David McKee put it this way: "To rush straight out on a limb, Douglas Moore's *The Ballad of Baby Doe* . . . is not just a great American opera but *the* Great America Opera. Its riches-to-rags story is quintessentially American."[47] But the quintessential specter of the mythic predatory female that drives the tragic opera must be maintained. When a 2001 New York City Opera production strayed too far from the Baby Doe of legend, it was criticized for portraying her "not as an ambitious gold-digger but simply a nice woman in a difficult position."[48] Beverly Sills still recalled in 2001 the animosity her Baby Doe generated: "There's no way to overcome the anger of women in the audience." Sills confessed she excised a line from the opera that suggested Baby Doe connived to seduce Tabor: "You have to play it as a chance meeting, a bolt of lightning."[49] The question of who seduced whom will never be known, for whatever early letters between Horace and Baby Doe that still existed at her death probably fell victim to the moralists' edict "Burn."

The Devils commenced to tear the inside out of the Tabor Grand Opera House.
. . . They are tearing his honorable name from his great Palace which started &
made Denver O the incarnate thieves & devils—August 29, 1921

In the early 1960s the Tabor Opera House and the Tabor block finally succumbed to urban renewal. Their decline had begun decades earlier, when the opera house was converted to show movies. By 1960 it was known as the Tabor Latin Theater, which showed primarily Spanish-language films. The huge opera house, once overflowing with crowds eager to view the infamous Baby Doe (and whatever actors were performing) was now a fifteen-hundred-seat dinosaur unable to survive into the enlightened era of protective historic preservation. Destruction of the old landmark, however, renewed interest in the colorful mining era and its wealthy monument builders such as Horace Tabor. Journalist Eva Hodges produced yet another series on Baby Doe in the *Denver Post*, and the Tabor saga lived on, despite the crumbling of their earthly empire. In 1962 English writer Gordon Langley Hall published a book-length biography, *The Two Lives of Baby Doe.* Although Hall did acknowledge the CHS staff, who "wheeled in the vast Baby Doe archives upon a large trolley," archivists recalled him doing only one day's research with those papers. His book included a hyperbolic suicide threat letter scrawled by Silver Dollar Tabor in 1914, plus a few dream excerpts by Mrs. Tabor. Hall also interviewed new oral history sources and brought to light a touching vignette about Widow Tabor's last years, written by the editor of the *Leadville Herald Democrat,* Henry C. Butler.[50] Despite Hall's obvious affection for Mrs. Tabor, and consideration for her sufferings in what he termed "The Greek Tragedy," he included many elements straight out of Caroline Bancroft's legend and in one case exaggerated the story further. Bancroft had written that the elder Tabor daughter, Lily, left Leadville and her mother for good when Wisconsin relatives assisted her escape. Hall added, "Lillie disappeared out of her mother's life forever, never replying to any of her future communications."[51] This is false, as more time spent with the Tabor papers would have proved, for Lizzie had preserved in her trunks several affectionate letters from her daughter Lily Tabor Last.

NEW SOURCES AND NEW INSIGHTS

In 1973 Duane A. Smith wrote *Horace Tabor: His Life and the Legend,* the first serious book to delve deeply into the now available Tabor papers. Smith, professor of history at Fort Lewis College in Durango, Colorado, had first been drawn to the Tabor story in 1956 when he saw the opera in Central City. Smith introduced Baby Doe halfway through his extensive biography and included excerpts of playful, affectionate letters Horace sent to Lizzie and his daughters, giving readers a sense of them as a family. Because Smith ended his book with Horace's death, he did not include Lizzie's "Dreams and Visions" or draw out the tale of her own impoverished demise. Smith's book is a traditional biography of a sometimes great man and centers on Horace's mining business conflicts and political career. It is also the first book to *remove* something from the Baby Doe legend: Smith is the only biographer *not* to repeat Horace's ostensible deathbed edict, "Hold onto the Matchless mine." In fact Smith did not find any reference to such a dying wish in the Tabor papers or in any of the news coverage at the time of Horace's death. He eventually traced the origins of Horace's purported last words to Baby Doe—words the legend uses to propel her actions for the next thirty years—back to their source: the colorful imagination of Caroline Bancroft. The elderly Bancroft staked her claim to inventing "Hold onto the Matchless" in conversations with both Smith and CHS historian David Hallas. But I suggest that the self-mythologizing Bancroft, in this case, claim-jumped David Karsner, whose 1932 *Silver Dollar* used the line twice and predated Bancroft's *True Story* tale by six years.[52] Bancroft was able to get away with her assertion merely because she outlived her rival biographer, Karsner.

Duane Smith also wrote a myth-debunking introduction to John Burke's 1974 *The Legend of Baby Doe*, a book true to its title that relied heavily on folklore, at the expense of complexity. "John Burke" was the pseudonym of Richard O'Connor, an ex-newspaperman and prolific writer who did not live to see his book published. Unlike his popular predecessors Karsner and Hall, Burke supplied rudimentary endnotes for his book, which reveal his heavy reliance on Caroline Bancroft and secondary sources rather than on the primary documents from the Tabor collection that were by then open to scholars. While Burke's fantasies about female sexuality during the good old days of the mining frontier (see the next chapter) are embarrassing by today's lights, he was a vivid writer. *The Legend of Baby Doe*, with the glowing Baby Doe portrait by Waldo Love gracing its cover, has been popular at the Colorado History Museum bookstore and at historic sites throughout the West.

May—5–1913 I dreamed this a.m. that my darling Lily was with us & that several times she fell backward in an unconscious condition & she look [sic] tall & sick but I thought that she would now belong to us & always be with us. . . . Funny why her father should look dutch in my dream O I suffered terribly for Lily & about her in the dream

The 1980s were a rich period for the New Western history, particularly women's history. Revisionist work, including two new books about the women of the Tabor saga, challenged androcentric stories of the Old West. Evelyn Furman, who had moved to Leadville in 1933 as a teenager and remained there as owner of the Tabor Opera House Museum, wrote *Silver Dollar Tabor: The Leaf in the Storm*. Furman did not present her work like a trained historian; half of the book was a reprint of Silver Dollar's pitiable novel *Star of Blood*, and many pages contained poorly reproduced holograph documents. But Furman's book for the first time utilized extensive excerpts of Silver's letters to her mother, as Silver gradually became the self-described "leaf in the storm" of nightlife, bad company, and promiscuity. Silver's descriptions of her dreams confirm the ethereal link that bound Lizzie and Silver together as codreamers. Furman also uncovered letters that show Silver's role as broker in the legend of the Good Daughter Lily deserting Baby Doe to live in the Midwest, a tale Furman debunks. The correspondence reveals that it was Lily who embarrassed her mother, not vice versa, by marrying her first cousin and giving birth to their child just six months later. Furman located a 1908 letter from Silver to Lily, urging Lily to remain in Milwaukee with her husband and child to avoid a scandal that would hurt their beloved mother. Silver wrote, "the newspaper reporters . . . will put a piece in the paper about Senator Tabor's daughter marrying her [———] and it will be heralded all over the U.S. and mamma will never rise to dictate and sign the last papers on the Matchless." The family later reconciled, as affectionate letters from Lily to her mother show. Lily noted that her daughter Jane had such big eyes she would surely look like her grandmother and then fondly recalled a 1917 visit Lizzie made to them: "the children talk of you so often."[53] Although Silver was the focal point of Furman's little-known book, passages from Lizzie's correspondence at last brought her voice as Mindful Mother to complicate the Baby Doe legend. This focus on Lizzie as Good Mother provided new information about the middle years, filling some of the gap between the two comfortably simple images of Baby Doe as young wanton and old widow.

In 1988 local Colorado historian Betty Moynihan published *Augusta Tabor: A Pioneering Woman*, drawing upon private diaries and papers loaned to her from Augusta's family. Books about spirited Anglo pioneer women were enormously popular, and Moynihan's study of Augusta Tabor documented the first Mrs. Tabor's considerable mettle. Moynihan benefited from pioneering feminist historians who insisted that women's ordinary work upon the frontier was worthwhile. She wrote, "The shared life of Baby Doe and Horace Tabor is tarnished tinsel. It is a tawdry tale sold with Hollywood hype to an unsuspecting public. The real romance in the life of the Tabors is the saga of challenge and discovery lived by Horace and Augusta as they forged new paths into the Rocky Mountain ranges." Moynihan also gave a compelling explanation for Augusta's obsession to "hold onto the Tabor name" after her divorce from Horace. Revisiting the well-educated Augusta's marriage to stonecutter Tabor, Moynihan notes, "As it did for every woman in those days, marriage robbed Augusta of her legal rights and individual identity. Signing the marriage contract was instant civil death for her. . . . In exchange, Horace gave her his name. At such a price, Augusta intended to keep that name forever."[54] Augusta's heirs provided Moynihan with a more youthful portrait of Horace's maligned first wife to show that Augusta was once young and soft like the photogenic Baby Doe. (Moynihan's less charitable perspective on Baby Doe and the gender trouble she generated appears in the next chapter.) A later biography of Augusta Tabor by Evelyn Furman continued to fill out the picture of this energetic yet vulnerable pioneer woman in order to undermine the image of the "vinegary" abandoned wife so crucial to the legend.

OBSESSED WITH BABY DOE

The ongoing vitality of Baby Doe's mystique has been good for the Colorado History Museum, for their Tabor exhibits remain popular and the Tabor manuscript collection is heavily used. Curious dabblers, scholars, would-be scriptwriters, and novelists have all made pilgrimages to the Baby Doe manuscript mausoleum held in the research library. Articles about the Tabors or Tabor buildings have since the 1930s regularly appeared in CHS's general history journal, *Colorado Magazine* (now *Colorado Heritage*). CHS staff attempt to correct misinformation about the Tabors whenever the legend can be interrupted by historical documentation. They have occasionally responded to inaccurate newspaper articles and made an attempt in 1994 to set the record straight concerning Horace's purported "Hold onto the Matchless" edict as one invented rather than uttered.[55] These ongoing debates about the Tabors, especially Baby Doe, serve both to reflect and to renew public curiosity. In 1992, the five-hundredth anniversary of the "discovery" of America by Columbus, CHS curator of books and manuscripts Stan Oliner took his curiosity about the fate of Baby Doe's famed Isabella diamond wedding necklace to the public. Oliner, with the assistance of the *Denver Post* and the local NBC television affiliate, showed photographs of the ostentatious necklace, last seen in Denver in 1954, and requested information on its whereabouts. Oliner believes one response was genuine, but the jeweler who told Oliner he had appraised the unforgettable stone would not disclose the name of its owner out of concern that anything associated with the Tabors would bring unwanted publicity, even though it was now fifty-seven years after the death of Baby Doe. As early as 1914 the *Denver Post* claimed that the diamond, which the Tabors had long ago pawned, brought bad luck to subsequent owners (Mrs. Tabor sent clippings of the article to both of her daughters).[56]

Colorado historians have also had fun with the Tabor tale, in keeping with the robust theatrical appetites of Horace. In 1992 they organized a modern-day "trial" of Horace Tabor on three charges: adultery, bigamy, and white male chauvinism. They conducted the trial, which was officiated by an actual judge, up in Leadville's Tabor Opera House. So many people showed up to view the living history event that the fire chief made many of them listen to the trial from outside. Dressed in period costumes, "Augusta," "Horace," and "Baby Doe" each presented their testimony from actual historical documents, along with many impromptu asides. To the hoots, cheers, and jeers of the audience "jury," Horace was acquitted. Subsequent trials have remained popular. The 2006 soldout version put "Baby Doe" in the docket on charges of "home wrecking, gold digging, adultery, child endangerment, trespassing, indecent extravagance, and panhandling." Colorado's popular historians Thomas Noel and Patricia Limerick performed as prosecution attorneys arguing before Colorado Supreme Court Chief Justice Mary Mullarkey. Over 125 years after she became a legend, Baby Doe can still draw a crowd.[57]

In 1995 novelist John Vernon created what I consider a drag-queen version of Baby Doe's voice in *All for Love: Baby Doe and Silver Dollar*, which *Publishers Weekly* praised as "literate and raunchy, wildly colorful and meticulously researched." Vernon's Baby Doe was described as "a selfish, sexually voracious, bitchy social climber." The book received a less enthusiastic review in the *New York Times*, particularly for its lack of attention to the inner life of Baby Doe. Reviewer Robert Houston found that the last chapter, in which Vernon had included several transcriptions of actual "Dreams and Visions," led to a sense of "tedium and puzzlement." Houston criticized the novel's imbalance, a product of the great attention Vernon paid to the licentious early Tabor days and Silver's gradual deterioration compared to the rushed glimpses of Mrs. Tabor's last years. Houston concluded, "What this novel needs is . . . more of those last 42 years of Baby's life, more invention. More lying, if you will, to fill history's blanks."[58] Houston and readers could not know from Vernon's book, overflowing with male erotic fantasies put into Baby Doe's mouth, that Lizzie Tabor had indeed attempted to fill history's blanks with thousands of her dream transcriptions, samples of which Houston found "disjointed" in *All for Love*, which quickly slipped into obscurity.

> *I am sick . . . with neuralgia & weak for want of strength food & worry about Sil & L & child and all no meat eggs butter milk or vegetable fruit only tea coffee. . . .*[59]

A more empathetic woman-centered approach to Lizzie Tabor is being undertaken by creative writer Kristen Iversen. In an earlier book, Iversen conducted research into primary materials from real-life Margaret ("Unsinkable Molly") Brown and Elizabeth McCourt Tabor about the contradictions between popularized images of them and their actual personal writings. Iversen noted, "I found that despite the fact that each of these women had left behind voluminous material stored in hundreds of files in archives . . . very few writers or historians had bothered to look at it." Iversen found that the stereotypes of a sexually loose Baby Doe and a garishly outrageous "Molly" Brown were more palatable to the public than the verifiable stories of two unconventional women interested in suffrage and, in Brown's case, public office. Iversen has turned to historical fiction in her book-in-progress, *Night Owls like Us*, to explore the complex mother-daughter relationship between Lizzie and Silver. Iversen's research about the conditions of Silver's death in Chicago will disrupt the "Bad Mother begets Bad Daughter" element of the punishing legend. Silver obsessed another writer, Jan Minich, whose poems form *The Letters of Silver Dollar*, published in 2002. Instead of distancing himself from Silver, Minich wrote, "Silver's thoughts found their way into mine, and I discovered in these poems in her voice to her mother, the book I needed to write." He saw Silver as bold rather than bad: "She could have had the safe and comfortable life of her sister, Lily, but she wanted more."[60]

Even though Baby Doe disrupted society in the 1880s, she has survived into the twenty-first century in ever-evolving ways. There is a Web site maintained by enthusiastic "Doe heads" (BabyDoe.org), which contains both the iconic photographs and a respectable suggested reading list. Baby Doe still acts as a lightning rod for contemporary feelings about women and power, as a documentary videographer David Wright noted in 2000: "You find people are really emotional about it. Was Baby Doe Tabor this ruthless *woman*, or a pretty sincere *person*?" (emphasis mine).[61] People throughout the West still know the Baby Doe legend, sharing with me their own vivid reminiscences or ones handed down through their families. While most of these reminiscences appear later in my analysis of gender fables built around Baby Doe, a particularly vivid one recounted to me in a Denver bar in February 2000 epitomizes the eroticism—or more accurately the necrophilia—in our ongoing obsession with Baby Doe. For it does become *our* obsession, a consensual act, when the speaker and listener collude in a recitation of the fantastical. To paraphrase the tale: a young boy was allowed by his father to go up to the Matchless mine on that cold day in March 1935 when they removed Mrs. Tabor's frozen body from the cabin. It was so icy and the body was so stiff that they had to use a sled to bring it into town. The fierce wind blew the hat off dead Mrs. Tabor's head, revealing the most beautiful long blond hair the little boy had ever seen on a woman. With one gust of wind, the threadbare hat so much a part of the penitent widow's costume was stripped away to bare the appealing hair of Baby Doe. Five years later, the story continues, when the body was exhumed in Denver so that it could be buried alongside Horace, the undertaker decided to open the coffin to confirm that it was Mrs. Tabor. There, on the undefiled corpse of an eighty-year-old woman, was the legendary beautiful blond hair of Baby Doe.[62] The obsession with punishing Baby Doe also lives on. After a recent lecture I gave on my Tabor research, a woman approached me from the audience and said her father had examined the body of Baby Doe in Leadville and that rats had eaten the nose off the corpse, horribly disfiguring it. Is it significant that a man told me the "forever young" tale whereas a woman told me about Baby Doe "forever punished"?

> *May 31, 1921—I dreamed . . . it was dusk out side I fell on side walk & struggled hard to get my cap on as it had come off & my black & white skirt was over my head. I got my cap on without moving my skirt off my head & then I got up off sidewalk & started home, several children were watching me it was dusk. . . .*

The consequences of the obsession with Baby Doe that led to the dismembering of the Tabor estate and the Matchless cabin in 1935 continue today. At almost every Tabor lecture I give, someone offers to show me an item they possess that they claim once belonged to Baby Doe, such as her little parasol. One woman invited me to stop by sometime to view two children's chairs she had purchased at a garage sale; they had once belonged to the Tabors, she was told. The woman lowered her voice and added, "Just as I bought them, a very old woman stuck her head out of the door and watched me. I wonder if it was Baby Doe herself." I regretted my role as the picky historian obligated to tell her that Baby Doe had died two decades before the date of the garage sale. The dissemination of Tabor memorabilia across the West in a virtual potlatch began when Horace sold off possessions to creditors in the 1890s. Then estate administrator McMechen conducted the well-publicized auction in the spring of 1935—and that fall conducted a mysterious private sale of more Tabor goods. Such wide dispersal of a legend means that Tabor relics could be anywhere and everywhere. Their locale and present-day ownership become symbolic of old frontier quarrels: a Denver woman told me after my May 2006 CHS lectures that "all those Leadville people" probably got to the Matchless mine cabin first and looted it.

Among the Baby Doe relics might be more papers. When Stan Oliner was CHS curator of books and manuscripts, he routinely received calls from people who had discovered writings by Baby Doe while sorting out the effects of deceased relatives and now wished to sell them. In some cases the heirs agreed to allow the items to be photocopied and placed in the archives, but no new purchases of papers have occurred. Leadville Tabor biographer Evelyn Furman told me in 1990 that she received a phone call every few years from a man on the West Slope who claimed to have a trunk full of Baby Doe's items for sale. When I asked her his name, she said she could not remember it. Those of us who are obsessed with Baby Doe share a haunting sense that more information could appear at any time—just as Mrs. Tabor anticipated that someday riches would emerge from the depths of the Matchless mine to reward her hard work.

Another frustrating dismembering is occurring amid the Tabor papers preserved in historical archives, where heavy use slowly erodes the collections. Lizzie's "Dreams and Visions," for example, are held in two repositories. The vast majority are at the CHS, but several others were bequeathed by Caroline Bancroft to the Denver Public Library. How Bancroft came to possess the papers is unclear, though I suspect they were among the "treasure trove of materials" she noted in her diary that she purchased from Mrs. Tabor's neighbor Sue Bonnie.[63] At the CHS library an entire folder of "Dreams and Visions" from the troubled year of 1914 is now empty. Mrs. Tabor's 1935 calendar—overwritten like a palimpsest with her final "Dreams and Visions," found on her cabin wall after her death—was photographed in the arms of CHS personnel for the October 18, 1953, *Denver Post* but has been missing for years.

If a reembodied Lizzie Tabor were to peer down upon the city of Denver today, she would find few reminders of her husband's edifices. The Tabor block and Tabor Grand Opera House are gone, although a large shopping center built in the 1980s near the downtown pedestrian mall is named the Tabor Center. The Tabor mansion is now dust, but the fine Capitol Hill house of Mrs. J. J. (Molly) Brown, who once came to the aid of Mrs. Tabor, remains a historical site. St. Mary's Cathedral where the Tabors were unwelcome has been demolished. The modest Sacred Heart, where Lizzie took her troubles to kindly Father Guida, is an energetic focal point in a multicultural urban neighborhood Lizzie would find unrecognizable. Would she be outraged or amused by the replica of the Matchless mine cabin that stands on a hill near the freeway? It housed the now defunct "Baby Doe's Restaurant," where customers walked through tunnels, crossed ore cart tracks, gazed upon photographs of the beautiful Lizzie, and dined in a copy of the cabin where Mrs. Tabor regularly faced starvation.

Dec 20 [1915] my Mother was frying a very largest platter of meat beefsteak piled high on it & fried potatoes & Rasfelt [Roosevelt] ate them I spred the white table cloth it was soiled & mussed he Presedent Roosfelt kissed me or I him & hugged each other he swung me around Tabor was there

Surely Lizzie would look down in pleasure at the huge golden portrait of Baby Doe that dominates the millennium mural spanning the entire outdoor length of the downtown Colorado History Museum building. Waldo Love's 1935 painting is vibrantly reproduced; its intense colors and placement as the leftmost item in the mural immediately draw the viewer's attention to Baby Doe. It has become Mrs. Tabor's portrait of Dorian Gray: painted during the year of her emaciated death at age eighty, Love's portrait perpetuates the stimulating fantasy of how gloriously lush she remains in perpetuity. This portrait has graced *The Ballad of Baby Doe* opera posters, the cover of *Life* magazine in 1959, and has been sold in the museum gift store on trinket boxes, refrigerator magnets, costume jewelry, and mirrors. Baby Doe's hypersensuality remains controversial. When CHS announced that the Waldo Love portrait would be part of its huge millennium mural, one irate member called the CHS president to complain about "that tramp" being honored. Yet as prominent Colorado historian Tom Noel told me, while we gazed up at the mural, "Ah, the snowy bosom of Baby Doe. Some people wanted to put Augusta up there as a true Colorado pioneer. But no, it's Baby Doe that will bring them into this museum."[64] The moral cost of such beauty is still inscribed once one enters the Colorado History Museum, however. Until very recently, schoolchildren visiting the museum would first encounter Baby Doe's bosom, but then they would be met by a stern "Augusta Tabor," as portrayed by a docent in period costume who guided them through the exhibits. Baby Doe might be the visual bait set to attract young people to history, but it is unthinkable she would ever be allowed to speak, to tell her side of the story. For children lured in by the warm portrait of Baby Doe in her décolleté gown, then lectured by Augusta in her prim starched blouse, the morality tale within the Tabor legend remains an uncomplicated one about a misguided millionaire's choice between two "types" of women. The mythic figure of Baby Doe, punished for flaunting her beauty, seductively greets the next generation.

CHAPTER 3

The Wanton

Sex and Power in the Mining Frontier West

July 24–1920 I had a terrible dream—I was in a house with several men
& Bill Courtney was hunting for me he kept passing by out side & looking
in all the windows for me up & down in all windows he was dressed very
fine & looked very fresh, white & pink skin, yellowish moustache & light
hair he was richly dressed—white tie. Then I was in the privey of our old
home in Oshkosh with Silver—we each sat on a hole—she said Courtney
looked handsome. Then I was rehursing to play on the theatre stage Men
were watching me act & Courtney was kissing my mouth as Tabor kissed
me (O nasty terrible dream it means trouble)

In this terrible dream, Lizzie is speechless as she appears on a stage for all
to see: vulnerable, sexual, and silent. In dream after dream Lizzie is unable
to speak or her words are ineffective. Being unheard is her worst nightmare. This woman who refused to shut up when alive, dunning wealthy people for loans, scolding her daughter's boyfriends, talking so loudly to spirits
in the night that hotel guests complained, was "shut up in prose," to use
Emily Dickinson's term—other people's prose as they built the legend of
Baby Doe. The characterizations and caricatures of Baby Doe in increasingly erotic and sadistic books, film, opera, novels, and visuals continue to
muffle Lizzie's authentic voice from her "Dreams and Visions." Onto this
mannequin Baby Doe, mouthing invented words, are inscribed each cre-
ator's fantasies and fears regarding female sexuality, the moral questions
that tease each generation, and our desire for an imagined West. We can
discover how much has been written onto the body of Baby Doe by first
probing the fissures in the legend's plot and then at long last adding
Lizzie's compelling revision of her life in her own words.

This inscription of personal and cultural values onto legendary figures is the engine that drives most biographers, subconsciously or consciously. In this era of reflexive biography, some authors confess up front that they are writing about themselves as well as about their subject, but the biographers of Baby Doe were not so transparent. An examination of the contradictory costumes in which biographers have dressed their subjects can speak volumes about each author's worldview. For example, Edith Gelles's survey of depictions of eighteenth-century figure Abigail Adams in her essay "The Abigail Industry" shows how in different eras Adams was seen as a heroic New England Madonna, a sexualized flirt, a political radical, and (predictably) a woman whose overmothering of John Quincy Adams caused his depressions. In the field of literary biography, Jane Tompkins in *Sensational Designs* demonstrates how various characterizations of writer Nathaniel Hawthorne—as inwardly depressive, sexually obsessed with Puritanism, or gregariously virile—have matched the cultural values of the times and maintained the artist's reputation by dressing him fashionably for each era. When these manipulations by biographers occur in our own times, however, they can evoke controversy and powerful divisions, for they reveal the conflicts in how we think history should be written. For example, critics railed against the biography *Dutch: A Memoir of Ronald Reagan* by Edmund Morris, who chose a bold strategy of interposing himself into exemplary Reagan moments, to "remember" events he never witnessed in order to propel his narrative. Morris insisted that he had ultimately created "his" Reagan after struggling with the insurmountable chasm between the public's affection for their imagined Reagan and the negative private anecdotes that surrounded this president. The highly nostalgic media depictions of Reagan's legacy after his death in 2004 show that Morris correctly assessed the mood of his audience.

The more notorious figures in America—Baby Doe Tabor, Marilyn Monroe, O.J. Simpson—seem to attract sensationalist writers and may never receive serious biographical treatment, but our ongoing obsession with them forms a subterranean biography of our cultural values. For the late twentieth century, O.J. Simpson was surely the strongest litmus test for unspoken assumptions about race, sex, and marital power. The warring visions of O.J. Simpson as sports hero, victim of racism, cuckolded husband, wife beater, either guilty or innocent of murder, revealed the racial chasm within America. More than a decade after the riveting trial for the murder of his estranged white wife, Nicole, Simpson is embraced by some, pitied by others, shunned by many who still consider him guilty. In late 2006, Simpson (or his misguided publicists) reignited this controversy with the promotion of his memoir, *If I Did It.* Public outrage caused his publisher to cease distribution of the book, and television interviews with O.J. were canceled. To me, this demonstrates that powerful (white) Americans still hold the power to silence those they judge to be beyond the bounds of decency. Toni Morrison's collection of essays presents Simpson as the nexus of institutional racism in the United States, a touchstone that reveals an abyss (hidden to many in the dominant race) between the ways in which African Americans and whites perceive justice. Will Americans one hundred years from now still be interested in the gruesome murder photos and the lengthy, internationally televised O.J. Simpson trial? Will Simpson's side of the story be available? Well over a century after Baby Doe committed the heinous crime of stealing another woman's husband and brazenly marrying him before a male-only audience, her story continues to seduce us, a touchstone for issues of sex and power.

In the case of Baby Doe Tabor, certain elements of the legend are uncontested, forming their own Stations of the Cross to be repeated in every version so that one can meditate upon her Passion: the irresistible beauty of Baby Doe; the loss of her first baby; the divorce from her first husband; the electricity between her and married Silver King Horace Tabor; the nasty divorce of Horace from Augusta; the triumph of the Washington wedding and the travesty of its moral controversy; the female shunning of Baby Doe; the doted-upon Tabor daughters; the appalling fall from wealth; temptations from other men, resisted by the transformed/reformed Baby Doe; Horace's dying edict to hold onto the Matchless mine; the sin and early death of daughter Silver; the increasing eccentricity and religiosity of aging Baby Doe; her faithfulness unto the mine; her lonely death and frozen crucifixion. The staying power of these elements and the variations and disputes within the legend tell us more about ourselves than about Baby Doe, who is relegated to the role of mute performer. In this chapter I penetrate the bedrock of the Baby Doe legend, suggest probable motives of the mythologizers, correct the story with historical data, and at last add Lizzie Tabor's "commentary" upon the events and people in her life from her Dreamworld writings that offer a counternarrative to the legend.

IT IS UNCLEAR: TURNING POINTS IN THE LEGEND

December 7, 1922—I had a grand dream of my Harvey Doe. He was with us in our home—my Mother was with us, dear Harvey sat at the Piano as he always did and all at once he sang a grand rich operatic great song his beautiful voice was

strong full and Rich and swelled out in great volume it was glorious we listened &
he sang a long time he was so happy handsome and grand he was so so happy &
we all were with him

Baby Doe: what's in a name? When I first began speaking to audiences about my research on the Tabors, out of empathy and respect I would use the name Mrs. Tabor, the name Lizzie preferred to use in public. When audiences looked confused, I would add, "Horace Tabor's second wife, the young one." Finally someone would enlighten the group (and me, as if I had not thought of it): "Oh, she means Baby Doe." We reveal our values by our choice of names: Is it Mrs. John F. Kennedy, Former First Lady Kennedy, Jacqueline Kennedy Onassis, or Jackie O? Mrs. William Clinton, Former First Lady Clinton, Senator Hillary Rodham Clinton, or Hillary? Mrs. H.A.W. Tabor, Elizabeth Bonduel McCourt Tabor, (my) Lizzie, Baby Doe? Especially in the case of women, a biographer's choice to use an intimate name (women's surnames are so impermanent in a patriarchal society) can signify a special caring relationship—or patronization. Although the name Baby Doe is universally recognized to indicate the second Mrs. Tabor, its origin is unclear, and each explanation of the source of the name establishes the tenor of the tale. If she was dubbed "Baby" by Central City miners because of her diminutive size and angelic doelike eyes, she was initially an innocent. If the name "Baby" was a shortcut for the disrespectful term "Babe," she was a mining-town tramp. When her first husband, Harvey, uses the term in a pleading letter it seems affectionate, but when the much older Horace writes to his "Baby" it seems suggestively Freudian. However, what if the name "Baby" were of much earlier origin, as several scholars suggest? Edgar McMechen argued that Lizzie's status as the babied daughter of the McCourts won her the name way back in Oshkosh. Musicologist Randi Lee Blooding claims the term was used by Lizzie McCourt's mother in correspondence, although I could not locate such a letter in the Tabor collection to confirm this origin story.[1] In an early scrapbook, young Lizzie writes of a suitor whose decoded name is Will: "Oh how he loved me. Yes, he worshiped me and called me his baby," making the source of the name Baby her private erotic secret. What's in a name? It could be family affection, innocent admiration, public leering, a private nickname from an old beau that Lizzie liked and told to Harvey. If the name came from the McCourt family or Will, Lizzie gains the agency of naming herself. However, once the name gains wider use in Colorado, it both distinguishes—and marks—her as a public woman. While some of Lizzie's letters to Horace are signed

"Baby" or "your Baby," I have not found one case of her using the term
"Baby Doe" for herself. Upon marrying Horace, she cherished the name
Mrs. H.A.W. Tabor and when widowed she used it like a knight's shield
when writing to enemies. But in the legend she is never renamed Baby
Tabor. The use of the euphonious Baby Doe forever links her with her first
husband, Harvey, perpetuating her status as a divorcée. In her Dreamworld,
Lizzie remarries Harvey Doe at least twice, while in contrast I found no
account of her famous Washington dream wedding to Horace. Harvey
appears in varying lights—sympathetic, pitiful, even erotic. Sometimes Harvey is in the same dream with Horace. Harvey appears as late as 1922 in
Lizzie's dreams, where she cross-references past specters of her first husband as if keeping tabulation. Thus, while Lizzie was never Baby Doe in her
conscious mind, she continued to dream of Harvey Doe. (One possible reason for Harvey's appearance in the Dreamworld was Lizzie's ongoing correspondence with Harvey's second wife, Ida. It seems Lizzie may have
requested financial assistance from the Does in 1915.)[2]

A next crucial turning point in the legend is the Central City estrangement and divorce of Harvey and Baby Doe. Historians have documented
the high divorce rate that characterized the mining frontier. For example,
Paula Petrik found government data showing one in three marriages failed
in Helena, Montana.[3] Mining was hard on all marriages, and the divorcing
Does were typical rather than unique. But the characterization of Baby Doe
as sinner or sinned upon in the legend depends on who is identified as the
adulterer. Was Baby Doe dallying with Jake Sandelowsky? Was unfaithful
Harvey visiting prostitutes? Or were both the Does philandering in the
morally lax mining town? Susan Lee Johnson in *Roaring Camp* documents
the numerous opportunities for extramarital socializing—and consequent
charges of adultery—in towns where men outnumbered women five to one.
In the Helena region, 25 percent of the husbands in divorce cases charged
their wives with adultery.[4] The fact that Harvey did not make this claim
against Lizzie speaks on her behalf. Lizzie's divorce claim of desertion, on
the other hand, was characteristic of a mining frontier in which women
were less tolerant of their husbands' shortcomings when so many other
men were available. The actual story of the Does is probably more nuanced,
a story of two mismatched people each looking for a misdeed by the other
as a means to end their marriage in an era before the concepts of incom-
patibility and no-fault divorce. But a good western legend requires a villain
and a gunfight (albeit marital), and so the legend writers choose sides on

behalf of Harvey or Baby Doe. This choice—to depict Baby Doe as either unfaithful wife or deserted wife—propels the morality tale. She leaves Central City for Leadville either as an adulterous predator seeking wealthy Horace Tabor and his sexual "appetites"—or a desperate divorced woman to whom Horace offers solace, rescue, and security.

The two earliest so-called biographers, David Karsner (1932) and Caroline Bancroft (1938), tackled the Doe divorce from very different perspectives. Mrs. Tabor and relatives of Jacob Sandelowsky were still alive when Karsner wrote *Silver Dollar*, so he steered clear of any suggestion of an extramarital relationship. Since Karsner's main interest was in the Silver King, he planted the attractive fantasy of Tabor in Lizzie's mind way back during her Oshkosh days when the newlywed Does contemplated the promise of Colorado: "Unbidden thoughts sprang into Elizabeth's mind about this nineteenth century Croesus. What was he like? she asked herself." Having already sinned by feeling lust in her heart for a yet unseen millionaire, Baby Doe is linked with original sinner Eve, while Horace becomes the tempting apple. Karsner describes her thoughts during her impoverished Central City days: "But Baby Doe was dreadfully unhappy. . . . It was all very well, this admiration of the mining camp, but she craved something more substantial, worthier of her beauty and spirit. . . . Baby Doe was a half century ahead of Hollywood and the night clubs, else these might possibly have furnished an immediate escape for her. What a dazzling picture she would have made, wearing a string of beads, a smile, and a leaf from Eve's notebook!"[5] Having undressed Baby Doe, Karsner sets her in search of her "Santa Claus" in the person of Horace Tabor and implies that it was Horace who helped her obtain a speedy divorce. Thus Baby Doe seduces Horace before she is even divorced, making her the adulteress in two triangles. She is the Evelike temptress who precipitates Tabor's fall from grace, therefore a woman who must suffer for her many sins.

In contrast Caroline Bancroft, writing in the voice of Baby Doe, portrays the Central City relationship with Jake Sands as a "very special friendship" that infuriates Harvey, an impotent provider. Harvey is depicted as a mother's boy who returns to Wisconsin, leaving his young wife alone during a long winter in which she discovers herself pregnant. However, Jake is there for Lizzie, and it is Jake who is by her side when she goes into labor: "My baby boy came July 13, 1879, and was stillborn. It was Jake who paid the bills and made all the arrangements. He was a marvelous friend."[6] By placing Jake's name immediately after the birth scene, Bancroft implies the child might be his, and narrator Baby Doe's use of the term "my baby" adds to the sense of paternal ambiguity. But Bancroft, like Karsner, was wary of impugning men associated with Baby Doe, as indicated in her 1937 correspondence with *True Story* magazine over who would bear liability should someone sue. For Bancroft, Jake's most important role is that of the transitional male who first mentions Horace Tabor and his fabulous wealth to the deserted Baby Doe and escorts her to Leadville. Bancroft renders Lizzie an innocent in the case of Tabor, for it is Jake in the biblical role of snake, who first plants the tempting seed of desire for the Silver King in Baby Doe's mind. Later writers speculated more openly that the baby's father might be Jake and in several cases portrayed both men keeping watch at the birth scene. Contemporary novelist John Vernon places both men at the baby's death scene, where they pose on both sides of Baby Doe to form a suggestive threesome while a photographer takes a portrait that includes the dead son.

Wed March 15–1922 I awoke to day with a sadness very great I worried because of my darling children & no money to start up Matchless Mine & no rent money and I asked our Blessed Saviour Lord Jesus Christ to give me wisdom what to do . . . & in a few moments I saw several Visions—I saw all so white & clear a young babys head & face with a small piece of white cloth in its open mouth. . . .

What did real-life grieving mother Lizzie Doe say about her child? Lizzie devoted a page in her mystifying personal scrapbook to her stillborn baby boy that mirrors the ambiguity of the Bancroft biography. Lizzie constructed a touching shrine to her loss, composed of visual and textual elements: it contains a cut-out Victorian etching of a musing angel, a picture of the Virgin Mary holding baby Jesus, a picture of an ivy-entwined cross, and one of the Sacred Heart. At top center is pasted a two-line newspaper announcement about the stillbirth to "the wife of Wm H. Doe." Four poems about a mother's loss and a baby's grave are pasted on the page. At center bottom within a wreath etching, Lizzie wrote her own announcement that omits any reference to stillbirth and claims her parentage:

My baby boy born July 13, 1879, had dark dark hair very curly large blue eyes he was lively. Baby Doe.

(The term "baby" for her child was typical of nineteenth-century naming practices.) In Lizzie's Dreamworld this child, whom she tenderly calls Baby Doe, and the second stillborn son she later bore as Mrs. Horace Tabor would be regular visitors. Lizzie's use of the singular possessive personal

Detail (lower right quadrant) of scrapbook memorial page Lizzie created about her first stillborn son, "Baby" Doe. Envelope with code on it is in lower right-hand corner. Courtesy Colorado Historical Society, Tabor Collection, FF 1438, Tabor scrapbook III, page 2. All Rights Reserved.

pronoun "my" teases us, as does the baby's curly dark hair, for Jake Sandelowsky was admired for his dark good looks. (A full-page picture of Jacob Sands was pasted in a far later scrapbook, next to an article about hidden love that Lizzie had clipped from a newspaper.) Lizzie probably placed real flowers on the page, as indicated by a card that partially covers two of the poems and uses code:

Flowers from my Baby's Grave given 72 by 7y 64v2 [me by my love] Sunday evening September 28ᵗʰ 1879. My sweet baby boy.[7]

This code led Caroline Bancroft to speculate about an affair in her 1955 *Denver Post* article, for secrecy suggests sexuality to post-Freudian minds. But many years later, Lizzie used code in her diary to indicate the beginning of "the change" (menopause), so her Victorian sense of what was private and therefore coded was different from ours. Lizzie also retained correspondence from her various 1870s suitors, including Jake, occasionally expunging sections in a complicated negotiation between saving and censoring. In a letter written her during the 1880 Leadville years, Jake is intimately familiar: "My darling Love. . . . I was up to Central [City] yesterday and thinking of the past made me verry verry sad, looking at the old windows from wich I received many smiles. And to day you would not look at me coming at your door babe I know you are awfull proud, but remember you must not throw such dreadfull blows upon me at once the man [two words obscured by xxxs] once and I believe with all your heart."[8] It is unclear if Jake had always been the unrequited lover who fell under the spell of Lizzie's beauty and did her bidding, or if Lizzie had responded to his passion at the nadir of her first marriage, for there is no record of her side of the correspondence. Jacob Sands is listed as a member of the Tabor Light Cavalry, and Sands was still corresponding with the Tabors in 1894, which indicates that Horace did not consider Lizzie's friend an enemy. In the "Dreams and Visions," Jake appears far less often than either Harvey Doe or Horace and seems to personify past wealth more than past romance. But even when she was sixty-one years old, Lizzie crossed out Jake's last name in an account of a seemingly innocent dream, which shows the ongoing danger of Jake Sands. The self-censoring also shows that Lizzie anticipated an outside reader might someday enter her Dreamworld where Jake could be viscerally vivid:

I fell asleep again & dreamed of lying in bed & looking through the door in another room & seeing my dear sister Tilly lying in a bed & Jake Sands came to her & stood by her bed & talked to her happily he looked fat & fine dressed fine light straw hat on & long gold & pearl earrings hanging in his ears he did not notice me until I called him & he came & sat on my bed I said O my what earrings you have & he laughed & said see they were horrid cheap brass worst kind 5c earrings to make him feel bad I said I am going to a convent he said O no they

should help you with your work. I said I have fixed all fine & taken care of all of
them & you too—March 27, 1918

In this dream, Jake's flashy earrings that Lizzie mistakes for fine ones
could signify both the illusive lure of his modest wealth during her lean
Central City days, as well as the forbidding exotic Jewishness of Sandelowsky, an ethnicity so devalued in mining towns that he anglicized his
name to Sands. She retreats at the dream's close from both Jake's Jewishness and his sensuality by mentioning a convent. In our culture's ideological dreamworld, permeated with misogyny and anti-Semitism, the legend
assumes that Baby Doe and Jake would be in bed together, rather than
merely in league together as a sexually charged but platonic team eager to
take Leadville by storm—she with her beauty and he with his business acumen. We fantasize that anything and everything could happen in the per-
missive mining frontier West.

By the time the legend places Baby Doe in Leadville, it really does not
matter whether she is separated, looking for a divorce, or already divorced.
Because of her beauty and her lack of a husband's supervision, she is a
dangerous woman. Her role in the Tabor triangle—as active predatory
femme fatale or passive tantalizing target for Horace's wanderlust—
depends on the depiction of each of the three principal players in the gender tale. In many ways the threesome in the Tabor legend are types straight
out of the classic western: Horace, the lone magnetic hero; Augusta, the
proper schoolmarm; and Baby Doe, the whore with the heart of gold—and
a lust for silver.

HORACE TABOR AND MASCULINE FANTASIES

We start with Horace, since the legend usually places him center stage. It is
Horace who bears the accolades of masculine power that attracts biographers, even if Augusta helped him earn them. Mayor of Leadville, lieutenant governor of Colorado, Midas of the Rockies, Croesus, Silver King,
Horace reigns, depending on the teller of the tale, as either the avaricious
empire builder brought down by his sexual appetites or, more benignly, as
a lucky millionaire unlucky in the consequences of falling in love with Baby
Doe. The trope of Tabor as gambler associates him with the "manly risk-
taking" of mining, albeit Horace's risk is financial rather than physical.[9] His
later bad investments become high-stakes gambles, with the odds against

him, rather than pig-headed bumbles. Horace's less compelling role as strikebreaking capitalist mine owner is downplayed by the popular biographers (except for Karsner, who had written about Eugene Debs and seemed to relish the irony of Tabor reverting to a job as day laborer). Horace is the personification of the unfettered Old West, rather than a representative of the new West of consolidated capitalism underwritten by an immigrant labor class. Even Duane Smith, who assiduously delineated Tabor's role as mine owner and labor suppressor, closes his study by calling Tabor a symbol of individual opportunity in the pioneer West. Smith, like the Denverites of 1898 he describes, seems willing to forgive Horace's shortcomings: "Purified by the fires of adversity and admired for his uncomplaining attitude, Tabor emerged as the Tabor of old, the fifty-niner, the patron of Leadville, Denver, and Colorado, and a man much beloved for all he had accomplished." Gordon Langley Hall, using characteristic hyperbole, calls Tabor "the kind of man who built empires."[10]

Many Tabor biographers seem drawn to Horace as emperor of a western mining frontier of unbridled male sexuality. In his 1932 book, Karsner portrays Tabor as "prodigal" (he had far too much experience with women to be cast as a naive Adam) and Baby Doe as a wandering Eve, rendering their inevitable mating almost biblical in Karsner's morality tale. In order to marry the sinful Baby Doe who becomes his downfall, Horace must reject smothering/mothering Augusta, which gives him potent pleasure: "He blurted out that he was not going to live with her any more. He had rammed that burning rod down her throat at last. Thank God he had got the searing thing off his mind and out of his hands."[11] Karsner depicts Horace as so sexually invigorated by Baby Doe that he engages in a Leadville orgy hidden from both his wife and his lover. Other male writers who address Horace's sexuality disagree over whether it was so potent that it attracted nubile Baby Doe or it was waning and so desperately needed her, but they all focus on his masculinity.

In the 1932 film, *Silver Dollar,* and in the 1956 opera, *The Ballad of Baby Doe,* Horace has such Freudian-inflected magnetism that both his ex-wife (who continues to try to mother him) and his new wife (who is young enough to be his daughter) join forces near the end to try to save him from economic ruin. In the opera Horace sings in a 2/4 "home meter" that lends a sense of impetuous energy even as he reels from bankruptcy. Tabor manages to stand before his magnificent opera house and sing, "The land was growing and I grew with it. In my brain rose buildings yearning towards the

sky." Penniless Horace, stripped of the capital that had once satisfied his prolific edifice complex, is still man enough to hold the love of two women. Historian Marshall Sprague characterizes the appeal of hypersexual Horace for
the opera creators (and I would argue for men trapped in the 1950s grey-
flannel-suit workaholic syndrome): "To them, Tabor was Everyman, with all
the pathetic dreams of glory of the average male, who had advanced at the
age of fifty-two from dreary subsistence and despairing nonentity to international fame, political power, sexual triumph and inconceivable wealth." Gentleman historian Edgar McMechen, on the other hand, steered clear of
sexual imbroglios and blamed Tabor's downfall on political enemies who
fueled anti-Mormon sentiments in their campaign against Horace as a
bigamist with two wives. (Since Tabor was American-born and not of demo-
nized ethnicity, his detractors were left with one of the few ways to tar a
native-born Anglo-Saxon: Mormonism.) To John Burke, writing in the unset-
tled era of women's liberation that threatened male privilege, Tabor represents the randy good old West: "It almost seemed—and this thought has
struck American men for continuing generations—that a man needed one
wife to help him through the early struggles and another to help him enjoy
his success." Tabor is the alpha-male match for pornographic Baby Doe in
John Vernon's 1995 novel: "His thick hairy body inspired disgust, but disgust
made Baby . . . amorously inclined. In his dirty ear she whispered atrocities.
She thought of the smell inside his pants." While male writers focus on
Tabor's money and sexual allure, Caroline Bancroft, writing her 1950 tale
from Baby Doe's perspective, targets Horace's rich (in both senses of the
word) personality as the key to love at first sight: "Always very well and con-
spicuously dressed, his personality seemed to fill any room he stepped into.
His generosity and hospitality immediately attracted a crowd about him and
he would start buying drinks and cracking jokes with everyone. 'That's the
kind of man I could love,' I thought to myself."[12]

   In Lizzie's Dreamworld, Tabor (or Papa as she often called him) appears
in myriad guises. He is a loving father to their girls, potentially incestuous as
he lies in bed with young Silver, rich, poor, stained with filth and dirty money,
worthy of a marble statue. (His various roles as comforter, guardian, and failure will be investigated as we enter Lizzie's Dreamworld in the next chapter.)
His palpable masculinity at times overwhelmed his dreaming widow:

*Friday January 24–1919—about 3–30 A.M. I had just got in bed for the
night—I could not sleep, in a moment I knew our Tabor was close to me on my
right, my husband Mr. H.A.W. Tabor who died on April 10–1899—he had his*

arms around my shoulders, his left arm around my shoulder in the back and his right arm acrost the front of my shoulders holding me tight his face was close to my face and his mustache long am [sic] beautiful as it was moved over my face. I could feel its hairs on my face and his breath only his same warm sweet breath with that same odor that only his breath had pleasing and sweet no one had that same breath, and his mustache on my face he held his arms around my shoulders the same way all the time, his presence showed health strength youth and a purified condition and state, he was so well and clear and his actions showed how loved and appreciated our love for him and the life and way I had lived and protected his name since he went home to live with Jesus Christ his Saviour. Still holding me around the shoulders his face close to mine his mustache always moved over my face and his breathing on my face, I knew God had sent our Tabor to me. So I spoke out very loud, thus—

> In the name of Jesus is this Tabor?
> In the name of Jesus is this Tabor?

In the name of Jesus Christ Who was Crucified and Died on the Cross for us—is this Tabor? . . . then I was certain it was Tabor—then I asked Tabor in a loud voice thus—Will our Child Silver soon come back to me? Quickly Tabor in a strong clear voice—"Yes"—then in a moment he said "Keep awake" in his own natural firm kind voice—he still held his arms around my shoulders and breathed on my face his mustache moving on my face,—Where my Spine meets my head a strong current made my head bend down on my neck on my right where Tabor stood holding me and my neck in the back pained and then Tabor our Tabor went to God. . . . I got out of bed at once—and my legs from my knees down seemed weak as if I must cross them to walk—this feeling was gone soon. Our Tabor only spoke twice as I have written above.

"FRIGID AND FRUGAL" AUGUSTA

If Horace is the model of a West open to (white) male risk-taking, freedom, and sexuality, poor Augusta Tabor represents all that is undesirable about a woman on the frontier: she longs to return to the East even in the midst of western bounty; she is so cynical she doubts the permanence of the Tabor millions; she is so moral she refuses to dress in glitter and rebukes Horace for profligacy; even as his fortunes rejuvenate him she has the misfortune to grow old. Augusta is the asexual "vinegary" middle-aged wife who constantly reminds Horace of their impecunious past; she signifies stasis while he sees

only the future. If Baby Doe is cast as a compliant Eve, was Augusta like
Lilith, Adam's first argumentative mate? In other words, Augusta has a dis-
tinctive voice: financially shrewd at first but parsimoniously shrewish at the
end, a most undesirable trait for a woman in a story about a man's man.
Thus Baby Doe represents the bad "other woman," while Augusta is the
stereotypical sunbonnet saint in the bifurcated myth of the frontier West,
where there is room for only two types of women. In the film *Silver Dollar*,
Horace's political advisors observe that "the boys" would eagerly vote for
Tabor, "but their wives won't let them." In John Burke's fantasy world of
lusty men bridled in by "biddies," Augusta symbolizes the sad effeminate
state of the former wide-open mining town of Denver: "Prunefaced dowa-
gers and grim female reformers seemingly had taken over and established
a neo-vigilante rule symbolized by the reticule and the rolling pin."[13]
Burke's simplistic division of mining frontier womanhood into two types
glosses over the many ethnicities and classes of women that actually operated in the West, enabling some miners to cohabit with women of color
while planning to marry a "lady" in the future.[14]

In the legend Augusta acts like saltpeter on robust capitalism, dashing
cold calculations upon Horace's throbbing dreams of more buildings, voic-
ing cautious misgivings about the real-life vicissitudes of mining speculation
that could return a man to dust. While money enhanced Horace's masculinity, Augusta was depicted as "frigid and frugal" in the 1935 *Rocky Mountain News* series about the Tabors.[15] I suspect the intelligent Augusta was also
frugal with her body as a way to limit her pregnancies, a birth control
method Daniel Scott Smith identified as "domestic feminism."[16] While most
biographers pay some lip service to her early years as a sacrificing, hardworking pioneer, Augusta's characterization rises and falls like a barometer,
measuring attitudes toward women in the West. In the 1956 opera, Augusta
recounts her sacrifices after she discovers that a pair of dainty gloves she mistook as a surprise for her are actually intended for Baby Doe. In a poignant
aria that reviewers noted was particularly appreciated by Coloradans at the
Central City debut, Augusta laments: "Look at my hands! . . . Hands rough
with working, Cooking, Scrubbing, Mending, Hands that even held an ax
and lifted rocks to build a home. Hands hard with labor. . . . No, they're not
pretty hands. Not like hers, Not like hers."[17] Nevertheless, Augusta's operatic
"home meter" is 4/4 time, reflecting her "foursquare outlook" and the
sometimes dissonant staccato notes render her voice particularly shrill when
compared to that of the melodic Baby Doe.[18] In Augusta's last scene with

Horace, she appears behind an apparition of his critical mother, a plot twist characteristic of the pop-Freudian anti-momism of the 1950s. Moore invented several encounters between Augusta and Baby Doe in the opera that continue to enthrall audiences with the old saw of a catfight between love-struck females. In the opera, as in the 1932 film, Augusta seeks out Baby Doe shortly before Horace's fall in one last attempt to save him from economic ruin. This undermines the notion of Horace's masculine agency and financial potency, for the two women are smarter than Tabor. This scene, however, also undercuts the historically documented financial success of divorced Augusta Tabor, who invested wisely and never looked back. Upon her death in 1895 she left her son half a million dollars—with no legacy for the faithless and floundering Horace. Augusta's financial steadiness is not dazzlingly operatic; it is Horace's meteoric rise to fame and his plunge into poverty that fuel the tragedy.

Augusta is also a cold reminder of Horace's climacteric age, which he tries to forestall through escapades with saloon girls before meeting Baby Doe. In its 1935 series detailing the ugly Tabor triangle and costly divorce, the *Rocky Mountain News* confirmed the fears of older women when referring to Baby Doe: "Encouraged Boyish Traits Augusta Had so Long Suppressed." Gordon Langley Hall, clearly himself in love with Baby Doe, sums up Augusta's problem: "How sour and dried-up she seemed, almost like a withered apple." In John Vernon's novel, an irate Baby Doe tells a wavering Horace to return to his "school-marm" wife.[19]

Whether Augusta's "tragic flaw" is her ugliness, dourness, coldness, or age, she speaks her mind to her foolish husband and ultimately to the public during the divorce proceedings. She embodies the risk women take when they demur, when they voice a critique of patriarchy. Hall writes, "As the years passed, Augusta was growing more tart and outspoken. Hod's [a nickname for Tabor] envious eyes strayed to the beautiful young creatures who had recently invaded the new town . . . and he looked critically at Augusta." As Jane Tompkins observes in her study of gender in westerns: "Because the genre is a revolt against a Victorian culture where the ability to manipulate language confers power, the Western equates power with 'not-language.' And not-language it equates with being male."[20] In the Tabor triangle story, manly Horace is nagged by Augusta's voluminous words, yet he is immortalized for only four words uttered at the very last to his beloved Baby Doe: "Hold onto the Matchless." How ironic that Lizzie, "the second Mrs. Tabor" also ended up being a stream-of-consciousness talker who conversed with spirits and compulsively wrote down long accounts of her experiences. One wonders if Horace had lived to be a doddering old man, unable to support his family, would Baby Doe still go down in history as his faithful wife—or yet another nag? Our cultural heritage is full of stories in which men command women, more or less successfully, to hold their tongues: Jason twits first wife, Medea, whom he has discarded for a younger woman, "You could have stayed in Corinth . . . if you had quietly accepted the decisions of those in power. Instead you talked like a fool; and now you are banished."[21] Shakespeare's shrewish Kate finds acceptance only when her feisty tongue is tamed. The Little Mermaid teaches our daughters that in order to gain his love, you may have to become mute.

Augusta's strong, level-headed voice was revived in 1988 by Betty Moynihan in *Augusta Tabor: A Pioneering Woman*. Moynihan was curious about this aggrieved woman in the Tabor triangle and could find only a tiny pamphlet, by none other than Caroline Bancroft, purporting to tell "Her Side of the Scandal." As part of Moynihan's research, she located Augusta Tabor's great-grandson in France, who showed her Augusta's diary. Taking on misogynist parts of the legend, Moynihan argues that Augusta married at age twenty-four (typical for women of her era) because she was wary of eradicating the civil and legal status she held as a single woman rather than because she was a desperate "flat-chested old maid," as characterized by Hall. The Tabor marriage vows were said for richer and poorer, but the richer Horace became the more he sought to discard Augusta, his mainstay when poorer. Moynihan cites the observations of a man who boarded with the Tabors in 1863: "You should see her place. Nothing slack or careless thereabouts, unless it is her husband. I cannot say that he does much himself, but he never makes fun of her, nor interferes at all and generally helps out when called upon, but he does not do anything on his own accord. As he says, he has to be prodded just like the ox they drove across the plains."[22] Rather than a model of individualism, this Horace is a likable but lazy man who is incredibly lucky. Moynihan creates evocative scenes from the early Colorado years: Augusta left alone on a windswept hillside in a small tent with her ill child while the men in her party go exploring for three long weeks, Augusta hiding gold in her petticoats during trips down to Denver so that thieves would not take it. Moynihan also refutes the association of Augusta with the East by demonstrating that she continued to buy land in Kansas after the Tabors moved on from there to Colorado, hedging Horace's bets on silver with her far surer investment in farmland. In the closing chapter of her revisionist biography, Moynihan describes the many social causes and charitable organizations Augusta Tabor supported after her divorce, turning readers' attention away from the mining-camp mystique of Baby Doe and toward the city-building citizenship of people like Augusta who helped Denver develop.

With the exception of the passage below, Augusta is virtually silent in Lizzie's Dreamworld, where she very rarely appears by name, although unidentified disapproving women form a chorus in a few dreams. In contrast, Augusta and Horace's son, Maxcy, appears more often in the Dreamworld. This near absence of Augusta in the Dreamworld, densely populated with minor figures such as day laborers, is remarkable and raises intriguing questions. Was Lizzie so furious at her social shunning, symbolized by Augusta, that she returned the insult by excluding the first Mrs. Tabor from the only world she could control, her Dreamworld? Was Augusta—in all her trappings of legitimacy as shown in the rare dream vignette below—so deeply threatening to Lizzie that she was a suppressed figure? Was poor Augusta and the adultery (centerpiece of the Tabor legend) so insignificant to Lizzie that she did not even bother to dream of her husband's first wife? This glaring absence undermines the very foundation of the legend of two women battling over one magnificent man, one that inscribes the precarious position of women dependent on male power and money.

> Oct 19–1919—I was on the street in this dream with Lily & Silver standing back of Papa who was talking with some church men in front of the Brown Hotel corners Pap said it was sweet of Augusta to give you this ground for your church & he was feeling kindly to her & I dreamed he was going to leave us & get a divorce we felt sad & terrible. . . . Then Papa Tabor had me on his lap he was sitting down in a big rocking chair he was holding me tight in his arms & kissing me I was lying in his arms & his head was bent down kissing me & he held his dear lips tightly pressed down on my lips all the time kissing & loving me we were so happy all of us he was hugging me & his breath seemed a little feverish not fresh

VISIONS OF BABY DOE AS FLOOZY AND FREAK

The mesmerizing figure of Baby Doe is the fulcrum upon which the entire western morality play balances. She is as complex and contradictory as her name: part innocent babe playing with fire, part ex–Mrs. Doe, prowling divorcée. If she is the sinful seductress of a married man, her fall is deserved punishment. However, if her only sin is her irresistible beauty, leading to ill-fated love, then her fall is tragic. Each person who attempts to tell her story—including myself—burdens Baby Doe with their ideologies regarding gender dynamics, the West, sexual power. Her comely silhouette acts like a Rorschach test administered to each generation, revealing which issues about female sexuality vex it. In her role as the younger woman, Baby Doe is Horace's (and every man's) dream and every wife's nightmare. For men, however, the nightmare occurs when a woman crosses the line between being the beautiful object of male desire and the threatening sexual female so vividly portrayed in the film *Fatal Attraction*. The Baby Doe in Karsner's 1932 book and the film *Silver Dollar* is a sexual predator—perhaps the tool of ironic fate—who ruins the fortunes of Horace Tabor. In depression-era America, hungry for the splendor the book and film depicted, it must have been satisfying to see a millionaire plummet into ignominy and his trophy wife become a penniless widow.

Caroline Bancroft's 1950 *Silver Queen* pamphlet introduces us to Baby Doe as a *former* wanton, a sweet-voiced old woman looking back upon her legendary life. Bancroft describes meeting the elderly Baby Doe in the company of Bancroft's mining engineer father, who was a longtime friend of Mrs. Tabor. While the two old-timers talked about the price of silver and the probability of restarting the Matchless, the teenaged Caroline's mind wandered: "I did not listen—to my shame, now." But Caroline recalled Mrs. Tabor turning her startling blue eyes upon her and observing, "And what a beautiful daughter you have! It is my lasting sorrow that the Lord's work has taken my own daughter." Bancroft returned this favor by creating a Baby Doe who was beautiful, with a "clear and bell-like" voice that would evoke sympathy.[23]

I believe Baby Doe became Bancroft's idealized mother as well as her idealized self: a woman both comely and independent, a woman with a way with words, a strong woman who could stand up to men (even abusive ones such as Bancroft's own father), a woman who would support Caroline financially by becoming her main literary subject matter for fifty years. In return Bancroft kept Baby Doe's side of the story alive throughout the West, helped establish the Matchless mine museum, and became known as the caretaker of the Tabor legend, especially regarding Baby Doe. By 1953, when Bancroft fired off a letter to the *Milwaukee Journal* after it reprinted the story of Lily (Tabor) Last denying she was the daughter of deceased Baby Doe, Mrs. Tabor was conflated with Bancroft's father: "My own father, similar in certain ways to Baby Doe Tabor, profligate with money, cracked about mines in the same way, but to the end rebellious, drunken and sadistic, was never denied by me. At the end of his life, completely ostracized by his own, and by my social set, he lived alone in the mountains and died under much worse circumstances than Baby Doe, Mrs. Last's mother. Baby Doe Tabor lived an exemplary last part of her life—devoted to her religion, penitent, brave, heroic." In response to a *Denver Post* article commemorating the centennial of Baby Doe's birth, Bancroft sent a letter saying that her own research indicated it was in fact Augusta Tabor who had been the gold digger. The 1983 edition of *Silver Queen* includes Bancroft's postscript defending Baby Doe—and herself as a historian: "In other histories Baby Doe had been given the brush-off; as a floosy, when young, and a freak, when old. The other authors gave their sympathy to Augusta, and their research was not too painstaking. My booklet was based on what reporters call 'leg-work'. . . . Among certain sectors, however, I was very much criticized for daring to defend Baby Doe and for writing fictional passages in this booklet for which I still have no proof. But oddly enough in some instances documentation later turned up for scenes that began as invention."[24]

By keeping alive public debate about Baby Doe and her era, Bancroft continued to pique public interest in her pamphlets. She thus memorialized the world of her miner father and her beloved mother, whom she termed "one daughter's fortress." Bancroft needed such a fortress, for in uncanny ways her family mirrored the Tabors. According to biographer Marilyn Griggs Riley, Bancroft's father was a mining engineer who inherited a fortune but eventually drank it away. Her parents' subsequent divorce battle, complete with tales of George Bancroft's infidelities, was fodder for newspapers in the 1920s. My empathetic interpretation of Bancroft's appropriation of Baby Doe contrasts with historian-novelist Kristen Iverson's view that "storyteller-historian" Bancroft "punished" strong-minded unconventional Colorado women Elizabeth Tabor and Margaret ("Molly") Brown in her tawdry booklets. In *Molly Brown: Unraveling the Myth,* Iverson argues that Bancroft and other stereotyping authors "freely amplified, exaggerated, and created their own morality plays about what happened to Victorian-era women who didn't follow Victorian rules."[25] In the case of "the unsinkable Molly" Brown, her bawdy buffoonery was actually invented, as a thinly disguised backlash against a woman who dared to run for public office. Mrs. J. J. Brown's social activism became misrepresented as unfeminine aggressiveness. (See chapter 4 for my own analysis of contrasting caricatures of Molly Brown and Baby Doe.) Admittedly, Bancroft's choice to begin *Silver Queen* with the grisly Matchless mine death scene seems like she is punishing the "formerly beautiful" woman for embodying gender trouble. But what if Baby Doe's "punishment" were read instead as Bancroft's use of "the authority of experience" about the disciplining that strong women—including herself—received in past and present patriarchal culture?

A similar case of female anxiety transferred onto a story occurred in the much publicized 1968 work of psychologist Matina Horner, who thought she identified what became popularly known as "fear of success" in women. Horner asked women to complete the story in a hypothetical scenario: they had just learned of being accepted into medical school and now told the news to their boyfriend. When most of the women created an unhappy scenario, they appeared to exhibit a "fear of success." However, in later studies, Horner discovered that what the women actually feared were the real-life ramifications of success for a woman: strained relationships with insecure males, questioning of their femininity, compulsory unfair choices between work and family. Perhaps Bancroft projected onto Baby Doe the repeated rebuffs and professional deaths she herself had experienced as a formerly beautiful, single, woman writer struggling in a man's world. By 1950 Bancroft was considered odd: a tall, middle-aged, unmarried female in an era when 70 percent of women wed before age twenty-four and unwed ones were "suspect." She still flirted with men but preferred the company of like-minded strong women such as authors Mari Sandoz and Marian Castle. The disproportionate attention she gives to tales of Lizzie's early beauty, which enabled her to snag the mayor's son and then attract Silver King Tabor, suggests that Bancroft understood the rules for ambitious women in the Victorian silver era, and still in the 1950s: gold digging was the only "mining" possible.

While the publishers of *True Story* required that Bancroft's original magazine version of "Silver Queen" use the first-person voice, her decision to retain the illusion that the elderly Mrs. Tabor was the narrator in her 1950 booklet was considered deplorable for a historian biographer. But it radically shifted the gaze away from Baby Doe as an object and let her sweet voice create far greater empathy with the reader than was possible in the other leering pseudobiographies. This retrospective "voice" of an aged Baby Doe offers speech as an antidote to the iconic photographs of the Tabor legend, which silently condemn the former beauty and force her into exile until she becomes the crazy crone. Bancroft undermines the anti-language, anti-woman code of the popularized wild West and compels us to listen to the wanton.

Since Bancroft could not read Lizzie's actual sealed-away words, she interviewed Leadville old-timers as part of her research; several of their letters about Baby Doe reside in Bancroft's papers. These letters display an unbridgeable gender gap that is a mere shadow of the heated emotions evoked by the living Baby Doe. Chief William E. Roberts, writing on behalf of the entire Veteran Volunteer Firemen Association, gave a three-page single-spaced defense of "Mrs. Doe." He recalled in vivid detail the first night he met her at a ball, heard her recite a poem, and was granted a dance: "Oh, what an armful of loveliness, no wonder men went crazy over her charms. She had It, according to the modernits [*sic*], but I say she had a personality that appealed to the male gender, that no other woman of her time possessed." Having befriended Baby Doe until her death, he observed: "As a youth, she may have made a mistake, but later on, she demonstrated beyond all doubt, that she was a faithful wife, a loving Mother, and so remained until the end of her life."[26]

On the other side of the gender gap, Florence Naylor Doty wrote Bancroft to criticize her respectful treatment of Baby Doe in *Silver Queen*: "It would seem there are plenty of deserving people to be lionized and historically publicised, but to take such an unworthy character who did nothing but squander Tabor's millions that his own wife helped him gain, and never put out a hand to help a single soul or to be honest with anyone." She then shared her own observations from 1915: "It was when I started living in Leadville that I got the lowdown on what Baby Doe really was . . . she was a Fifth street woman meaning (Red Light) . . . nobody and I mean NOBODY in Leadville would have anything to do with that 'Fifth Street woman.'"[27] Not one woman's account retained by Bancroft defends Baby Doe. Two elderly women who saw Baby Doe when they were young talked to me after a lecture and confirmed the shunning (to the point of stoning) that she endured. One woman recalled how she noticed, when a young girl, that people would part on the sidewalk to let Mrs. Tabor pass. They stared but never spoke to her. She recalled discouraging a boy playmate from casting stones at the elderly Mrs. Tabor. The other woman wrote: "When I was a child (I am 87 now) she certainly wasn't mentioned in front of young girls!"[28] This wall of social erasure—to have one's very name forbidden in polite conversation—has to my knowledge no parallel in contemporary America.

Aug 25–1921 I dreamed again of taking off my waist & my family was there & that devil of a Mrs. Nellie Irons [?] & when I took off waist it showed all the sores on my back and sholders, I was ashamed

The Tabor Story, published in 1951 by Bancroft's nemesis Edgar McMechen, also opens by inviting readers to gaze upon Baby Doe. But rather than depict her aged corpse as Bancroft did, he describes her beauty as she enters the Tabor Opera House in Denver for the first time as Horace's new wife: "Then a whisper, faint but insistent, ran through the house. It resolved into two words—'Baby Doe!' . . . A woman in deep mourning, devoid of diamonds or ornament, stood there momentarily. . . . Her lovely face and sparkling blue eyes gave a piquant air to the black poke bonnet nestled upon her golden hair. So this was Baby Doe, the mysterious siren of the eighties." McMechen's earlier description of the 1936 CHS museum display that included "intimate" toilette items was almost erotic: "It is as though a faint incense—the essence of Baby Doe's vital spirit—hovers over the cases."[29] His intimate details about the items from her trunks that he had clearly touched several times in his role as estate administrator lend credence to McMechen's claim that he was "half in love" with Baby Doe. By the time I heard of Edgar McMechen in the late 1990s, the story had evolved to claim that McMechen and Baby Doe were lovers, to which I responded in disbelief because he was thirty years younger than she. But this addition to the legend both undermines McMechen's motives for defending the Tabors and resexualizes Baby Doe as a woman who not only seduced Horace, a man old enough to be her father, but then as an aging widow became the lover of a historian young enough to be her son.

The booklets by Bancroft and McMechen were part of a flurry of productions about Baby Doe Tabor in the 1950s that started with the highly successful novel *The Golden Fury* (1949), included a new *Denver Post* series in 1954, the opera in 1956, and a 1959 *Life Magazine* article on "The Frontier's Fabulous Women" that featured Baby Doe as cover girl. Why was the Tabor legend retold in so many forms during the 1950s? I suggest that the subtext for renewed interest in Baby Doe (or more accurately the two Baby Doe's, one an adulteress, the other a faithful old guardian) was the larger culture war over the role of women in post–World War II America. The 1930–1940 era of the strong heroine in popular culture was over, as Betty Friedan demonstrated in her analysis of women's magazines in *The Feminine Mystique* and as Marjorie Rosen showed for films in *Popcorn Venus*. Even in 1950s westerns based on strong historical women, such as *Annie Get Your Gun* (1950) and *Calamity Jane* (1953), "women had to dress down their own independence and dress up their bodies to get their man."[30] Thus while lush Baby Doe graces the cover and interior of *Life*, the text lauds the faithful "Mistress of the Matchless" who followed Horace's orders until she froze to death. Amid the colorful 1950s *Life* ads that link men with alcohol and women with the home, Baby Doe is put in her place: the tiny domestic space within a crumbling cabin. Another cause of gender trouble in the 1950s and 1960s was the Kinsey report findings that females had sexual needs like males and a seemingly endless ability to feel pleasure. Baby Doe was a fascinating embodiment of voracious sexuality so disruptive that it ruined the Tabor marriage and shook staid Denver. Unknown to those who wrote about Baby Doe and read about her, Lizzie had recorded personal, passionate, sometimes embarrassing dreams about herself as a sexual being.

July—21–1913 I dreamed Smith our 1tt4r82y [attorney] wanted to [———] & kept kissing me. . . . I think the dream means trouble

By the 1960s the sexual revolution had begun, and women's bid for sexual freedom and equality brought about a backlash of "punishment" films, according to Rosen. In movies such as *Hush, Hush, Sweet Charlotte,* formerly beautiful actresses portrayed elderly women for whom "sex has failed and dementia has set in."[31] Hall's book, *The Two Lives of Baby Doe* (1962), fits this pattern of disciplining a woman for inordinate sexuality by making a spectacle of her deteriorating old age. The book's color cover contrasts a large Baby Doe bedecked in an ermine cape with a diminutive figure of the baggily dressed older Mrs. Tabor. As Foucault observes in *Discipline and Punish,* in order to be effective as spectacle, the penalty meted out by a culture must exceed the advantage gained by the offender. Thus Baby Doe must be banished from Denver and "sentenced" to thirty years' solitude, a longer time period than the decade she enjoyed as a millionaire's wife from 1883 to 1893. In his chapter "The Greek Tragedy," Hall uses excerpts from Mrs. Tabor's tortured dreams, most of them drawn from previous newspaper accounts, to accentuate her suffering. But Hall, like McMechen before him, does not condemn Baby Doe for destroying the Tabor marriage, which he claims was already on the rocks. Hall says her sin occurred when she married Horace in a Catholic ceremony: "Baby Doe was to spend years as a penitent to expiate what she later believed to be a great sin—the deception of her Church." Hall's generation of biographers could not claim to have seen or met Baby Doe personally, so they relied on oral histories and reminiscences as substitutes. Hall closes his book with one that draws together the two Baby Does, the beauty and the beast. He recounts the tale of the crown of uncorrupted youthful hair on Mrs. Tabor's corpse (which I also heard vividly repeated in 2000) and adds his own moral lesson: "The most amazing thing about her appearance was the mass of red-flecked golden hair carefully arranged like a young girl's about her shoulders. Luxuriant as in her heyday, it still retained the original color, with hardly a gray hair. Baby Doe had spoken the truth when she told Theresa O'Brien, 'When one is a penitent, one must hide one's beauty'."[32]

What is missing from the necro-obsessive visions is an account of all the years in between the "two" Baby Does, years that Lizzie documented in her diary, letters, scrapbook, and dream accounts. When paging through these scrapbooks, I discovered a photo, never before reproduced, that shows her as a middle-aged woman and begins to fill in the blanks of the biography. Lizzie appears to be somewhere between forty and fifty years old. The ringlets of hair on her forehead and her tilted head resting upon a hand make her seem coyly familiar with admirers. Yet her large eyes look tired, as if they have witnessed sorrow as well as divine dreams and visions. Lizzie described some of her visions in letters to dear John Guida, the priest who remained loyal to the Tabors and who wrote back tenderly even as they fell into bankruptcy, "Not a day passes—not one—in which I do not offer my poor prayers for you every one of you in the holy sacrifice of the mass." Clearly Lizzie made amends with some in the Catholic Church, for she recorded in her diary that she attended Communion and received kindly letters from a Father Keenan of St. Patrick's Church in Fon-du-lac, Wisconsin. However, she also pasted in her scrapbook a tiny letter from a priest, James O'Mally of Oshkosh, stating in 1883 that since Miss McCourt and Harvey Doe were married in a Catholic ceremony and Harvey was still living, the church considered her marriage to Horace "illicit and nowise sanctioned."[33] In her middle years Lizzie Tabor, as represented by her scrapbook, is complicated and unfixed, not simply a repentant wanton. No longer Eve, hardly a saint, she is as complex as was Mary Magdalene.

One former Leadville resident's reminiscences of Baby Doe's middle years, as told to him by his father, provides intriguing anecdotes about the previously elided period between biographers' depictions of the Wanton and the Madwoman. The writer, whose father was a business associate of Mr. Zaitz, the kindly merchant who provided Mrs. Tabor with goods on credit, complicates his 1973 letter on Harvard Observatory stationery with this disclaimer: "I am sure I have not manufactured the incident, though I am rather vague as to when it actually occurred." The letter describes how Baby Doe, tired of using a "long steep ladder" to access her mine, tried to restart

Lizzie Tabor in midlife photo found in her scrapbook. Courtesy Colorado Historical Society, Tabor Collection, FF 1438, Tabor scrapbook IX, page 212. All Rights Reserved.

a hoist engine. This resulted in billowing smoke that drew a curious crowd of Leadville residents up to the Matchless, where some men dismantled the device to save the day. However, Baby Doe considered this a plot against her. Even more intriguing is this observation: "Because of my father's close association with Mr. Zaitz, I am in a privileged position to know something of this relationship. But he came home from time to time, recounting to my mother something of 'wild parties' in Baby Doe's cabin at the Matchless. . . . The biographies of Baby Doe all seem to picture her as sitting around, during the Leadville period after Tabor's death, mourning him and dreaming about the past. The records indicate that she was a far more realistic, resourceful woman."[34]

In the 1970s the second-wave feminist movement fueled a national debate about women's power—sexual, reproductive, financial. In his 1974 book, *The Legend of Baby Doe*, John Burke clearly prefers the legendary bawdy old western mining camps to the changing urban West symbolized by "the Denver matriarchy." His book co-opts the twentieth century's sexual revolution and applies it to the frontier, for Burke clearly admires how Baby Doe sexually "liberated" herself from Victorian convention. He faults Horace not for his lust but for his bad gamble in misjudging the moral climate of feminized Denver: "Tabor would have a hard time adjusting to the difference between mining-camp mores and the hypocrisies of a more settled community."[35] Burke argues that the double standard that tolerated other rich men's covert adulteries would not tolerate Horace's attempt to legitimize Baby Doe as his wife. I propose that the transgression that infuriated Denver was not the assault on its moral standards but the one on social class. Western memoirs are full of tales of prostitutes who made their fortune in one camp and then left their past behind to marry a nice man elsewhere, a story that reinforces the bogey of the sexually duplicitous woman. Baby Doe, however, had the nerve to stay in place and embody the social mobility of a divorced woman who regained the privileges of marriage—albeit without its social acceptability. With her ostentatious carriage, her brazen appearances at the Tabor Opera House, her displays of her daughters, she held her ground in Denver—just as she would hold it later at the Matchless mine.

I had the worst & most terrible dream my mouth was full of human dirt of 2 kinds. I thought I would die trying to swallow it I finialy did in agony. . . . August 27, 1919

In John Vernon's innocuously titled 1994 novel, *All for Love*, Baby Doe has a very dirty mouth as well as uncontrollable sexual appetites, which she bequeaths to her tawdry daughter, Silver. Vernon's story strangely mixes Currier and Ives moments taken straight out of Bancroft's book, such as an Oshkosh skating contest scene that first attracts Harvey, with scenes in which Baby Doe uses language inauthentic for a nineteenth-century woman. For example, as she breaks up with Billy Bush, with whom she has been cuckolding Horace, she says, "Billy, go ram a needle up your ass." The novel brings the depictions of Baby Doe full circle, for Vernon is the only person since Bancroft to attempt extensive first-person narrative in his exploration—and exploitation—of Lizzie's sexuality. Vernon's inclusion of a few "Dreams and Visions" reveals his interest in Baby Doe's interior life, to which he laid claim in his author's note: "my subject is the inner life. To base a novel like this one upon fact is to reserve the purest trespass for oneself. The inner life begins where historical knowledge ends, and utterly transforms that knowledge." Lizzie's rich descriptions of her inner world—complete with colors, characters, and surrealistic settings—would have made the novel a radical experiment rather than a male-centered fantasy about the sexual acts of Baby Doe. While Vernon's novel has been blasted by serious Tabor scholars, it does suggest that, rather than being simply crazy or senile, Lizzie inhabited a complex cosmos in which past and present existed simultaneously. In a sensitive passage buried in all the muck of *All for Love,* Vernon tries to imagine the terrain of Baby Doe's mind: "What was it, years later, that made her think it was a dream? Fifty years or so after the fact who could distinguish dreams from memories, or memories of dreams from dreams of memories? Everything happens eventually, even dreams. Nothing stays the same, nothing changes, everything flows in the granite of history."[36]

Baby Doe continues to obsess us in the twenty-first century in various forms—documentary films, Web sites, books—for we remain intrigued with female sexuality that both empowers and endangers. At least three other women writers besides myself are currently working with the magnetic "Dreams and Visions" of Baby Doe.[37] Tolerance for nonrational writing, opened up by the transnational success of magical realism and postmodernism, invites explorations of Lizzie Tabor's Dreamworld. However, simple dissemination of more "Dreams and Visions" does not guarantee greater empathy or understanding of Lizzie Tabor, for we dogged few who are familiar with this "text" from her mind have considerable powers of selection. For example, in choosing which dream of a baby to include in this chapter about the Central City stillbirth, I could have used one in which a woman grabs a dead baby from Lizzie and proclaims to the world, "She has killed one," which could imply that the untidy pregnancy of a child of unknown parentage was terminated by a panicked Mrs. Harvey Doe. Or I could have selected one of the loving dreams of nursing babies, to emphasize the ubiquitous shadow of loss in Lizzie's Dreamworld. I chose to transcribe the dream of the baby with dark curly hair as one that would intrigue, yet not prejudice, readers. Likewise, the "Dreams and Visions" without commentary that I include in the epilogue highlight the visitations from beneficent and horrible spiritual figures that Lizzie Tabor experienced. For each reader, they may confirm that Baby Doe was a veritable madwoman or an aspiring religious mystic. My power, as I stand behind the curtain of the Dreamworld deciding which of Lizzie's visions to bring to light, will be explored later as we enter that world.

THE PLOT TURNS

Sept 22–1921 our Beloved Tabor was up high standing in an open door he was looking down on me as I was walking to Matchless Mine with a working man on a lower road and Tabor strong grand and handsome jolly gay & laughing at us he called at me and said in a gay voice O my sweetheart I wish I were going with you I called back & said I wish you were my sweetheart & he answered O yes my sweetheart & we were so happy loving each other

The fateful meeting of Baby Doe and Horace is the catalyst of the Tabor legend. Who seduced whom? Who is the sinner? And what is the sin? The earliest "biographers" place Baby Doe and Horace at the same Leadville restaurant, where their eyes meet, Horace invites her to his table, and the rest is history. Whether Baby Doe intentionally places her nubile body within sight of Horace's notorious wandering eye depends on the writer's own view of Baby Doe as actively predatory or passively predestined. In Karsner's 1932 book, Baby Doe "had come to this very hotel to seek out the Great Spender, and she had captured him."[38] In contrast, a claim that Horace was the initiator of the affair appeared in Forbes Parkhill's 1951 book *The Wildest of the Wild* and continued into the 1990s with Clark Secrest's *Hell's Belles.* They purport that Horace paid Harvey Doe $1,000 for an introduction to his lovely wife, which would render Harvey both pimp and cuckold in the very wild West. It really does not matter who was the first sinner, for the time-proven outcome when mature male power encounters youthful female sexuality is inscribed in our drama, opera, psyches: Caesar unrolls the carpeted Cleopatra; David gazes upon the naked Bathsheba; Henry VIII is amused by girlish Anne Boleyn. Such powerful men can thrust aside wives and morality in pursuit of lust, but the beautiful young women are vulnerably culpable.

Only Horace and his Lizzie knew the details of their early courtship. Their secret will never be known, for there is a dearth of documentation. Lizzie clearly had an affection for love letters; she retained several from Harvey Doe, Jake Sands, and other admirers. But the CHS archives hold no such letters from Lizzie's most famous lover, the still-married Horace Tabor, until after his divorce. In early 1883 when he was a senator in Washington, D.C., Horace wrote of their wedding plans and gushed, "I love you to death and we will be so happy. Nothing shall mar our happiness for you are all my very own and I am yours from hair to toes and back again. I love you I love you

Kiss Kiss for ever and ever."[39] Horace referred to receiving correspondence from Lizzie, but remarkably few of her letters exist today. While Lizzie saved letters from her lovers, her husband, and later her daughters, Lizzie's letters to Horace seem to have been discarded. Did Horace destroy Lizzie's early missives when he was still married because they were evidence of his infidelity—or was he an insensitive man who simply threw away her love letters? Or were the letters in which Horace and Lizzie documented their illicit passion marked "Burn" and thus purged from the CHS collection before processing?

The question of whether it was Horace or Baby Doe who was the troublemaker continued to interest newspaper reporters, for Lizzie documented in her scrapbooks her contemporaries' confusion over her role in the ongoing debacles of new husband Horace. She pasted glowing accounts of her legendary beauty next to her wedding invitations, but she also saved newspaper articles that condemned her character. During the nasty lawsuit battle with former business manager William (Billy) Bush that revealed Horace's tawdry tactics in pursuit of a divorce from Augusta, the press blamed Baby Doe as instigator of the rift. It was rumored that Bush had once turned the impoverished Baby and Harvey Doe out of their Central City rooms, a wrong she could not forget. Reports converted the blushing young bride into a ruthless harpy: "She is having her revenge now & she will make Tabor pursue Bush to the bitter end. . . . As the Roman poet puts it, 'Dex femina facti'—a woman is at the bottom of it all."[40] Depicted as both beautiful and cruel, Lizzie seemed to enjoy being an enigma to her contemporaries, much as she is today.

FROM RICHES TO RAGS

The legend of Baby Doe recounts in sensual detail the lavish glory that was Tabor: the huge mansion, the beautifully appointed carriages, the splendid gowns and jewels that graced the Silver King's lovely new wife and his darling daughters. The greater the ostentation, the more dramatic the fall. In contrast, biographer Duane A. Smith, whose 1973 book utilized the Tabor archives, told of the millionaire's generosity. For example, Horace opened up the Tabor Grand Opera House during Christmas for children's shows. Lizzie Tabor gave sizable donations to various Catholic churches and colleges in Colorado and Wisconsin and regularly sent funds to Sacred Heart's kindly priest John Guida. But the earlier mythogenic works on Baby Doe inscribed the rags-to-riches-to rags tale without any complicating details of the ill-fated Tabors' social contributions, and they remain obscure.

The denouement of the irresponsible love of Horace and Baby Doe is the fall of the tainted house of Tabor. It is Horace's death that ends the opera, and even a 1978 book dedicated to legendary women of the West effaces Lizzie's years of legendary steadfastness, proclaiming that the saga of Baby Doe ends with the death of her husband "although she lived on for another thirty-six years."[41] The universal cause of the Tabor tragedy is bad judgment. However, the trail then diverges, for some blame Horace for bad judgment in the realm of money, while others say his mistake was in loving Baby Doe. If Horace had remained with Augusta as his ballast, she would have nagged him into saving his money. Irving Stone, on the other hand, argues that Baby Doe's youthful, almost virile, vigor sustained Horace as his fortunes waned: "She was in the full flush of her own maturity and strength, a tower of resolution alongside the crumbling wall of H.A.W's anxieties and desperation."[42] Undoubtedly Tabor's extramarital escapades helped dash his overblown political aspiration, but his financial ruin was of his own doing. The love story was not sad at all for Horace: he was tacitly admired among men for his new showpiece wife, sexually revitalized, the father of a second family of doting daughters, and mourned at death by a gorgeous widow whose decades-long vigil then made the Tabor name legendary. The bitter residue of the love story fell upon the two women: Augusta, who was publicly thrown aside in divorce court, and Baby Doe, who was left a penni-less widow with two young children. In this cautionary gender tale, Baby Doe is blamed or pitied for choosing the wrong prince, Silver King Tabor, as if a divorced woman, new to Leadville, had vast career options or much power to choose. Our culture perpetuates for young women the myth that being beautiful can attract the right prince, as it does for Cinderella and Sleeping Beauty. Yet today's daughters also know the tragic story of real-life Princess Diana of Britain, a woman who "chose" so badly that in fleeing the boring prince (in the car of a playboy prince) she lost her life. Older women recall Jacqueline Kennedy, whose Camelot-like existence all came tumbling down with the assassination of her husband, who was later revealed to be no prince at all but an inveterate womanizer. Do the sagas of unlucky princesses Baby Doe, Diana, and Jackie teach girls that they should rely upon themselves—or that they should become so beautiful (even if it takes surgery to become The Swan) that they will attract a large pool of princes from which to choose?

> *Saturday Nov 1ˢᵗ 1919 I dreamed we had build a house on Matchless new pine for the men to cook & eat in O so many men were there & my Mother & Tilly my Sister we were around such long table I was standing up & was cooking so much bread & dough-nuts & such lots of things in such great quantities & mother said that Tabor made water & so many kinds of minerals came out of him. . . .*

In the Tabor legend fraught with bad choices, the dying Silver King leaves Baby Doe with some very bad advice: "Whatever happens, hold on to the Matchless. It will give you back all that I have lost."[43] The submissive Baby Doe retreats to the Matchless mine, where she will live on and on in fealty to her flawed prince, unhappily ever after. This deathbed edict attributed to Horace is one turning point for the conversion tale of Baby Doe: all of Denver expected the former mining-town tramp to find another sugar daddy. But instead, she obediently returned to Leadville, site of her adulterous conquest of Tabor, where she abided in a cabin on its outskirts as a chaste widow. Those who portray Baby Doe as a sinner depict her conversion as an involuntary one resulting from the economic downfall that was a moral curse upon the errant Tabors. Her long sojourn in the Matchless mine cabin is her penance. More romantic writers attribute Lizzie's conversion to the true love she found with Horace and her daughters, symbolized by her faithfulness to her husband's dying wish. Baby Doe is redeemed through her deference to the great man. As the *Rocky Mountain News* said, in its 1935 series summing up her life and death: "Augusta assumed a dominance. But Baby Doe allowed Tabor to dominate."[44] Thus elevated, Baby Doe joins other self-sacrificing legendary women who symbolically immolate themselves on the pyres of their love: Dido, Cleopatra, Alcestis.

"Hold onto the Matchless," the bedrock of the entire second half of the Baby Doe legend, was probably never uttered by Horace, nor even his idea. Neither respected Tabor biographer Duane A. Smith nor I in our separate research could find any newspaper references to the edict during the 1899 extensive coverage of Horace Tabor's death. Given the detailed journalistic attention to both factual and fantastical information about the Tabors, this absence of Horace's most notable utterance undercuts its credibility. However, when Baby Doe died in 1935, her brother Philip McCourt told a reporter: "Tabor used to say, 'We must keep the Matchless, Phil. There is still money in it.' And that's what he said when he died. Did you know that? When he died he told Elizabeth to hold on to it."[45] Did the aged Phil remember correctly—or were his recollections permeated by David Karsner's book and film of 1932 that first revealed Horace's dying words? Historians who do know myth from reality at the Colorado History Museum still display Horace's purported last edict by his portrait, although they also display storyteller historian Caroline Bancroft's name below as a signal that the quotation is probably fictional. This gesture of both undermining yet still playing with the linchpin quotation of the Tabor myth is surely lost on viewers who take the museum's version of Horace at his (last) word. While the Matchless mine had long been a favorite of Horace's, would he actually request that Lizzie live on the Leadville property, even during the deadly winters?

Within the multitudinous papers of Lizzie Tabor, I have found not one explicit reference by her to any such "Hold onto the Matchless" plea by Horace. While widowed Lizzie often evokes Horace's name in her business correspondence via her signature, Mrs. H.A.W. Tabor, she affirms *her* rights to her property. When she has visions of hosts of devil-men lurking by the No.6 shaft to threaten the mine, it is lone heroine Lizzie who prays to save the Matchless. In the Dreamworld, the Matchless is represented by a young girl dressed in gingham, rather than Horace. What is clear—in the diary, the correspondence, the "Dreams and Visions"—is Lizzie's unflinching determination to hold onto the silver mine for herself and for her heir, Silver. When we enter the Dreamworld in earnest, deeper mining will show how the Matchless evolved to symbolize motherhood to Lizzie, not an inheritance from her husband. It turns the focus away from fealty to Horace and toward a woman-centered tale of an embattled mother and her daughters. I posit that the staying power of the legend's dogged insistence that it was Horace's idea that propelled compliant Baby Doe toward her final fate exposes our bedrock notions about proper widowhood and our lack of imagination regarding women's agency. It is we who hold onto the Matchless edict, as doggedly as we hold onto the idol of (dying) masculine power.

CHAPTER 4

The Bad Mother and Good Widow

"Much Madness is divinest Sense"

> *Jan 31–1918 I dreamed of being in a church & as I went to the Alter I
> passed some of my family standing there a few other people were scattered
> about. . . . O the grand Alter was so big & high and every bit of it was bur-
> nished Gold & in the nitch over the blessed Sacrement stood the Virgin
> Mary and on her beautiful head was draped all the point lace which was on
> Lilys and Silvers christning robe & it fell down over part of the gold Alter
> & the Virgin Mary was alive and it was my child Silver or my Sister Mag-
> gie who was standing in the nitch to represent the Virgin Mary. as I walked
> past our folk I was ashamed for I looked so cheap & poor looking*

Former siren Baby Doe, steadfast during the Tabor bankruptcy, ordered by
dying husband Horace to "Hold on to the Matchless mine," retreated to the
silver mine up in Leadville. But it would take thirty-six years of isolation for
the "conversion" of the Wanton into the Good Widow to be complete. The
sequence of punishments Baby Doe endured in the Tabor legend endgame
makes transparent the vindictiveness of an androcentric culture intolerant
of powerful women. The provocative body of Baby Doe underwent several
conversions: the beauty became the crone; the Denver social interloper
became the Leadville madwoman; the earthly sinner became the costumed
penitent.[1] The still-silent beauteous object underwent metamorphosis,
becoming the pitiable abject. This process of conversion, however, required
a ten-year-long sojourn in a personalized purgatory wherein Lizzie suffered
as the tormented mother of her bad seed, a wanton child. Ultimately, the
redemption of Baby Doe was gained only by sacrificing the pearl of greatest
price, her daughter Silver. After Silver's untimely death in 1925, Baby Doe
was allowed to slip into benign madness as the woman who never admitted

her daughter was dead. Two drawings that appeared in the 1935 *Rocky Mountain News* series on the Tabors illustrate this conversion. In the first, interloper Baby Doe meets gaunt Augusta and it is the wanton's fetching face we are privileged to view. In the second drawing, we gaze upon the face of the lovely Virgin Mary statue and it is pear-shaped elderly Baby Doe in rags who has her back turned away. She prays alone to the Virgin Mary for comfort. The viewer too is comforted—Baby Doe is at last kneeling in humility.

Two Wives of Tabor Met

© Colorado Historical Society

Austere Augusta, the middle-aged wife No. 1 of H. A. W. Tabor, performed the duty of a formal call upon the second, girl-wife Baby Doe. Augusta's calling card remains in Baby Doe's memoirs.

Illustration accompanying the 1935 *Rocky Mountain News* series about the Tabors. Caption reads, "Austere Augusta, the middle-aged wife No. 1 of H.A.W. Tabor, performed the duty of a formal call upon the second, girl-wife Baby Doe. Augusta's calling card remains with Baby Doe's memoirs. Courtesy Colorado Historical Society, Tabor Collection, FF 1438, Ellis scrapbook, page 15. All Rights Reserved.

Second illustration accompanying the *Rocky Mountain News* Tabor series. Now it is penitent Baby Doe who faces away from the viewer. Courtesy Colorado Historical Society, Tabor Collection, FF 1438, Ellis scrapbook, page 20. All Rights Reserved.

107

When eighty-year-old Baby Doe Tabor died in 1935, she was finally trans-
muted into the Good Widow. What is a good widow? She is female, for widowhood seems one profession ceded to women. For most of the professions,
the female practitioner is still the aberration: she is the act*ress*, the aviat*rix*,
the woman doctor. The assumed gender of the widow, like that of nurse, is
female. Widow*ers* are rare and valued commodities whereas most women
are mere vestiges of what was once a couple. The good widow is obedient,
which Baby Doe was to a fault, going up to Leadville in irrational fidelity so
fierce that it may have driven her mad. But what if the pat legend were disrupted by speculating about other reasons for the retreat of widowed Baby
Doe to the depleted silver mine?

THE SHUNNING

*. . . the woman dressed very low necked & elegant sat on the porch with me talk-
ing lovely & O such a friend I lifted up my clothes & showed her my naked thin
legs & said ["]I lost my flesh after the trouble of Silver's when I looked they were
not as thin as I thought." February 2, 1916*

What if Baby Doe were virtually exiled from the city of Denver by moralistic
shunning so icy she was driven away to the social purdah of the Matchless?
The length of time a disruptively beautiful woman must endure being
socially ostracized before earning public pardon is a measure of the outrage
generated by the woman's "crime" and also a mirror reflecting society's
changing values. For example, in the late twentieth century, the earlier marriage-wrecking sins of beautiful Elizabeth Taylor were mostly forgiven when
her aging overweight body, marked by drug abuse and surgical scars, performed as a spectacle of suffering. When one man heard jokes about Taylor
becoming fat (and old), he observed, "They're really making her pay for
having been so beautiful." Film scholar Caryl Flinn has observed that we
have a necrophilic fascination with the death of female beauty, which fix-
ates upon the inevitable decay of sexual icons like Greta Garbo and Elizabeth Taylor. Young and old contrasting photos show them stripped of their
power—their beauty. Thus two Garbo photos fascinate us by being "face to
face with the holocaust of her legendary beauty, which lies exposed for
everyone to see and gasp at like a disaster photo of a plane crash or natural
catastrophe."[2] On the other hand, president-wrecker Monica Lewinsky can
be seen on late-night television as a saleswoman rather than a woman
shunned. Will photographers hound her as she ages?

In the legend Baby Doe moves up to Leadville almost immediately after Horace dies, but Lizzie's correspondence and diary show that she tried at first to stay in place in Denver in order to conduct her business and quietly raise her children. By most accounts, Baby Doe was still an attractive woman in 1899, as we can see by the single midlife photo of her, unearthed from her scrapbook. Her tilted head and luminous eyes are still inviting. Even after Lizzie first moved to Leadville, her correspondence and diary for several years mention trips to Denver for business and social events. Her brief role as a Merry Widow is elided in the legend, which makes only passing reference to wealthy men who made advances to the Widow Tabor and were rebuffed. Lizzie's more active role as unattached widow seeking society and investment support from monied men surely threatened Denverites. If Baby Doe would only go away to Leadville and its seemingly endless winters, she could no longer trouble those who had voyeuristically consumed her voluptuousness while Horace was alive. A modest memoir written by Leadville resident Theresa O'Brien quotes elderly Baby Doe as saying, "I was only forty-five when Mr. Tabor died. I still had my beauty. I could have created many a scandal for that elite who snubbed me down there (Denver), but my faith restrained me."[3]

At last Lizzie Tabor's words speak to the Baby Doe legend. This comment—with its self-consciousness of the power within penance, showing Lizzie's knowledge of her own disruptive presence that required self-restraint—was what intrigued me to know more about her. If we view her as a shunned woman in exile (or self-exile), Baby Doe joins a lineage of other banished female troublemakers: Medea, who killed her father, her brother, and perhaps her sons; Anne Hutchinson, who challenged Puritan patriarchs. In some interpretations of the Medea tale, she represents primitive magic as a dark "other" who threatened to pollute the coalescing Greek state and thus was purged—or even framed for murdering her children by Corinthians who eradicated all of her kin and then paid Euripides to depict Medea as a Bad Mother. To Denver urbanites at the opening of the twentieth century, Baby Doe no doubt evoked memories of a primitive, immoral mining-frontier past they preferred to forget. By shunning her, they could drive the mining-town tramp back to the virtual ghost town of her origins. The harsh winters that made travel almost impossible rendered Leadville ideal for banishment. How ironic that Leadville's remoteness, which allowed Horace Tabor to carouse with Baby Doe in the 1870s, now enclosed her. For her enemies, the Matchless mine up in Leadville became metonymic for the Widow Tabor: barren, isolated, exhausted, forgotten, contained.

THE RETREAT

I dreamed Lily and Silver and I went today with sister Tilly we knocked on the front door & Tilly came walking up the hall to us & she said "O the whole family" I got insulted & the children & I sat down on the side of the steps & after a little the children went in & I left & went to a room I rented & Andrew Haben [brother-in-law] he looked well & strong & fine came in my room & said "May be you will go in a convent." I said no I would not stand to be under anyone but I will live for the poor & I would want my wine etc. . . . May 3, 1915

It is just as possible that Lizzie Tabor had a mind of her own and chose to go to Leadville on her own initiative. Rather than being driven from Denver, Lizzie may have seen isolation as a relief from the big-city fools who had misjudged her motives for marrying Horace and now underestimated her mettle. There could be multiple motives for this decision by Widow Tabor to seize agency in her own fate. If Lizzie chose to spend the last half of her life in religious seclusion, she would welcome the flood of "Dreams and Visions" that put her in touch with the divine and would consider it her calling to transcribe these visitations for future readers. As early as 1906 Lizzie's unique religious state was described by her daughter and fellow dreamer Silver in a letter to Father Guida. Silver recounted her mother's accidental fall into a mine shaft at the Matchless that was witnessed by a man helping them. Silver wrote, "Mr. Atkins was so horror struck that he could not move. He could see her going down fast. Mamma was lifted right out of that hole and placed on the boards beside it and no one knows who did it or how it was done but we know that it was our blessed Saviour."[4] In a 1912 letter to Father Guida, Silver described her mother's miraculous recovery from her sickbed after calling out the name of Jesus and having a vision of a deceased nurse descending from heaven to save her. Silver's letter also provides another powerful motive for Lizzie Tabor's retreat to a religious life, one that is much more believable than that of penance for past "sins." Silver recounts her mother's sadness over the realization that her two daughters were not going to "live for our Savior alone and with her always. . . . Mamma says that all the same this terrible presumption of hers has broken her heart but it now looks as if God is going to give her a chance to serve Him Him [*sic*] in this life."[5] In the cloisterlike Matchless cabin, Lizzie could indeed serve God by recording the exceptional dreams He sent her.

Tuesday Dec 2–1924 . . . O our Blessed Saviour gave me the grand blessing of dreaming of Papa Tabor my darling—husband he came & got in bed with me, he

*said—can't I squeeze in here with you I was in my cot & it was right & modest
he had on his underclothes & he lay there with me & never did I feel in such lovely
Peace with God & all the world O such quiet [unclear word] gentle & peace
Peace had at last come.*

Another possible motive for Widow Tabor's choice to be alone in Leadville revolves around her perception of herself as a mourning lover paying
tribute to her beloved by withdrawing from the world. She had pasted newspaper articles and editorials about her great affair with the Silver King into
her scrapbooks, interspersed with love poems that took her fancy. Clearly
Lizzie was in love with love. The Tabor affair that shook Colorado and the
Washington wedding that gained national notoriety surely linked Baby Doe
and Horace with the world's other legendary misunderstood lovers. Particularly suggestive is a book list found among Lizzie's papers that includes
Abelard and Heloise. It is not clear that Lizzie ever read the book, but her interest in these ill-fated medieval lovers speaks volumes. As a result of Heloise's
pregnancy, she and her tutor, Abelard, are secretly married, despite Heloise's
fears that this will ruin his career. When their love affair is discovered,
Abelard is emasculated and Heloise retreats into the life of a nun. Despite
their separation, their letters to each other overflowed with passion. Lizzie
emulated this faithfulness as a still-beautiful widow who lived in nunlike aus-
terity at the Matchless mine, a site that represented her husband's glory
years and vigor, writing about her beloved's visitations.

When Lizzie Tabor is viewed as a willing isolate, motivated by either religious calling or romantic love, her extraordinary efforts to protect the
Matchless mine become understandable: she demonstrates almost manly
determination rather than madness. There exists a long tradition of religious women achieving an unsexed status, and feminine wives such as
Christine de Pisan and Kate Chopin becoming professional writers when
young widows—ostensibly to support their children. Lizzie Tabor, with two
daughters to support, dedicated herself to what she termed "my important
writing," her "Dreams and Visions."

MANLY-HEARTED WOMAN

Widowed Baby Doe Tabor could not be meek, for she needed strength to
defend her interests. Her rare public writing defended either her daughters
or her property. In her fourth year of widowhood, Mrs. Tabor wrote an extensive letter for publication in the *Denver Post* that drew upon her status as a

beleaguered widow and mother of innocent young girls. She was respond-
ing to the newspaper's report of a lawsuit against Mrs. Tabor, in which she
was depicted as "hollering" from the back of a courtroom. She wrote, "Since
I have had to battle alone with the world and provide for two young children and sustain the sacred name bequeathed them by their honored
father, I have had to do much against great odds, with only good health and
high hopes to support me. I have not carried my grievances into the newspapers, and would not now were it not solely in the interest of my children.
For their sake the public should not be left in a moment's suspense as to the
stain so heartlessly and untruthfully put upon their mother. When I saw their
swollen eyes this morning I then knew that not another day would go by
without the public being apprised [*sic*] of the vile slanders which were wring-
ing their hearts almost to despair." At the end of her long and detailed
description of the fraudulent attempts of her mine lessees who took her to
court, she signed her name "Mrs. H.A.W. Tabor." She employed time-proved
sentiment for orphaned children and a desperate widow to defend herself
against the claim that she was irrational: "instead of 'hollering' from the
back of the room, as represented, I simply answered when I was called upon
to verify a question put to me."[6] It was rare for a woman to speak and write
so forcefully in public, especially a pariah like Baby Doe, but Widow Tabor
again defied gender conventions. Her letter demonstrates her sense that
justice was due her, as well as her refusal to silently bear injustice. This probably only hardened Denverites toward the former hussy who had defended
her marriage to a millionaire on the grounds of love and was now defending her widow's right to his defunct mine as a badge of honor.

Manly-hearted Widow Tabor dressed in a combination of men's and
women's clothing, evidence to onlookers that she had clearly lost her mind
and all sense of feminine propriety. The gender transgressor whose sensu-
ous dresses once accentuated her femininity now wore transgender garb.
When she had long ago donned overalls to help Harvey Doe at his Central
City claim, Baby Doe was admired as feisty. Now dressed in workmen's
clothes, she was pitied as an aging woman who had gone mad. Lizzie most
probably wore men's clothing because she was active at the beginning of
her widowhood in trying to operate the mine herself and later supervised
an array of men who leased options to work the Matchless mine—until she
suspected them of fraud and drove them away. At last, in 1928, another
strong and popular Colorado woman who was familiar with mining came to
her defense. Mrs. J. J. ("Molly") Brown, when questioned by a *Denver Post*

reporter in 1928 about the eccentric costume of Baby Doe, replied in her characteristic straightforward manner: "She is a miner at heart, a miner in manner, and so why not a miner in dress?" Mrs. Brown pleaded for support of Mrs. Tabor, describing her "religious fervor" and the faith that radiated from her "beautiful face." Yet Mrs. Brown also made it clear that she did not know Baby Doe during the time they both lived in Leadville, for that would have reminded Coloradans they were both former mining-camp women.[7]

Baby Doe and "the Unsinkable Molly Brown" were outrageous women who tested public tolerance, but they have received different treatment in the gender morality tales surrounding them. While public sympathy for Baby Doe was widespread only after her death, the conversion of sentiment toward "Molly" Brown occurred when she "earned" respect through one heroic action. Prior to the fateful 1912 *Titanic* sinking that catapulted Brown to fame, she and Baby Doe were both tarred with the same brush: public disdain for "the Irish." For example, during the 1880s Tabor divorce scandal, Baby Doe was depicted as an Irish gold digger who intended to move her large Catholic family of ten surviving siblings to Denver as dependents—while the fact that Protestant Augusta Tabor also came from a family of ten children and had been accompanied west by her brother was never noted by the press. Although Margaret Tobin Brown was thirteen years younger than Lizzie Tabor, both were cast as the same caricature straight out of anti-Irish lore: bawdy, beautiful, social buffoons despite their crude attempts to become proper ladies. Both women married older men who became Leadville millionaires more out of luck than hard work, and both were ostracized by Denver's social elite. Baby Doe's role in the divorce scandal justified her being snubbed, while "high-spirited bosomy" Margaret Brown was simply too boorish, too loud—too Irish—to be accepted.[8]

Margaret Brown biographer Kristen Iversen uncovered another crucial trait these two women had in common that irritated their contemporaries: "Women who lived relatively independent public lives—and stood for the cause of suffrage, as both Margaret Tobin Brown and Elizabeth McCourt Tabor did—were cast as aggressive, flamboyant, 'unnatural' women whose physical characteristics were described as overtly masculine or excessively erotic." Iversen notes that Elizabeth Tabor was a member of the National Women's Suffrage Association, and in 1893, her last year as a wealthy woman, she donated office space to the association in the Tabor building. Iversen speculates that Margaret Brown, who was a member of the somewhat elite social circle of Lizzie Tabor's brother Peter McCourt, must have met Baby Doe. But Mrs. Brown told the *Denver Post* in the 1928 interview that they did not meet until 1927—after Brown's own conversion into the beloved heroine of the *Titanic* tragedy gave her enough social cachet to champion the infamous Baby Doe.[9]

The events surrounding the *Titanic* catapulted one of the two plucky Irishwomen onto a divergent path. By the time of the 1912 *Titanic* tragedy, Baby Doe Tabor, swept away from Denver to remote Leadville, was a footnote in history. Margaret Brown's acts of bravery, on the other hand, made her an international heroine of such stature that even Denver's social leaders were compelled to accept her. While Brown was converted by her actions into an acceptable woman, Baby Doe was seen as an inactive widow, waiting pitifully at the Matchless mine for silver that would never reappear. Brown had the sense to successfully abandon ship and row a lifeboat to safety, but Baby Doe figuratively went down with the ship and joined her husband as they sank into poverty. Brown's post-*Titanic* fame provided an entrée into polite society and softened public gossip about her separation from her husband, J. J. Brown, in an era more tolerant of divorce than the 1880s of the Tabor ugliness. Margaret Brown had her share of problems with her children, but the family reconciled in 1925, the year Baby Doe was fending off reporters' questions about her notorious daughter's death. In 1932 Brown died of a brain tumor, which may have contributed to her increasingly alienating eccentricity. She had only $25,000 left from her earlier millions. In that same year, Widow Tabor suffered agonies over a scurrilous book and film purportedly based on her life, *Silver Dollar*.

Margaret Brown was not victimized by biographies during her lifetime, perhaps because of her social standing, public popularity, her articulate public persona as a former political candidate, and her network of accomplished children. The mythic biographies appeared shortly after her death when she was dubbed "the unsinkable" Mrs. Brown by writer Gene Fowler and then popularized under that moniker in a pamphlet by none other than Caroline Bancroft. Even though the Brown children attempted for years to counteract the growing legend of their mother as a bawdy Irishwoman, which began as a radio play and then continued as a Broadway musical and finally a popular film starring Debbie Reynolds, the legend also proved unsinkable. In contrast, Mrs. Tabor did not pursue a lawsuit against the *Silver Dollar* producers—which only reinforced the image of her as the passive widow. Today, many people learn about "Molly" Brown through the light musical comedy whereas Baby Doe warrants a tragic opera. The beautifully restored Brown mansion is a Denver historical landmark whereas the Tabor mansion long ago disappeared. Baby Doe's home is immortalized by a reconstructed shack in Leadville, a shack as fabricated as the Tabor legend.

Yet the paths of "Molly" Brown and Baby Doe merge in the larger cultural legend that invalidates women as they age, no matter how famous or infamous. Iversen writes, "Our last image of Molly Brown is of an overdressed, overeducated woman who can speak five languages sitting in a gaudy room, despondent and alone. And of course, none of this is true."[10] It is also untrue that Baby Doe sat alone awaiting death at the Matchless mine. In truth, Lizzie Tabor exhibited extraordinary heroism as a Mindful Mother who faced a Dreamworld inhabited by demons—and two difficult daughters.

THE MINDFUL MOTHER OF LILY

Wed Mar 27–1918 I dreamed to day of being in a house and on a big sofa sat Lily and Silver, Lily was about 7 years old and Silver about 2 years old or less she was sitting close to the right hand arm of sofa & Lily was close to her Silver wanted Lily who was care careing for her & loving her to put some pink silk ravlings around her neck for a chain Lily held the ravlings in her finger she would not put them on Silvers neck for fear it would hurt Silver I said that is right don't then went out in the hall & sat down on the floor & cried because Silver was not as she used to be before she left the cabin. . . . In my above dream of Lily & Silver it seemed so lovely to see Lily with Silver for when she was about 7 years old she would be with Silver every minute & Lily would always say "Silver is my baby God sent her to me she is my baby not Papa's & Mamas only mine all mine she is my live doll["] & she would hold her & hug her tight O how Silver would not leave Lily for us—they loved each other so

The legend of Baby Doe is particularly cruel and obvious in its fairytale-like depiction of the two Tabor daughters—Lily so good that she fled her tainted mother and Silver so bad that she died in a flophouse. Biographer John Burke wrote almost gloatingly of Silver, "she would make her mother envy Horace for having been the first to die. And she would present her mother with a tragic riddle: which gave the more pain, the unloving daughter who went her own way, or the loving daughter who resembled her so much it seemed like a Biblical vengeance?"[11] However, Lizzie's correspondence, diary, and spiritual writings vehemently disrupt this image of Baby Doe passive before the punishment meted out to her as a Bad Mother. They instead show the tireless attempts of an active mother who fought with all her resources to save her girls. Lizzie did suffer, especially from unbidden "Dreams and Visions" about Silver, but she also went far beyond the expectations we have of mother-love. In fact, the dominant theme of the Dreamworld is the fight of the Good Mother on behalf of her children. This may be Lizzie's prime motive for saving the accounts of the explicit tortures she endured: to record her meritorious motherly efforts. Lizzie interpreted her nightmarish dreams as portents of danger to her daughters, which compelled her to act. These omen dreams motivated seemingly irrational actions of the Leadville madwoman, who would rush to the telegraph office to demand messages from Silver or to wire money to "Mrs. Ruth Norman" and a dozen other false names Silver employed. And just when the agonizing "Dreams and Visions" threatened to exceed human endurance, God would send a beautiful vision of the Blessed Virgin to lend Lizzie strength. She was solaced by visions of Mary, the mother of Christ, which Lizzie took as a sign of God's compassion toward her as another suffering mother.

In the legend, the eldest daughter, Lily, is cast as the good child in the Tabor morality tale about doomed offspring of sinful parents. It is Lily who, accustomed to an indulged millionaire childhood, rebels at the hard life her mother must offer in Leadville. This mother-blaming Catch 22 in the legend condemns Baby Doe first for being too doting when rich and then for being too destitute. Lily sought out the quiet middle-class life offered by midwestern McCourt relatives and secretly arranged to leave Leadville. The 1962 Gordon Langley Hall version of the legend is the most extreme in depicting this rupture: "Baby Doe could hardly believe her ears when she heard of Lillie's [sic] decision to desert her. . . . Lillie disappeared out of her mother's life forever, never replying to any of her future communications."[12]

> June 18–1918 I dreamed of being with Lily my lovely darling child & my dead sister Maggie she said Lily's Legs are the most wonderfull & beautiful legs in the world but they are not about brain & then she said something about twins & Lily. I am worried about this dream for to dream of Maggie has always meant sorrow to me, & this is the 3 times lately I have dreamed of Lily's legs. Lily had the greatest brain & she is the smartest & best child in this world. . . .

In reality Lily's move to the Midwest was both gradual and consensual. According to biographer Evelyn Furman, Mrs. Tabor and her two daughters traveled to Wisconsin and Chicago in 1902 to visit their McCourt kin. The family concurred that eighteen-year-old Lily should stay in Chicago to help care for her ailing grandmother. As Lily's absence from Leadville length-ened, Lizzie's favorite brother, Stephen, wrote to her, "I am so glad you went to Chicago and you will be glad that you left dear Lily as it will do a world of good and Lizzie, it is real noble and brave in you as I know just how you worry."[13] In the Dreamworld, Lizzie was indeed worried, battling with all her powers against attempts by brothers Pete and Phil McCourt and her sister Claudia to "steal" darling Lily from her. Lily's "visit" continued for years, despite her regular letters to her mother indicating she wanted to come home. At one point when Silver wrote that their mother was sick, Lily even offered to sell her jewelry in order to have money to return to Colorado.

Then in 1908, Lily wrote startling news from Chicago. She had secretly married "the best man in the world," Jack Last, her first cousin. Jack Last was ten years older than Lily and the son of Lizzie's beloved deceased sister Nealie, which must have made the secret love affair seem all the more like a betrayal. Lily wrote seven months later that she had given birth to a baby girl, revealing the reason for her hasty marriage. In contrast to the legend of the Good Daughter Lily being embarrassed by being a Tabor, it was Lily who Silver and Lizzie feared would taint them. Silver wrote Lily on behalf of their mother: "She is praying every minute that you will not leave Chicago to make a visit to Green Bay or any small city or anywhere when [sic] we are known." Lizzie soon wrote a conciliatory letter that insisted, "Come home to mamma and Honeymaid at once do not delay you and dear Jack must always live with us."[14]

The legend's punitive depiction of Baby Doe as rejected mother became "truth" over many years of retelling because no one until the 1960s had access to the Tabor papers documenting the affectionate mother–daughter letters. Their correspondence shows it was the scandal-phobic Widow Tabor who initially asked daughter Lily not to return to Colorado. It took until 1982 for Evelyn Furman's little-known book to deconstruct the Bad Mother image of Baby Doe. Despite the fact that Lily married her cousin, her mor-tified mother soon rallied to send her daughter advice on family planning. Silver wrote, "mamma is in bed prostrate with grief because your baby is weaned. . . . Even though you had very little milk for her you should have partly fed her but still nursed her, her second summer may be a very sad thing for you and us all and mamma is wild with grief because you are prob-ably agin [sic] in the family-way and mamma says it will be but a repetition of her martyred Sister Nealia, one child in her womb, one nursing at her breast, one on her lap, one on her dress at her feet, four scarcely able to

walk, consequently her blood was impoverished and she went to a prema-
ture grave."[15] This advice shows Lizzie an assertive mother providing information she may have learned from her association with the women's rights
movement. It illuminates a candid and frank relationship between a pro-
gressive mother and her daughters as they discussed how to control fertility
despite being Catholic.

In 1911, when Lizzie and Silver paid an unannounced—perhaps uninvited—visit to the extended McCourt family in the Midwest, it took them
over a month to locate Lily in Chicago, where she was living near her Aunt
Claudia. Lizzie wrote in her diary, "Lily did not know Silver & Silver said she
was so changed that I fell sick & could not go to Lily until May 30 I did
not want Lily to see me suffer." However, the eventual mother-daughter
reunion lasted three joyous days: "We spent the evening with our darling
Lily last evening with our pet." Lizzie kept in touch with Lily, sending her
letters, newspaper clippings about the Tabor family, and a book about Saint
Rita. After a 1917 visit from her mother, Lily affectionately wrote, "the children talk of you so often. They don't forget you and often say they wish you
would come again."[16] As late as 1925 Lizzie mentioned in her diary receiving a Mothers Day card from Lily. While Lily's children may have wished to
see more of their Grandmother Tabor, I found no evidence that Lily ever
visited her mother in Colorado, which probably gave the gossips the satisfying impression that Good Daughter Lily had made a complete break with
her Bad Mother.

Lily inhabited a liminal space between Lizzie's Dreamworld and her waking world, especially in the unsettling years of Lily's marriage and sequence
of pregnancies. Lizzie interpreted Lily's presence in her "Dreams and
Visions" to be an omen. She combined a real-world experience of hearing
a loud voice call "Ma" on August 7, 1912, with a vision she recorded on
August 15. Lizzie considered this experience to be very important, as signified by her full married signature and closing annotation:

> *Between 1–2 AM this morning Aug 15–1912 I saw in the dark after I had just
> gone a-bed & I called to Silver & said to her "I just saw in the dark in very white
> letters in writing the name Lily or Lilly very plain & bright & so white in the
> dark.["] Silver & I had just a few moments before put out the light & retired. She
> said O my whats going to happen I wonder why I have seen that Beautiful Vision
> of Lilys Baby & heard the voice call ma & the next day I dreamed Lily Baby
> called Mama just like the voice I really did hear & then to really see the name Lily
> in the dark Mrs H.A.W. Tabor Note all dates*

Lily regularly "visits" the Dreamworld in two different contexts. If she is a young child in the Tabor family, "Papa" and Lizzie reliably rescue her from disasters. However, when she appears as an adult, she is pathetically thin and surrounded by children. As late as 1920 Lizzie was still tortured by dreams of her malevolent brothers Peter and Phil "stealing" Lily, an outrage that had occurred (at least in her opinion) eighteen years earlier. She tried to interpret the cause for her midnight anguishes, which sometimes resulted in what she called her "terrible condition" (probably diarrhea). Lizzie's commentary at the end of the following transcription refers to a marvelous dream she had also recorded for that day about Silver and herself seeing the beautiful heavens open up.

Sept 17–1920 this evening Friday O the devil in his rage put a terrible dream on me . . . my dear brother Phil . . . was in a long black over coat & black hat all black his hair & eyes looked very black . . . he said "lily had a baby it was not quite living ["] or something horrible like that & she is leaving with the Red Cross as soon as they get passes & going to some far off barbous country like Rusher. . . . I stopped walking & fell flat on my back arms outstretched on walk. . . . I said when did you know all this, he said O we got a letter from Lily to day & she told us the whole thing in letter, I nearly died in this devilish dream with grief. Then the devil put that terrible loathsome condition on me & God Jesus saved me O Bless You Saviour our only Lord The devil was mad because God had blessed us with the Stars & Blue sky & White clouds—Peace at last.

Lizzie distrusted her brother Phil, especially in his dealings with young Silver, and her brother Peter had long ago been relegated to what she called her "living dead" in the Dreamworld because he had refused to help Horace avoid bankruptcy. Then Lizzie had a vision, in 1912, of what she called "Lilys sad and living grave" in her poem "Dawn of Sorrow" (excerpted as Lizzie's "aria" in chapter 2). Did some rift—so hurtful that the Mindful Mother destroyed epistolary evidence of it—render Lily dead to Lizzie? (This would explain why Lily Last, when hounded by reporters in 1935, denied she was the daughter of the infamous deceased Baby Doe Tabor.) Lily had long ago joined the host of Lizzie's "living dead," which may explain Lily's waning presence in the Dreamworld as Silver began to dominate it.

SILVER'S "UNFORTUNATE DISPOSITION"

Saw Silver come down a light colored stairs and when she got in the middle she fell in a heap. Silver dreamed she had a basket of grass & a lively green garter snake

was in it & a chicken & put the basket with them in under her pillow to sleep on—
January 16, 1911

In the legend beautiful, doomed daughter Silver Dollar Tabor embodies the sins of her parents, and her death becomes the ultimate punishment for their illicit passion. She is the willful daughter who catapults her Bad Mother Baby Doe into madness. Silver's own words in the pitiable novel she wrote, *Star of Blood*, seemed to foreshadow her predestined demise: "The sins of the father and the mother shall be visited upon the children, even unto the fourth and fifth generations."[17] Silver is by far the most prominent figure in Lizzie Tabor's diary, correspondence, and Dreamworld. Good Mother Lizzie also recorded dreams that her daughter experienced, such as the one above when Silver was twenty-one. Their special relationship as codreamers made mother and daughter particularly close. The Tabor papers show that, even after she had moved away, Silver mentioned her dreams in the letters she wrote to her mother. The papers also document in excruciating detail the long downward journey Silver took through love affairs, dubious careers, and terminated pregnancies before her painful death. In fact Silver is the one actor in the story who is less sensationalized in the legend than she was in real life, as her mother's records candidly reveal. As early as 1913 Lizzie's sparse diary recounts her anguish at Silver's growing rebellion:

> *for fun I rubbed the handle of my old pen knife on the cats back & O my God what a howl she made & what a scene she [Silver] threw herself on the bed & vowed she had no home & what she would do, well this is the last of such treatment I am ever able to endure & God don't intend me to live this life home all day & only watching to see if I could give her a comfort of any kind, she says to me so often shut up stop talking don't talk & such abusive language I never dreamed could be meated out by any one bad or good I shall ever pray for God to change such an unfortunate disposition poor child & how I love her & O God I have taken such good care of her & O my & God has blessed her with Visions to save her forever May 20, 1913*

Lizzie clearly wanted to keep a written record how much her daughter suffered—and how much she herself endured as Silver's grieving mother. Lizzie's candid papers erode the mythic figure of the Bad Mother. They recount her vengeance as she followed and harassed Silver's lovers, the battles she fought with her fast daughter, the trip she made to Indianapolis to rescue Silver from a "miscarriage." Her papers document the devastating results of shunning upon a widow and her daughter. This mad woman named her daughter's seducers, whom she somehow hoped would be brought to justice by those more powerful than a penniless widow. When we enter the Dreamworld in the following chapter, the complexity of Silver and her multiple roles in the "Dreams and Visions" emerge, along with the powerful narrative contained in her letters home, which influenced her mother's spiritual experiences.

Silver's death at age thirty-five is the event to which most of the Baby Doe biographies attribute Baby Doe's conversion to excessive religious devotion and madness. Depending on each biographer's taste for scandal, Silver's drunken death due to scalding is set in a boardinghouse or a brothel. Each generation of male biographers has upped the ante against her, with novelist John Vernon ending Silver's life in the most sadistic scene: "The flat was full of steam. . . . In her brassiere and slip she looked red as a lobster. As she tried to climb onto the bed she slid down, but the parboiled skin of her arms was still wet and stuck to the wet sheets and pulled, turning white."[18]

Kristen Iversen, who is completing a novel called "Night Owls like Us" that is sympathetic toward Silver, examined actual police reports and news coverage from Chicago to both critique the legend and show how it grew in the press. In a small September 19, 1925, *Chicago Daily News* article under the headline "Woman, Scalded, Dies of Gas," the cause of death of "Miss Rose Tabor, a nurse" was attributed to asphyxiation. Iversen suggests this scenario: when the water Silver was heating on her stove boiled over onto the gas burner, it doused the flame, while fumes continued to enter the room. When Silver tried to turn off the stove, she was overcome by the gas, and as she fell, she pulled the scalding pot of water onto herself. By September 21, the *Chicago Daily News* had discovered that the "cabaret zone" victim was the daughter of a famous woman: "Mrs. H.A.W. Tabor has just learned of the most recent tragedy of her tragic life." It called Silver the "estranged" daughter of "her forgotten mother." The article characterized Baby Doe as having been an actress when Horace met her and as not opposing her daughter's stage life.[19] The *Chicago Tribune* located Lily, the other daughter of Baby Doe, who confirmed that the dead girl was her sister, Silver, but disclaimed any similarity to the tawdry side of the Tabor family. By the time the news reached the *Denver Post*, the headline befitted the still evolving misinformation that kept the Tabor legend alive: "Silver Dollar Slain by Fiends of Chicago Slums."[20]

No wonder Mrs. Tabor adamantly denied that this woman who died under questionable circumstances was her daughter. The legendary madness of

Baby Doe is "proved" by her insistence that Silver was still alive in a mid-western convent. Some suspected that Baby Doe was not mad, but crazy as a fox in her attempt as Bad Mother to camouflage yet another Tabor family scandal by denying the death of Silver. If Silver's character was indeed a "biblical vengeance" on her errant mother, Lizzie's belief that her daughter was not dead could be an apostolic act of faith. Within the Dreamworld is evidence that the careworn mother had far more complicated interpretations of Silver's fate, for like Persephone, Lizzie could bring her daughter back from the underworld.

Writings about the Tabors offer a wide range of interpretations for Silver's tarnished character, emblematic that attitudes toward women had changed from the Victorian pure-or-profane binary that categorized Baby Doe. Silver was characterized in the *Chicago Daily News* article as an artifact of the Old West, for with the daughter's passing "went the last type of beauty that had made her mother the idol of Denver." For Tabor biographer Hall, Silver was typical of the Lost Generation, a New Woman who wanted both a career and love, love that she lost when her beau was killed in the Great War. For sexually obsessed writers Burke and Vernon, Silver was both a nymphomaniac who fulfilled their fantasies about female passion and a self-destructive victim of her own unbridled eroticism. Although Lizzie made a note in her diary to look up the definition of the term "nymphomaniac," she had a forgiving mother's interpretation of her daughter's misdeeds. She attributed Silver's mistakes to seductive men who "hypnotized" her innocent daughter into demonic behavior. The "Dreams and Visions" show the extent to which the dreaming mother, through sheer subconscious willpower, recast her nightmare child into a Dream Daughter. But by 1919 even her mother could not deny Silver's cravings for sex, drugs, and alcohol. In the Dreamworld, however, Lizzie still occasionally cast Silver in the role of the dutiful daughter. The ambiguous ending of the following vision account reveals that, while Silver was idealized, she was inexorably moving away from her mother:

> *Aug 12 Tuesday—1919 I had a beautiful Vision today of my darling child Silver she was riding in large carriage going backwards from me she sat alone in the carriage all in snowy white dress & white lace & white lace like cap with light blue flowers around her face her face was beautiful & lovely & her eyes were the brightest she was smiling & holding out both her arms & hands to me smiling keeping her arm & hands held out to me all the time & the carriage was black & going away from me. This was a strong long Vision*

THE GOOD WIDOW

Although Silver's death confirmed that Baby Doe was a Bad Mother, Lizzie's guardianship of the Matchless mine earned begrudging admiration for her tenacity. She did indeed "hold onto the Matchless," even when it was legally no longer her property. The *Rocky Mountain News* reported in early 1934, "Mrs. Tabor, who has kept her lonely vigil at the mine for many years, last Saturday drove away three men who were planning to inspect the property preparatory to its reopening."[21] Sadly, the three men were missives from her benefactor, wealthy banker J. K. Mullen, whom Mrs. Tabor had approached in 1926 on behalf of her Matchless property, which was $14,000 in debt. She told Mullen, a devout Catholic, that she had seen a vision of large hands signing a document and the Catholic clergy with whom she shared her vision led her to him. According to historian William J. Convery, Mrs. Tabor appeared at the banker's home on the night of a terrible snowstorm and regaled him with her tale while fondling and kissing the oversized crucifix she wore. Shaken by this specter and her story, Mullen arranged to pay off Mrs. Tabor's debt in return for her promise to give him the mine title as security. However, she cleverly avoided ever giving Mullen the title to the property. So he eventually foreclosed on the mine and allowed Mrs. Tabor to continue living there under the illusion she still owned the beloved Matchless. Her torturing dreams of dark men skulking around the mine property show how she continued to fret over possession of the Matchless. In 1928 Mrs. Tabor again appeared as a midnight specter clutching her rosary and speaking of God—but this time to Margaret "Molly" Brown, who tried to rally support for the poor widow in a *Denver Post* interview. While the Mullen and Brown efforts to aid Baby Doe were touted in the newspapers, they did not ease the besieged mind of Lizzie, who had dreamed of great things for her mine:

> *December 15–1916 I dreamed today that my darling Tabor threw his clothes pants & vest & clothes on a rocking chair & he said "life with out you is unbearable" ^or impossible^ & he disapeared from me he had gone I put my hand in his pants pocket & pulled out two grand pure gold round pieces one was like a gold pendant about 2 in acrost & thick glittering gold the other was about 2 in acrost & had Mexcan figures on it it was so bright & grand and was round another gold article I can not describe Then my darling Mother came in & around her neck was that gold grand neck chain that Tabor gave me & on one side from her neck down hung Tabor's Fob gold & grand & glittering to her waist. . . .*[22]

Beneath the legend of ungrateful Lily and immoral Silver slowly pushing their Bad Mother toward madness lies a heartbreaking explanation documented by Lizzie in her writings: starvation. The widow wrote in her 1921 diary:

> *This 13 day of December I have nothing to eat not a cent & no rent money God don't let me get hungry—I have had very little to eat lately. Bless God forever*

Many other entries and explicit visions of delicious untouchable foods form a poignant leitmotif in the Dreamworld. Buried in Lizzie's papers that no one could access at first—and no one cared to alter—is evidence that the widow banished by the Denverites was literally starving. This sin of omission is underplayed in the biographies, but it is omnipresent in Mrs. Tabor's writings. Reporters who entered the Matchless mine cabin just days after the death of Baby Doe printed her "weird diary" notations scribbled on a February calendar: "Oh terrible. No food left. On my hands and knees. Need bread. Cold. Suffered alone. Awful blizzard. I saw purple near the ceiling."[23] The town of Leadville cut off water service to the cabin when Mrs. Tabor did not pay the bill, so Lizzie may have gathered her water from the flooded Matchless mine shafts—water steeped in lead. Rather than attribute the growing strangeness of Widow Tabor to malnutrition and lead poisoning, both caused by a community's cold ostracism, the legend focuses on Baby Doe's sensational failure with Silver, turning the blame back onto the easy target: the Bad Mother.

"MUCH MADNESS IS DIVINEST SENSE"

Despite all her trials, Widow Tabor did not sit quietly by her cabin door thinking of Horace, as suggested by the opera *The Ballad of Baby Doe.* I believe Lizzie embarked on a risky path of *strategic madness* in order to achieve her ends.[24] It served society's need to punish Baby Doe so well that it gave her wide freedom from the madding crowd and provided hard-won privacy. In turn Widow Tabor might receive aid from people who stared in horror and pity at the madwoman, just as they had once stared at the beautiful Baby Doe. In his history of insanity, Michel Foucault describes the "ships of fools" that held threatening mad people at bay during the Renaissance. Likewise, when Coloradans deemed old Baby Doe mad, it justified her exile up at the mining cabin, where she could serve out a "life sentence" of solitary confinement. Moralists judged that the hypersexual Baby Doe at last fell victim to her ungoverned desires. Madness was long considered the result of too much passion; for example, "self-abuse" (masturbation) was one route to insanity. Madness was also seen as the inevitable price of tragic love (Tristan and Isolde) or of evil behavior (Lady MacBeth, King Lear). Tragic love and evil adultery were the defining themes of Baby Doe's life. On the other hand, madness could result from excessive religious devotion or obsessive anxiety over one's salvation. Surely Baby Doe's growing religiosity—fueled by her guilt over her sexual trespasses inscribed onto errant Silver—was driving her crazy. The mad person was considered undisciplined, for while all people have "insane" dreams, the sane know how to govern themselves and how to distinguish between dreams and reality. But the madman, according to Descartes, "believes he sees when he imagines." Baby Doe's imagination was so vivid that she conversed with spirits, according to the O'Brien memoir of Leadville days. Theresa O'Brien's mother managed the Leadville hotel where old Mrs. Tabor occasionally stayed. "Mother would scold, 'Goodness, what am I going to do with that old woman? She comes here for the express purpose of renting rooms 1 and 2, where she talks to someone in the spirit world all night, making the roomers very unhappy.'"[25] Old age has also been associated with dementia and madness. Passionate, lovelorn, religious, guilt-ridden, undisciplined, old: everything about Baby Doe, it seemed, destined her to insanity.

July 15–1915 I had a Vision to day of some one holding a gun to shoot some one & of many faces & of many Skulls some laughing & showing teeth & laughing O so many skulls death was all around I hope God will spare all all I fear for the family

It was this kind of mad vision that shocked and puzzled me when I first encountered the writings of Baby Doe Tabor. I had always wondered how a legendary beauty, who had already paid the high price of being ostracized for the love of Horace, would voluntarily give up her seductive power over men so dearly bought, and shut herself up in a cabin. I theorized that her "penance" was actually a feminist performance that formed a daily living rebuke of the treatment she had received. If Coloradans wanted a former bad woman to gawk at in self-satisfied disdain (reminiscent of Hester in *The Scarlet Letter*), then she would provide it with stunning theatricality, dressed to the hilt as their madwoman from Leadville.

When my theory encountered Lizzie's writings, however, I became convinced that she truly entered the Dreamworld of temporary madness and that her religiosity was far more complex than either a calculated public performance or abject penance. Even after thirteen years of immersion in Lizzie's

Dreamworld, I find that she refuses to "stay in place," to be fixed within any theory. She vacillates between mad "delirious discourse," as she records her "Dreams and Visions," and rational commentary, when she emerges from the Dreamworld to pen a description of her experiences. She dresses and behaves at midnight like a lunatic, yet she conducts her mining business in daylight with clever sanity that utilizes her reputation as a touched (and therefore untouchable) crazy old woman. Her scrawled, error-filled hand-writing seems like a madwoman's rant, yet her correspondence in the large looping script typical of an elderly person is perfectly legible and logical.

She joins a lineage of functioning mad people: Margaret Cavendish, known as "mad Madge" for her crazy costumes and the crazier idea that a woman could write in the seventeenth century; or the raving and brilliant Marquis de Sade. Lizzie's madness reminds me of Dr. W. C. Minor, mur-derer and lexicographer, who was the subject of Simon Winchester's *The Professor and the Madman*. Minor, longtime resident of an insane asylum in Victorian England, conducted perfectly rational correspondence as a pro-lific contributor to the *Oxford English Dictionary*. When Minor's situation was revealed, he became internationally renowned as "poor Doctor Minor." Like poor Baby Doe, Minor's madness gained him sympathetic notoriety and precious privacy so that he could continue his writing project.

Lizzie deployed strategic madness when necessary. In her diary notes she described feigning a fit of madness in order to get Silver to leave a lover and care for her raving mother. (In later years, Silver's own sensational mad fits showed that she had learned this lesson well from her mother.) Yet Mrs. Tabor feared appearing too mad, lest villainous plotters could use madness against her as an excuse to wrest the Matchless mine from her. Her "Dreams and Visions" show that once Lizzie "exited" the Dreamworld, she was able to write her logical interpretation of a dream. After troubling visions of Silver, Lizzie noted, "I must get to her" or "This means I must help Honeymaid." Thus she distinguished between the madness within the Dreamworld and the real-world actions she must take as a consequence: writing letters, send-ing a telegram, wiring money. Lizzie's code-switching muddles the border between the rational and the irrational. In some cases, such as this record of 1914, Lizzie drew a literal dividing line between the two worlds:

Dec 21–1914 I saw in a Vision a man reaching to get my bundle but I got it first

---

I was followed by a tramp this evening & barely escaped him this part is real not a Vision

By 1920 the line between the two worlds had become increasingly blurred. Was Lizzie finding a way to integrate her worlds, or was she losing her mind?

> *Then I saw another Vision of two small new pine houses on Dankin Mine (that is telling me they are shipping Matchless Ore.) In my coffee cup to-day I saw a big goat with horns. God help us*

> *July 9–1920—this really happened The enemies sent this eve—about 7–30 2 two murderers to kill me at mine they then hid up near RR Tressell God saved me*

> *Yesterday and to-day the 9 July I saw so many round purple danger lights—and loud knocks on door*

Lizzie was able to escape the Dreamworld when she could not endure its torments by asking for God's help or by performing a religious act such as finding her crucifix, which returned her to the real world and her task of recording "Dreams and Visions." There were times during torments by Silver, however, when Lizzie sought solace from the real world by long excursions into dreams, as we shall see.

THE MADWOMAN IN THE CABIN

The performance of outrageous madness as a personal statement of outrage has a long tradition. Foucault argues that madness is the ultimate rage against an intolerable society: "And this madness that links and divides time, that twists the world into the ring of a single night, this madness so foreign to the experience of its contemporaries . . . makes possible all contestations, as well as total contestation."[26] The madwoman who raves against patriarchy, whether she be Charlotte Perkins Gilman's heroine of "The Yellow Wallpaper" or Mary Austin's "Walking Woman," is central to second-wave feminist literary theory. A host of wild literary figures were examined by Gilbert and Gubar in their classic book *The Madwoman in the Attic.* Their study of nineteenth-century female writers who created fictional madwomen to speak for women mad at their social invisibility was pivotal to my initial interpretation of older Baby Doe. Surely she was not mad, but a real-life mad woman who could no longer tolerate the hateful snubbing she endured from those who would not meet her eyes, yet rudely leered at her. If the face of youthful Baby Doe mirrors our fantasy of powerful beauty, her haggard face reflects the anger of older women as they become powerless social dross.

Three twentieth-century women, in exceptional dissent, wrote empathet-
ically on behalf of beleaguered Baby Doe. The first vote of empathy
appeared in a 1938 letter by Sister Florence, formerly of the Leadville
Catholic hospital where Mrs. Tabor stored trunks containing her "Dreams
and Visions." Written to another nun, it is teasingly discrete, for Sister Florence was sworn to secrecy as Mrs. Tabor's confidante—and she knew how
potent anything said about Baby Doe could be. Sister Florence observed,
"Too well I knew how men treated her—men cheated her right here in this
city (Denver) and the less I say about it the better off the Sisters of Charity of
Leavenworth will fare."[27] In a 1948 magazine editorial, Dorothy Hendee was
bold enough to defend Baby Doe. She depicted the embattled widow
through the eyes of Frank Waters, who had waded in knee-deep snow to
bring Mrs. Tabor oranges in 1934. Tabor's weak, thin voice and frightened
demeanor showed how society's scorn had turned the widow into a hunted
animal. Hendee decried the attempt to humiliate Mrs. Tabor in old age by
the filmmakers of *Silver Dollar.* "With what shall we charge her? Husband-
stealing? No. The charge will not stand. Bad taste and ostentation? Yes. She
was guilty of both upon occasion. Beauty? Yes. Beauty is always suspect especially by those who are without it. But are these crimes deserving persecu-
tion?" Hendee closed, "Thus ends the drama which began a hundred and
five years before. A drama with no hero and no villain; a drama with a cast of
human beings, even as you and I."[28] The third woman to closely identify with
Baby Doe was, of course, Caroline Bancroft, who as she aged became
increasingly appropriative of all things Tabor. Ironically, when she was quite
elderly, Bancroft suffered a sad experience that mirrored her opening scene
in *Silver Queen* featuring the prostrate corpse of Baby Doe. Bancroft fell in
her home, where she lay alone for days, unable to reach anyone for help.

> *Dec 21–1915 I was with out a cent & I did not know where to get food or food
> money but I left it to our Blessed Jesus our God and our Saviour & He sent a
> Lady acquaintance to me & she offered to loan me & I borrowed two dollars from
> her she said I could have more O how good and merciful God is blessed be God &
> His Holy Name I always pay her more than I borrowed.*

Shunned as a wanton, barely tolerated as an aging object of scorn,
Widow Tabor had to perform extraordinarily well as the madwoman in the
cabin to earn a modicum of sympathy from her contemporaries. Consciously or subconsciously, she became a spectacle that satisfied moralists.
As Foucault says in *Discipline and Punish,* "It is the fact of being constantly
seen, of being able always to be seen, that maintains the disciplined person

in his subjection."[29] People who have shared their memories with me tell of being pushed toward Denver store windows when they were young children and told by their parents, "Look, look! Baby Doe is passing by." One woman told me her parents warned her that Baby Doe was a witch. Accounts flourish of people who remember climbing the mountain road to catch of glimpse of Baby Doe at the Matchless. Perhaps some of Lizzie's visions of devils peering in at her from corners of the cabin were actual voyeurs whom the delusional starving woman mistook as spirits.

In turn, the benefit the madwoman gains from "constantly being seen" is that she is not forgotten: always in sight, she is always in mind. Thus Baby Doe is sister to another powerful madwoman, La Llorona, a figure who has for generations haunted Mexican folklore. La Llorona, according to the legend, is doomed to weep and walk along rivers forever as punishment for having drowned her children on behalf of a lover. Like La Llorona, Bad Mother Baby Doe had lost her children and now roamed the streets of Leadville at midnight. La Llorona is said to still inhabit lonely places and to speak with those in need of solace from the weeping woman. People have told me they have seen Baby Doe, years after the date of her death, ignoring my historical objections and insisting on their sighting. She is always seen. This strategic madness gained Widow Tabor some physical aid and perhaps friendship. One woman told me that, when her father offered Baby Doe new shoes, she declined, saying she preferred to wear rags on her feet. If her power came from performing the penitent madwoman, new comfortable shoes would not do. I have been told by numerous individuals that their families anonymously left food at Baby Doe's doorstop. Given Lizzie's litany of hunger in her writing, I wonder if some of these memories are revisionist views of what people think they should have done for an elderly widow. Others insist that trying to assist Mrs. Tabor was futile because she would take no charity.

The debts Widow Tabor accrued and could not repay were one form of indirect charity. Several notes of indebtedness signed by Mrs. Tabor for hotel rooms in Denver were submitted after her death by claimants on her estate. One particularly poignant letter from a family stricken by the Great Depression shows how the appeal of the widowed Baby Doe extended beyond Colorado. Mrs. Clarence Boerner of Ohio wrote the Leadville judge supervising the Tabor estate, "One day I read an article in a newspaper about Mrs. Tabor, stating what a poverty stricken, lonely life she led, realizing myself what it meant to be poor, although having never been lonely, I wrote asking her if she would mind if I wrote her friendly letters and if we

could we would send her a little money to help her. She seemed delighted
to be our friend and stated if we would help her she certainly would repay
us for our kindness." The three-page letter describes the collect telegrams
they received from Mrs. Tabor asking for money. Bills are attached to the
claim, as well as a typed letter with Mrs. Tabor's signature thanking the family for $40 sent to the Denver storage company and the $10 sent directly to
her. Mrs. Tabor wrote, "We expect to open the mine very shortly now and I
will make arrangements to have you hear from me in a very substantial way,
for your wonderful kindness." Boerner's letter closes with a request showing how the legendary mystique of the Matchless mine infected creditors
who grubstaked old Baby Doe: "P.S. Judge Evans, would a person be allowed
to search for silver in the 'Old Matchless' now that Mother Tabor is gone?
Does that belong to the state too? Could we work the mine and search for
silver, will you tell us if we would be allowed or how we could get permission
to do so?" Mrs. Boerner received $10.20 for her claim and no response
about access to the mine—which in actuality had for years been owned by
J. K. Mullen.[30]

As Mrs. Tabor's age and poverty became etched on her face, she gradually earned respect for being a tenacious mining-frontier survivor. People
tell of risking gunfire to visit the guardian of the Matchless and to hear her
story. In 1932 author David Karsner, who had almost completed his book
Silver Dollar (without consulting Mrs. Tabor), made the pilgrimage. "In Denver I was apprised of her peculiarities, and in Leadville they told me she was
a good shot." It took several attempts to gain entrance from the wary widow,
who peered at Karsner with "a wild watery blue eye." By the end of the visit,
however, Karsner was more sympathetic toward Baby Doe and closed his
book with her words: "'Well, Mrs. Tabor,' I say, to make more conversation,
'it must be fine to live away up here in the Rockies, with the gilded sky
almost within reach of your hand, and this mine of silver beneath your feet.'
'Yes, it is,' she says. 'But you have forgotten something.' 'What is that?' I ask.
'God in my heart.' She touches a cross dangling on her tattered blouse."[31]
If the end of legend is dead wrong, if Baby Doe is viewed not as a crazy former hussy but rather as a harassed elderly widow, a woman starving for conversation, family, friends, who met only scornful or curious stares, a woman
literally starving for food despite living in a tight-knit community, the end of
the saga of Baby Doe is shameful. Shameful for those who saw, for those
who "were only following orders" from their parents to stare at—and
shun—an old lady who fifty years ago had been tarred as a Wanton.

I am all alone this Xmas & heartbroken

Xmas Dec 15–1920 I dreamed of great big pieces of the redest freshest juiciest Beef quarters of beef cut in half so even & the butcher kept cutting me of the thickest steaks at least 3 inches thick & all solid meat with small streaks of white fat thru them he cut in to the Liver that formed part of the last steak & part of the Liver was on the red juicy steak the grandest I ever saw. . . .

At the bitter end, Lizzie Tabor may have succumbed to actual madness. The remnants of her last "Dreams and Visions" suggest she could hold the demons at bay no longer. Yet these are only fragments of fragments, because the Matchless mine cabin was repeatedly ransacked after the death of its guardian. Mad or sane, she continued to write. Her final scribbled descriptions of devil visions were written on a large calendar, pictured in the 1935 *Denver Post* but now missing from the CHS archives. At the time of Baby Doe's death, the short samples of her tortured visions printed in newspapers verified the recluse's sleepless suffering and perhaps aided her conversion into the Good Widow. By dying "on duty" at the Matchless mine, Baby Doe Tabor at long last earned the respect she was denied in life. Adjectives such as "faithful," "proud," and "tragic" were added to the moniker "Baby Doe." Leadville memoir writer Theresa O'Brien recalled her mother saying, "Isn't it strange, children? Mrs. Tabor wanted to be famous. Look! Now she IS famous the world over, and the elite are gone and forgotten."[32] The positive spin put on the entire Tabor saga, in which Horace and his "Baby" were now symbolic of the pioneering mining spirit, would have thrilled Lizzie. How she would have loved to paste into her beloved scrapbooks the numerous articles and pictures from the 1935 newspapers about her heroic widowhood. At long last Baby Doe was converted into the stalwart, beloved "Mistress of the Matchless Mine" by poet Clyde Robertson, known in the East as "the Bret Harte of the Rockies." The long poem, illustrated with a line drawing of an elderly woman praying before a pot-bellied stove, closes:

A wildcat wailed on Fryer Hill—
A woman sighed—then all was still.
The last coin of her golden store
Fell from her hand; across the floor
A pilfering pack rat slyly stole
And dragged it off to his robber hole
Still the faithful fingers cling

To a rosary—a knotted string.
A knotted string, where a prayer still lingers,
Clasped in calloused, quiet fingers.
A gutted candle, black in the socket—
A man's face in a tarnished locket—
A lean rat making ready to leap—
A woman, open-eyed, asleep.
She who could write with a scholar's pen—
She who had shone like a jeweled plaque—
Dead with her dreams in a mountain shack.
Holy Mother, grant her peace;
Grant an uncontested lease
Beyond the Great Divide's dark line
To the Mistress of the Matchless Mine![33]

Converted Good Widow Baby Doe now became symbolic of the admirable risk-taking mining frontier for her biographer John Burke: "if Baby Doe Tabor is a legend to match Horace Tabor's it is not because of her dazzling beauty but because of her quest, full of loneliness and privation, for that ephemeral fortune under Fryer's Hill. That search, too, symbolized something about the Old West. It wasn't what you found, but the mystique of the search that was important."[34] Baby Doe was transformed to fit the mystique of the early 1859 individualistic miner—despite the fact that she arrived in Colorado too late, with the wrong husband (and herself the wrong gender) to undertake such a quest. Burke even admiringly linked Baby Doe to another legendary delusional dreamer, Don Quixote.

FROM BABY DOE TO "JACKIE O": PROFESSIONAL WIDOWHOOD IN AMERICA

On May 2, 1919, Widow Tabor wrote indignantly in her diary:

Again this eve they persicute us they Refused to let me take a book from the Public Library because I have no property & our Blessed Father & Husband is the Father of Colorado. God help us.[35]

Was it the denial of library privileges that infuriated Lizzie, or the haunting fear that her husband Horace Tabor—and therefore she as his widow—was being forgotten? To be the Good Widow of a Nobody was (and still is) the obscure and impoverished lot of many women, but this was not the fate

Lizzie Tabor intended for herself. She therefore embarked on the time-proven path of "professional widowhood," which bequeathed a prominent deceased man's honors to his wife. Baby Doe was achingly poor, but rich in recognition everywhere she went as the woman for whom Horace Tabor had risked all. Divorcée Baby Doe knew when she married Silver King Horace Tabor that association with a wealthy husband was her best means of livelihood in a male-dominated culture. After Horace's impecunious death, the only capital she had left was his name and legacy.

Placing Lizzie's experience as Mrs. H.A.W. Tabor in context with that of two other extraordinary widows—Mrs. George Armstrong Custer and Mrs. John F. Kennedy—provides insight into her choices and strategies. Custer and Kennedy form the bookends of widowhood: Libbie Custer embraced the role of Victorian widow as an empowering one, whereas Jacqueline Kennedy eschewed becoming "the Widow Kennedy" and tried to escape that fate. The options and obstacles these three widows encountered form a telling triptych about widowhood in America, a role that most married women inevitably inhabit.

In the case of the second Mrs. H.A.W. Tabor, Horace's famous name—first famous because of his wealth and then infamous when linked with her name—was her widow's dower. By performing extraordinarily as a Good Widow, via the sheer longevity of her role and the degree of her physical suffering, Baby Doe ensured that Horace would go down in history as a man worth her sacrifice. By keeping the name of Horace Tabor alive in the public's mind through her eccentric miner's costume, Lizzie guaranteed that his adventures would be known by twentieth-century post-frontier people. Although after only ten years of widowhood, Mrs. Tabor could not even check out a library book using Horace's name, she was in some ways a "professional widow" who received some advantages as the spouse of a once famous man. For example, Mrs. Tabor lived rent-free on the Matchless mine property eventually purchased by former Tabor associate J. K. Mullen. Lizzie benefited in her final role as Mrs. H.A.W. Tabor from the social tradition of respect given faithful widows, which reached its sentimental pinnacle in the era named for the ultimate widow, Queen Victoria.

In some ways widows had more freedom of action than wives, who were expected to defer to their husbands. If a widow were left penniless, it was acceptable for her to earn a living, as did the successful and beloved professional widow of the nineteenth century, Mrs. George Armstrong Custer, affectionately called Libbie by her biographer Shirley Leckie. Widowed since

George Armstrong Custer's death at the Little Big Horn in 1876, Libbie Custer provides an interesting study in what might have happened to Lizzie Tabor had she been given access to power and a public audience instead of exile. Like Baby Doe, Libbie Custer found herself destitute after George's death, for he had both defaulted on his life insurance policy payments and accrued secret gambling debts. However, charitable contributions from a public sympathetic toward the soldiers Custer fatefully led against the Sioux provided her a modest bridge income. Libbie then faced the crucial juncture in her widowhood. She could follow the traditional route of quietly earning a modest income from acceptable female occupations such as sewing or teaching school and fall into respectable obscurity. Or she could pursue a "career" as "a hero's widow," as suggested by her cousin Rebecca: "When I read in the papers the brief line saying you were in the hospital ministering to the wants of the wounded I thought the mantle of your heroic husband had fallen upon your shoulders. Wear it, Libbie, for his sake!"[36] Thus the "plucky widow," as General Sherman admiringly called her, embarked on a steadfast life course. She created, publicly disseminated, and defended her image of George Armstrong Custer as a golden-haired heroic boy general. Leckie's book wonderfully details the various strategies Libbie employed to become what Custer herself termed "the widow of a national hero," a role she would play until her death at age ninety-one. Libbie dressed herself as a traditional old-fashioned widow, and her ruffled Victorian costume became her armor, much like the outrageous transgender costume became Baby Doe's. It was unthinkable for a gentleman to offend such a widow, so George Custer's contemporaries did not voice their critique of him as an unwise and disobedient soldier. Only after Libbie's death did the iconoclastic studies of General Custer begin, but by then Custer's peers who could have provided damning evidence of his ineptitude were dead. The dutiful Libbie had served as Custer's guardian for fifty-seven years, outlasting them all.

How did Libbie Custer rise from the ashes of her husband's death and debt, while Lizzie Tabor sank? With no children to support, Libbie had more physical mobility. She also had access through family and powerful eastern friends to publishing, which gave her social mobility. Nine years after the Little Big Horn battle, Libbie published her first memoir, *Boots and Saddles*, which she told from the perspective of "the only officer's wife who always followed the regiment." (The fact that Libbie followed the regiment in order to keep an eye on George and curtail his legendary womanizing was not mentioned.) By depicting herself as the boy general's partner, rather than in the paramour role Baby Doe could not escape, Libbie earned comparison to the honorable widow Queen Victoria by one book reviewer. Libbie wrote and published two other memoirs; Baby Doe was busy with what she called her "important writing" and although there are indications that she hoped some day her "Dreams and Visions" would be published, they appeared idiosyncratic and mad. Libbie Custer embarked on a successful speaking career for female lyceum audiences, whereas Lizzie's speaking engagements were limited to midnight conversations with a host of specters. Libbie, through her public speaking, good works, and efforts to erect monuments in lovely sites on behalf of Custer, became known as a beneficent angel, while few people would even talk to outcast Baby Doe, who was herself in dire need of benefactors.

In their old age, however, the two widows' experiences sadly converged: like Lizzie Tabor up in her cabin, elderly Libbie lived mostly in the past, alone. She wrote in a recollection for family, "The hours that one sees people and keeps up the farce of perpetual happiness are few compared with the never ending hours when one is alone with the past, and all those who were nearest have 'gone to the country from which no traveller returns.'" Libbie died at her home on Park Avenue in 1934 and left an impressive estate of over $113,000. Her death was treated with dignity, unlike the publicity surrounding the frozen body of Baby Doe. Libbie was buried next to her husband at West Point. Leckie found it telling that Libbie's flat grave marker was overshadowed by George's obelisk, but this signifies, Leckie says, the cost of Libbie's decision to live a "reflected life." Widowed at age thirty-four and known as quite a flirt, Libbie could easily have remarried. But as her cousin observed, "how much rather would you be the early widow of such a man than the life-long wife of many another."[37] What mortal man could compete with the mythic blond hero Libbie had laboriously constructed of her first husband as she carefully edited their love letters for inclusion in her publications?

Given what we today know about arrogant General Custer, Libbie's task of fending off military critics and creating a monumental hero seems no harder than Lizzie's task of fanning the embers of support for deceased Horace, which began shortly before his death. Penniless Horace received the appointment as Denver's postmaster because of the lobbying of men who affectionately remembered the former Silver King. His funeral was enormous. Was it the lack of access to publishing and a public forum that curtailed Lizzie Tabor's chances of leading the successful life of Libbie

Custer? If Lizzie had chosen to write "The Memoirs of Baby Doe," she surely would have made a comfortable income. But Lizzie's choice—or calling— was to write her puzzling "Dreams and Visions," which only priests could read and only she could understand. Her challenging roles as a Mindful Mother defending her daughters' reputations and as guardian of the Matchless mine foreclosed the route of promoting herself on a lecture tour. She avoided the press and usually did not write for a general audience as Libbie Custer did, and this undermined her efforts to resurrect and re-create Horace for public consumption. Or perhaps within Lizzie's mind there were conflicts about Horace's character that she could not overcome in order to promote and market her husband. Libbie's biographer Leckie had similar misgivings: "I found myself wondering whether she was a masochist, a saint, or a person who had exploited her dead husband's memory in order to sell books and derive income from her speeches."[38] The "Dreams and Visions" that comprise Lizzie Tabor's "memoir" show her as masochist, saint, heroic mother, and much more. The differing fates of the two widows Libbie and Lizzie show how powerful the onus remained of being the unforgiven Baby Doe, former home wrecker and gold digger, a role that trumped that of widow of a famous man.

> Sept 8–1919 I dreamed I was with Mr. L28s28 h2 h5g2d [Lensan he huged] me he kissed me & wanted me & pressed me to him & I felt terrible he said I am going on a trip to California come with me. I said I could not but that I loved him I had that f2638g [feling] very hard 48 72 [in me] & we made love
>
> Blessed God don't let the devil make such dreams come to me I loathe them O my Blessed Saviour I adore you spare me from bad dreams

As Lizzie's reaction to the dream above attests, it was difficult for a beautiful widow to be chaste. Young widow Jacqueline Kennedy's transformation into remarried "Jackie O" illuminates one path available to a widow of high social and economic class. This route was foreclosed to Baby Doe by social opprobrium and her own dedication to Horace. Lest expectations for a Good Widow's behavior be considered a relic of the Victorian era, the life of Jackie Kennedy provides a case study of patriarchy's efforts to control its unattached women. Jacqueline Kennedy, the woman who refused to become our "national widow," became almost another entity as "Jackie O" until converted at the end back into the Widow Kennedy. Like Baby Doe, well-coifed debutante Jacqueline Bouvier had expensive tastes: fine horses, beautiful costly dresses, wealthy men. Jacqueline's mother proved in her second marriage that a woman's route to power and security was through a rich husband. Like Baby Doe, the beautiful Jackie Bouvier Kennedy became the focus of national attention as the lucky wife of the handsome and youthful U.S. president. Unlike Baby Doe, Jackie's social class, sophisticated education, and money enhanced her husband's status.

Tragically widowed in 1963 at the age of thirty-four with two young children, Jacqueline said, "I am a living wound. My life is over."[39] Like Libbie Custer, Jacqueline faced a life decision: she could continue to perform symbolically as the nation's widow, the comforting role she had offered to the deeply troubled country for five years. In return, the nation would hold her in deep affection and respect for the rest of her life. This was the route followed by Corretta Scott King, whose husband was assassinated in 1968. Mrs. King continued to mark the anniversaries of her husband's birth and death, lobbied on behalf of a national civil rights holiday of commemoration, protected her family's interests in Martin Luther King Junior's papers, and defended her husband's reputation. Like Coretta Scott King, Mrs. Kennedy in the role of the beloved president's widow could appear at public occasions for decades to come and declare that her husband was a saint. But Jacqueline knew, as the world soon would know through publications surely as hurtful to her as *Silver Dollar* had been to Baby Doe, that her husband was no saint. After the 1968 assassinations of King and then John Kennedy's brother Robert, Jacqueline feared for the lives of her children and decided she no longer wanted to live in the United States. It could be dangerous being a Kennedy, where she felt the pressures of "the world's obsession with me." So she charted a bold course, moving beyond the shadow of her famous husband to prove that her life was not going to be a reflected one. She told confidant Theodore White, "I'm not going to be the Widow Kennedy."[40]

Jacqueline, sometimes called America's queen, married handsome virtual prince John F. Kennedy, and together they reigned in an ephemeral Camelot. The second time around, Jackie chose a froglike man, Greek millionaire Aristotle Onassis, who had earlier jettisoned his first wife in order to pursue an affair with opera star Maria Callas. Now he (temporarily) dumped Callas for the luminous Jacqueline Kennedy. The world was shocked by this marriage between a thirty-nine-year-old beauty and a philanderer twenty-three years her senior. Some called her a bartered bride. Jacqueline was accused of being a gold digger, much like Baby Doe, and earned a new nickname from journalists, "Jackie O," probably a salacious reference to the hypersexual heroine in *The Story of O.* The world's obsession with Jackie did not end, however. Tormenting paparazzi sold photos of her recumbent in a bikini that fueled public disappointment in the former First Lady's new life as a remarried merry widow. But Aristotle Onassis had the money that could provide for the beleaguered Jacqueline what she craved: he owned an island to which they retreated. Jackie said, "I have a tendency to go into isolation when I'm sad," and thus her heavily guarded island home served as a retreat similar to the cabin of Baby Doe. For Jacqueline Onassis, enormous wealth bought the isolation of the "eccentric," whereas for Baby Doe poverty rendered her a madwoman. And Jackie with her new-found resources eventually emerged from her grief with a mobility that penniless Lizzie Tabor could not imagine. She began to spend time yearly in her beloved New York City and on occasion visited her first husband's grave or directed plans to build his monument, the Kennedy Library. There she housed family papers that will be opened only after the death of her surviving daughter, Caroline; they may contain her version of her life story in the educated, lisping, melodic voice we have come to love as uniquely Jacqueline's. Rather quickly, she and Onassis separated. He died alone in 1975. Jacqueline Kennedy Onassis was again a widow—a very wealthy widow.

The last two decades of Jacqueline Kennedy Onassis's life were productive on many fronts. She overcame her loathing of public scrutiny and championed numerous historical preservation causes. She nurtured books as an editor for Doubleday where her education, taste, and social connections were invaluable in her quest for outstanding manuscripts. And she found love a third time with Maurice Tempelsman, whose situation as a married man was underplayed in the press. But photographers hounded the once beautiful Jacqueline until the end of her life. In fact, a *National Enquirer* cover photo of her in a shapeless stocking hat, her face puffy from chemotherapy, arrested my attention when I spotted it at a supermarket, for she reminded me of Baby Doe. The headlines declared, "In Last-Ditch Bid for Happiness . . . Jackie O to Wed. Pals Say Lover Will Pay Millions to Get a Divorce."[41] The interior story prose, complete with fabricated quotations, was every bit as sensational as the 1938 *True Story* tale of Baby Doe and was the genesis of my meditation on widowhood in America.

After Jacqueline Onassis's death in 1994, the Sothebys auction of her possessions allowed the public to "dismember" her in their lust for relics, just as they had Baby Doe. The items that brought the highest bids were associated with the Kennedy era. Jacqueline's body was transformed back into that of the Widow Kennedy: she was buried in Arlington National Cemetery next to her first husband, President John F. Kennedy. Finally in place and respectable, the Widow Kennedy is no longer referred to as "Jackie O," and my students are puzzled when I mention the name Onassis. In some sense, the Widow Kennedy never left America. While "Jackie O" was cavorting in Greece, we retained Mrs. Kennedy as our Celluloid Widow whose agony was replayed on every anniversary of the presidential assassination: Jackie walking with Robert Kennedy behind the funeral cortege; John-John saluting the coffin of his father as it passed; Jackie benumbed yet beautiful in her widow's veil. How merciful that Mrs. Kennedy died before the 1999 plane accident that killed her beloved son, John. This mercy was not granted to Lizzie Tabor, who, for over a decade in her Dreamworld, foresaw her daughter Silver's endangerment and her glassy eyes as omens of death. In that netherworld, Lizzie brought all her powers as an experienced dreamer to bear on her greatest challenge: a defiant and increasingly promiscuous daughter. As a woman excluded from all social networks and distrustful of her siblings, Lizzie faced a widowhood far less comfortable than the one Libbie Custer constructed and Jackie O uneasily inherited. Lizzie believed she could only call upon God and memories of her beloved Horace as she went on steadfastly alone.

> *Easter Sunday April 12–1925 I am living alone on Matchless mine in Cabin I dreamed early this a.m. in the night of being on a Rail Road track & Rail Road rails & brown ore like earth I had with me a tall rich Oil Painting of Jesus nailed to the cross crucified & a gilt frame about the shape & size of the Painting given to Papa Tabor by citizens of Denver at the Opening of Opera House & I had hard work to handle alone on R.R. Track the Painting of Christ in its heavy frame in my dream early this a.m. Easter I kept dreaming the above all night over & over again all night*

CHAPTER 5

Entering the Dreamworld

Lizzie Tabor Speaks

> God made me stronger and gave me nerve to night to start my important
> writing for months I have had no peace or way to write important things

The face and body of Baby Doe are part of the visual bedrock of western mining history.[1] For 125 years, her limpid eyes have stared out from newspaper clippings, the ubiquitous Caroline Bancroft pamphlets, the opera posters, and now the Colorado Historical Society entryway mural. In this chapter, the authentic voice of Lizzie Tabor speaks from the papers she faithfully preserved. What did Baby Doe's voice sound like? Biographers and oral history informants are unanimous: it was melodic and kind, even in old age. Perhaps she had a voice like F. Scott Fitzgerald's fatal beauty Daisy, a voice that sounded like money. But the voice that emerges from Lizzie's "Dreams and Visions" is fervent, repetitive, and demanding attention. At first, to me, it sounded like the voice of a madwoman. Now it sounds plaintive and urgent, yet interrupted. Lizzie's intense voice is compromised by frustratingly unreadable handwriting, words spelled multiple different ways, and unidentifiable proper names, as if she were speaking from a bad cellular phone connection. Her taunting use of her idiosyncratic code at the most important junctures in her narrative raises both curiosity and irritation, for these are crucial words. There remain only fragments of Lizzie's writings from the last decade of her life, which essentially breaks off the connection and leaves no conclusion. As someone who emotionally stands resolutely in Lizzie's corner, I want her complete story, yet all I face are jumbled fragments.

Fragmented, jumbled, compromised, interrupted. These are telltale signifiers in the history of women's writing. Illiterate medieval mystic Margery Kempe narrated her tale of divine visions to religious scribes for "her" book (a book she could not read), in which she was portrayed as "this creature." Seventeenth-century nun Sor Juana Inés de la Cruz embedded her critique of patriarchy in clever verses, until her plainer prose provoked a bishop to ban her from ever writing again. Emily Dickinson warned, "Tell all the Truth but tell it slant—" and closed Poem 1129 with this lesson: "The Truth must dazzle gradually / Or every man be blind—."[2] Lizzie Tabor, however, wrote with blinding white-hot intensity in her effort to tell all her truth, which survived only in fragments. In geological parlance, however, fragments are exceedingly interesting phenomena. They indicate disruption is happening, that something is undergoing dissolution. How fitting, then, that this disruptive femme fatale left her legacy in fragments that disrupt the legend of Baby Doe.

"MY IMPORTANT WRITING"

Lizzie Tabor left multiple clues within her "Dreams and Visions" that she intended her "important writing" to be read eventually by others. This concurs with the account of a Mrs. Boehmer, who told the *Denver Post* in 1935 of a visit she made to elderly Baby Doe at the Matchless mine. Boehmer recalled that Mrs. Tabor pointed to two paper bags on her cabin shelf and said, "In those sacks are my notes of the past, little stories and explanations of countless visions I have experienced. They are truly my memoirs."[3] While the morass of fragments in no way resembles a "memoir," within its apparent madness one can ascertain the method of an author and editor. For example, Lizzie sometimes worked from sketchy notes en route to developing a final draft of her "Dreams and Visions." Some of her most carelessly scribbled "mad" visions turn out to be first drafts, which became separated from her second versions before my research assistant, Patty Pokigo, and I reunited the two texts. Hours of reading seemingly repetitive "Dreams and Visions" revealed this revision, in which Lizzie first captured the immediacy of a divine experience in a sketchy note and then later rewrote it to her satisfaction. These rough drafts help explain the mystery of her two types of handwriting, one of them a maddening scrawl and the other quite lucid. Perhaps she scribbled drafts in the dark, convinced that the time-consuming process of lighting her lamp would dissipate the power of her dream experience. In some cases, as shown by the photograph of a draft laid upon its more developed dream (page 143), the second account was developed from a tiny first-draft scrap. But in the example below, Lizzie's early draft of a vision appears quite complete—until it is compared to her later version. In this final draft, Lizzie elaborates on the setting, accentuates the narrative's tension through her choice of verbs and adverbs, then adds description to help a future reader visualize her terror. Clearly this is a writer honing her craft.

> *[Version one] Monday morning about 2–30 AM while kneeling close to bed saying my prayers I heard outside my window from low down 2 terrible heartbreaking very loud cries one right after the other very pearcing & sharp from no living person it was a spirit crying it was the Banchee. . . .*

> *[Version two] Sept 13–1920—Monday morning about 2–30 I was kneeling down by the bed praying—and all at once I heard down outside of my window as if low down—and all was so still not anything stirring I heard a loud pearcing heart-rendering shreaking cry so sad and awful, then in a few seconds about a minute it gave out the very same loud terrible cry so sharp so agonizing pearcing the night & so mournfull only twice It cried I got to the open window before the 2nd cry was finished O it was unearthly like the Banchee-Cry. . . .*

In some cases, Lizzie went beyond words to assist her reader's visualization. She drew primitive pictures of demons, of the Virgin Mary playing the piano, of an angel hovering above a mountain in the Dreamworld. Lizzie's work in revising the most vivid "Dreams and Visions" and in illustrating them shows how she utilized two media to re-create her experiences.

The "Dreams and Visions" contain other markers typical of seemingly "private" writing that is intended for other eyes. For example, some Victorian women's diaries contain bracketed explanations for "characters" within their texts, a sign that future readers are anticipated. Thus Lizzie's clarification within an account—"Dr. Kirkpatrick, Dr. Fantz's friend"—signifies her attempt to identify individuals for other readers. In Lizzie's case some dreams, coupled with the diary, form a *testimonio* of wrongs committed, which shows her clear motivation to clearly name the wrongdoers. Lizzie also labored to identify recurring figures in her Dreamworld, such as the little Matchless Mine Girl costumed in her signature gingham dress. Yet sometimes Lizzie carefully coded the names of pivotal people in both her

Thursday March 3 - 1921 - I had a terrible —
dream to-dey I was in a room (cheap) & on the
window sill was a cup with small brown —
papers & each paper had dope in it, the little brown
papers were in a little white cup. I heard my own
dear Boining Phil come to my door so I quickly
locked it for I knew he was coming to get the—
dope out of the little brown papers in the cup & he
knocked & tried to open door but he could not then
he climbed up to break in the transome then
I opened the door & poor dear Phil fell down
in the room on the floor his poor face was
as white as snow & his hair & eyes were so
black he looked terrible he had a little black
satchel in his hand — Some one I dont know
who, had put the dope on the window sill
& it belonged to them it was theirs —
O I am so sad about this terrible dream
of Phil God protect him for us all, Dear God

I also dreamed of having a beautiful
new kind of white writing paper it
seemed transparent but for writing, only
a small few pieces like an long envelope
& several more " but lovely something
so new - then I had a common white
long envelope

march 3 - 1921
dreamed of Phil
dope in little brown
papers in cup
Phil fell in door
white after
dope

Draft (lower triangle-shaped paper) and revised version of a 1921 dream.
Note that Lizzie wrote "copied" twice on the draft. Courtesy Colorado Historical Society, Tabor Collection, FF 994. All Rights Reserved.

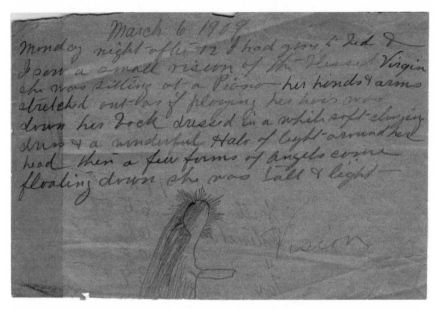

Drawing of blessed Virgin Mary from 1909 account of a vision. Courtesy Colorado Historical Society, Tabor Collection, FF 922. All Rights Reserved.

diary and spirit accounts. This suggests that Widow Tabor knew her writing was not only important but would be endangered if it were to fall into the hands of those she suspected of plotting against her. Her coding—of vowels as sequential numbers (a = 1, e = 2, etc.) combined with a slightly inconsistent coding of consonants—rarely hides an identity. Rather, the code actually highlights a name by arresting the reader's eye, piquing her curiosity, teasing her to decipher the name. Such coding, used by diarists from Samuel Pepys to "ordinary" pioneer women to today's sexually active teens, is another indicator that the writer anticipates a future audience with whom they can match wits. In Lizzie's text, her use of the obvious "S36v2r" to indicate daughter Silver doing shameful acts in the real and Dreamworlds, stops the skimming eye and calls attention to Silver's misdeeds—and therefore to the Good Mother's burden. If our dreams themselves are codes that attempt to tell us psychological truths obliquely, as scholar Janet Jacobs suggests, then these codes-within-codes conceal—and beckon one into—the labyrinth of Lizzie's mind.[4]

A final sign that Lizzie felt her writing had significance was her assiduous attention to the date and time in which a dream or a vision occurred. She

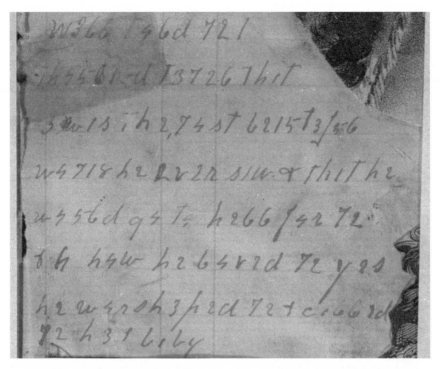

Coded page detail from Lizzie's scrapbook: "Will told me a thousand times that I was the most beautiful woman he ever saw & that he would go to hell for me. Oh how he loved me yes. He worshiped me and called me his baby." Courtesy Colorado Historical Society, Tabor Collection, FF 1438, Tabor scrapbook VII, page 10. All Rights Reserved.

was determined to record the accurate sequence of events within the two worlds she inhabited, especially when she took a dream to be an omen concerning the future. She made notations on both the dream account and the diary entry, cross-referencing the connection between the two, in essence "validating" her ability to foretell the future by attentiveness to her dreams. In a world that Lizzie perceived as increasingly hostile, the need to document every threat by shadowy evildoers—corporeal and spiritual—must have fed upon itself. Although life-writing scholar Jennifer Sinor has convincingly argued that ordinary journal writing need not "story" in order to be valuable, Lizzie worked hard to create a logical story out of her extraordinary, seemingly illogical Dreamworld experiences.[5]

June 12–1915—I went to the Post Office after 12 P.M. [A.M.] as I neared the corner of 9th St where Lamie the black cat died I saw a spirit of a man standing

under the Electric light & it quickly vanished before my eyes I said O that tells me
there is danger ahead of me but I said I am not afraid. . . .

If Lizzie burned to tell her story, her "Dreams and Visions"—written on flattened brown paper bags, the backs of telegram forms, the margins of newspapers—frustrate the reader. Lizzie's physical poverty was at war with her writing project, for as Virginia Woolf sagely observed in *A Room of One's Own*, great works of writing may seem ethereal, "but are the work of suffering human beings, and are attached to grossly material things, like health and money and the houses we live in."[6] Like desperate diarists on the Overland Trail or aboard missionary ships, Lizzie lacked writing paper, and this compromised her work. Transcriptions dated 1915 and 1917 exist on a single page, suggesting that Lizzie had writings covering several years close at hand, perhaps rereading them for omens and portents she hoped to understand in retrospect. It seems inconsistent that this maligned woman would laboriously write and revise thousands of "Dreams and Visions," only to leave them lying around in her vulnerable cabin. Lizzie had cheated death by starvation and by accident so many times that these miracles may have convinced her she would never die. Perhaps Lizzie believed she had time enough to write her memoirs, even as she approached age eighty. As her distrust of outsiders grew, Lizzie may have trusted only God to protect her important writings, just as He had oftentimes preserved her.

Did Lizzie develop a filing system for the "Dreams and Visions" that she was recording sometimes at the rate of 350 a year, a system destroyed in 1935 by pilfering treasure hunters at the Matchless? Posthumous inventory reports concerning the possessions Mrs. Tabor left with nuns at Leadville's St. Vincent's Hospital describe "bundles" of papers. I wonder if the papers she had put into gunny sacks stored there were originally tied in chronological bundles, for Lizzie wrote "copied and filed" on the back side of various fragments. Perhaps Lizzie Tabor, like secretive Emily Dickinson, created "books" out of twine-bound bundles in an attempt to guide future readers. The posthumous dismembering of Dickinson's hand-bound body of work by editors may have occurred also with Tabor's bundles when well-meaning archivists organized them by genre. Lizzie's papers in the Tabor Collection are orderly now, separated into traditional categories: correspondence, miscellaneous writing, photos. But Lizzie's life, like any life, was messy, happening on multiple planes simultaneously. Thus, the chronological order that Lizzie tried to impose on the wide variety of her writings—an order that linked her Dreamworld encounters with real events, merging letters, newspaper clippings, and visions—was probably destroyed when sorted into traditional archival files. Lizzie's mind resisted such categories: the hybrid nature of her writings shows how she could slip—or purposely glide—from her dreams to her diary, all within one page.

It required tremendous patience to reconstruct even a short period in Lizzie's life *as she experienced it* because the boxes that hold—and separate—her papers by category must be viewed singly at the CHS library. As a case study, the laborious reintegration of Lizzie's Dreamworld writings about daughter Silver with correspondence from Silver reveals direct connections between Lizzie's seemingly irrational dreams and the real-life letters that stimulated them. They show that it was Lizzie's papers that were disintegrated by archivists, rather than her mind that was disintegrating. Reintegrated, the writings speak to each other and suggest one function for the "Dreams and Visions": they were Lizzie's internal journal about the Dreamworld in which she processed horrific news regarding Silver.

A brief scan of possible motives—sublime and mundane—that propelled Lizzie's graphomania provides a sketchy map of the Dreamworld. Lizzie credited God with sending her the most beautiful of her "Dreams and Visions" and may have felt a religious obligation to record these visitations. On the other hand, if Lizzie were a compensatory writer (to use Robert Fothergill's term for a person motivated to journal by their quarrel with the world), she would have an earthly audience in mind.[7] She may have hoped that her adult daughters would be more sympathetic to her plight than those who shunned her. Silver, in fact, had some experience as a newspaper writer. Perhaps Lizzie, who denied Silver was dead, may have expected her to find a way to organize and tell her mother's story to future generations. The "Dreams and Visions" could be the isolated Lizzie's long "letter to the world" from which she was banished or had retreated.

In this Dreamworld, she created an alternative community, much as medievalist Christine de Pizan did with her visionary City of Ladies. While Pizan created a utopian community, the geography of Lizzie's Dreamworld ranged from her idealized Wisconsin home and lavish Denver mansion to dark dystopian bug-infested houses. The Dreamworld citizenry included her beloved deceased family, estranged kin called "my living dead," her husbands, hosts of mysterious babies, and ubiquitous devilish men. The Dreamworld became an elaborate structure built within the mind of a woman who needed someone to talk to—even if they were demons—or she would go mad. The "Dreams and Visions" in partnership with the diary form the record of a woman whose mind was harassed by poverty, family tragedies, and hunger. Lizzie crossed off the days on the calendar that hung in her cabin, an indication that she was determined despite her isolation to know the correct date. Perhaps the notations "copied" and "filed" were a demented woman's attempt to meld together her waking and sleeping experiences because she realized her short-term memory was fading. Especially as she spent more time among her "living dead" in the Dreamworld, Lizzie may have used her writings to anchor time and space, which would explain her concern with dating her scraps. Lizzie needed to know what day it was when she emerged from her journeys within the Dali-like flowing time of the Dreamworld in order to protect her interests in the real world. Most likely, Lizzie Tabor used her writing for multiple purposes: to record, to testify to both earthly bedevilment and heavenly visitations, to give herself something in old age to reread with delight and horror, to proclaim "I exist" to those who wondered if the madwoman in the cabin was still alive.

SILVER AS CODREAMER

The dominant figure in the Dreamworld is Lizzie Tabor's youngest daughter, Silver, sometimes called Honeymaid. Because Silver lived with her mother intermittently until 1914 and then, when away from home, wrote letters that her mother preserved, it is possible to partially recapture the relationship between some "Dreams and Visions" and the events that stimulated them. Silver's life began like that of a fairy princess swaddled in the wealth of her father, Silver King Horace Tabor. But by age nine, Silver had only her mother to rely upon as together they descended into poverty that led them to rented homes and hotel rooms. Silver adapted with spirit to life in Leadville, however. When Lizzie decided to move into a shack on the Matchless mine property, Silver for a brief while helped her mother search for ore. She and her mother became codreamers, codefenders of the mine, and probably codependent. This is where we enter the Dreamworld. In 1905, when Silver was fifteen, mother and daughter shared with each other tales of their pleasant dreams, such as this one signed "Lizzie":

> The night of Wednesday June 7th—1905 I dreamed I saw Tabor & Rosenfelt [Theodore Roosevelt] the president & another man sitting on a bench together the President was in the middle & in a large Hall & I had honeymaid with me & the

President was talking to her & a lot of other [unclear] stuff the next night Honey
dreamed the wonderful dream of the Blessed Virgin

Five years later, Silver actually did meet Theodore Roosevelt during his visit
to Denver, and Lizzie must have felt confidence in the power of her dreams
to foretell the future.

On some occasions, mother and daughter experienced the same dream,
confiding in each other, deepening their bond and, in this case, their
thwarted hopefulness:

Leadville [no month indicated] 5 1908 Last night I dreamed that the loan on
Matchless was made & so did Honeymaid dream the same I woke so Happy &
so did Honeymaid & I felt so happy this morning & it has been a day of bitter dis-
appointment all day. . . .

This was the idyllic period in which Silver wrote to her Aunt Claudia in the
Midwest to assure her that Leadville was a suitable retreat for the eccentric
mother-daughter twosome: "No one knows where mamma and I are. We have
a very quiet secluded little spot and it has been the only place for momma
right now and it is very lovely. It seems that the Angels must have taken us to
it so please dear Aunt Claud do not mention our names to any one in Denver." But in July of that year, Mrs. Tabor learned from seventeen-year-old Silver that she had received two proposals of marriage. The shock of Lizzie's
realization that her confidante Silver had a love life beyond her scrutiny is
recorded in her diary of July 14, 1908: "Today is one of the saddest days of my
life for several reasons then this evening Honeymaid told me she had two
offers of marriage one from Mr. Miller and the other from Mr. [———] she
kept the secret from me and I could have sworn that she told me everything
as I did her it is breaking my heart Gods will be always done."[8] A dream from
1910 shows Lizzie and Silver still linked, although they are endangered by an
old enemy of Horace's who is desirous of their other silver:

Tuesday Nov 15–1910 I dreamed or had a vision this morning & saw a tall &
short man hit Silver in the neck & head & crush I think the life out of her then
they were all at me we were walking on the street stores all along the way they
over powered us in the shadow just before we got to a lighted store then later this
morning I had a dream of Silver & I being struck down by one in our own room
near the [unclear] and to day Moffatt sent the Sherif to serve papers on us Mr
Rufner & he served them on Silver they are trying to rob us of the Maid of Erin
& Hinerill

Ten days earlier, Lizzie had suffered from a dirty dream of snakes that she associated with Moffat, whose name she had read in the newspaper.[9] Thus memories of past wrongs to Horace that probably arose when Lizzie read about Moffat became living Dreamworld threats toward her Silver/silver.

Silver was increasingly attracted to wildness, as evidenced in a poem she sent to be copyrighted in 1910 called "The Dare-Devil." The poem's praise of a masculine devilish figure echoes the controversial desires of another mining town rebel, Mary MacLane of Butte, Montana. MacLane's 1902 diarylike book repeatedly called upon the Devil to ravish her—and made the first-time author a rich young woman. Silver's poem was less professional, but implicitly passionate: "And life with it's [sic] beggars, young and old; / Loves a Dare-devil—deviant and bold."[10] Lizzie recorded Silver's defiance—and her successful disciplining of her daughter—in a March 1911 diary entry: "Silver and I went to confession and the priest told her not to read bad books. She fell on the floor and screamed in rage, and acted terrible. I scalded my foot through the mercy of God because Silver would not go to communion and I said I will go on suffering with this foot if you don't, for we must not let the devil conquer after much trouble. She got up and went to communion and conquered the devil. I shall never forget my sorrow and heartaches by the way she acted."[11] Lizzie's diary notes for the next few years mention Silver's loud voice and her "determined disobedience." However, the two remained codreamers, occasionally sending accounts to Father Guida, who responded in 1913, "I congratulate you on your beautiful dream of last month and I long to hear more about it."[12] Thus the codreamers became coauthors, even if their only audience was Father Guida—whose praise surely encouraged them to dream on.

THE TROUBLE WITH SILVER

The hellish period from March 1914 to February 1915 is where we enter the Dreamworld in earnest, integrating materials about Silver from Lizzie's diary and correspondence. In the Dreamworld of 1914, two characterizations of Silver war within the psyche of the anguished mother: the good Silver, usually signified by a young nonsexual girl, and the troubling sexual Silver. While the usual characters continue to circulate within the Dreamworld—Horace (Papa) Tabor, Lizzie's mother, evil unnamed threatening men—three newly appearing figures warrant attention. The first is Stephen, Lizzie's beloved deceased young brother who is always portrayed in a positive light, compared to the ambiguous and contradictory depictions of Lizzie's other relatives. Stephen, who had studied to be a priest, clearly represents something reverent—perhaps religious forgiveness. Second, Saint Rita enters the Dreamworld, where I believe she functions as a surrogate suffering mother. The story of Saint Rita's life, similar in uncanny ways to Lizzie's, appears in the last chapter, in which I suggest possible functions for Lizzie's rich "Dreams and Visions." The third figure is a baby, who seems to mature in Lizzie's dreams until she is a toddler and then evolves into the propitious Matchless Mine Girl who is so welcome in the Dreamworld. However, figures of discarded, ill, and dead babies also haunt Lizzie. The babies' symbolism is connected to a coded and complex 1915 calendar, a visceral inscription of the dreaming mother's worst secret. We progress toward the calendar in Lizzie's dark Dreamworld, illuminated by her words and my interpretations, but ultimately unsure of our step.

Saturday April 11–1914 at 7:15 I heard a heavy long breath drawn, yesterday was Good Friday & the anniversary of Papa's death 15 years ago I was deserted by S36v2r last month I am alone [sideways on sheet:] S36v2r called to day

In 1914 a rift between Silver and her mother gave birth to hateful, emotional letters from the daughter, and powerful dreams for the aching mother. Silver became romantically involved with a young man named Ed (sometimes spelled Edd) Brown. The ever-vigilant Mrs. Tabor suspected that Ed was after both of her prized possessions—her daughter Silver and, through his relationship with Silver, access to the Matchless mine. Silver threatened in a letter, "But if Ed does not get the Lease [to the Matchless mine] I am going to leave town," which presented Lizzie with a bleak decision: retain either her mine or her daughter. Silver also complained about her impoverishment and drilled to the core of her mother's fantasy: "And I through the years have waited for the time when the Matchless would yield the means of pleasure and happiness to me."[13] Thus the mine bore enormous symbolism in the Dreamworld: if it could be returned to production, Silver might find life with her mother bearable and return. However, the mine was also a burden, because of the myriad threats to steal it that Lizzie furiously recorded. Silver broke with her mother in a characteristically dramatic way. She wrote "A Statement" in the large handwriting characteristic of her most desperate correspondence:

To whom it may concern and the Authorities and the Coroner: I—Silver Tabor, this March 17, 1914—at 2:40 a.m—state that I may be going insane or something else. If I am insane place me in a Catholic institution and under a quiet and peaceful influence I will regain my mind

for it is the mastery over me and exasperation that is day by day taking
my mentality. And when I am in a place where I am not insulted and
exasperated and forcibly mastered I will become sane again as when I
am with anyone but my mother. I am gay and strong and perfectly normal and will be again. My head is covered with self-inflicted bruises
and my heart is weak and my lungs congestive for I am a frail girl, a
nervous wreck from the life I live. . . . And I am sure that if I lived a
month or perhaps a week more with my mother that I would be hope-
lessly and permanently insane and the only chance I have is to be
seperated [*sic*] from her as I try all the time to kill myself. And she says
I am possessed of the Devil—which before God—I am not for I am an
earnest Catholic and sane and sensible and gay and strong among all
other people.[14]

Silver then left home, claiming that her mother so harassed Ed with her
threats to disinherit Silver and her fury over the twosome's news that they
had set a date for their marriage that he fled. This act likely confirmed Mrs.
Tabor's fears that it was the mine Ed actually desired. Silver's letters to her
mother were both desperate and pitiless in their warnings about what
would happen if Mrs. Tabor continued to scare away Ed Brown: "And how
dare you interfere in my love affairs. What would Papa say if he knew what
you did to his Honeymaid. . . . I will never see you again by my efforts. . . .
May God pity you when you face him in the other world. . . . I will not take
your letters from the Post Office and all messages which come to me from
you I will refuse to accept. And if God does pity you and you ever see Papa—
tell him that you sent his Honeymaid adrift in the world." Silver signed this
nine-page letter "A Leaf in the Storm." This letter sets up a particularly
cruel link that Silver would invoke during the next decade—for Silver knew
her mother's religious vulnerabilities, mind, and dreams as did none other.
Silver connects her fate to a final judgment of Lizzie's mothering to be
determined by God and Papa Tabor in heaven. Thus the more Silver
descends into a hellish lifestyle, the more Lizzie is compelled to do extraordinary "dream work" in order to plead her case as a Good Mother. Equally
cruel was the irony, perhaps not lost on Lizzie, that Silver desired the same
"gay" life that had once been the milieu of Baby Doe. Now it was Lizzie,
rather than Augusta, who was accused of being a humorless taskmaster.
Three days after Silver left her devastating letter, Lizzie described a mirror
breaking and an alarm clock spontaneously ringing twice as Silver left to go
to a dance with "Edd" Brown: sideways in the margin of the diary sheet, per-

haps an indication that she returned to her diary to search for portents, Lizzie wrote, "April 23—Looking glass broke and clock rang April 23–1914 Silvers in Vendome Hotel."[15] The Vendome Hotel, where Silver briefly boarded, had in the glory days been the Tabor Grand. Lizzie may have feared Silver's move as symbolic of her deep wish to return to her father, his fortune—and his legendary profligate Leadville lifestyle.

In early May 1914 Lizzie had a powerful vision that vividly described Ed Brown's villainy, while depicting Silver's sexuality "slant":

> *Sunday May 3 or Monday May 4 1914 I had a Vision first I heard Silver say "Wait I want to bid you good by," then I saw her in the whitest dress O so white and the front of it was all covered with blood very red then I saw her face then I saw her on the Matchless Mine near the water boxes & I saw a tall young man the form & size of Ed Brown throw her hard & terrible down on the ground & he stood over with his hands pushing as hurting her & he was leaning over her it was terrible. [Followed by loving vision of Silver's Lamie cat that had died.] These visions must mean something terrible for my poor Honeymaid all to the fault of the dirty filthy Brown family She is surely cursed to ever have met them that dirty devilish Edd Brown thug came to us in the Keystone Hotel. Poor Honeymaid.*

Silver's white dress, a symbol of her purity, is bloodied by devilish Ed Brown as he holds down the passive girl, probably sexually assaulting her. The fact that Lizzie saw this vision of rape occurring on the Matchless mine property shows how closely danger to her daughter was associated with danger to her property. No blame in the vision is laid to Silver, a sign that in the Dreamworld the mother brought all of her powers as an experienced dreamer to bear on her greatest nightmare: a rebellious, sexually active daughter.

> *May 27–1914 today I dreamed that Silver came & laid very near me on the bed & kissed me on the mouth she was by my left side I heard to night about her having all that money paying for everything God help me h4rse.*

In Lizzie's Dreamworld, as in much of classic mythology and Christian theology, evil appears on the left side and good on the right. Even as she described the warm embrace from affectionate Silver, Lizzie saw within the dream a bad omen and switched to a diarylike account of news she later received about Silver having money to support a white horse, which Silver rode wildly through Leadville, making a spectacle of herself, according to the Tabor biographers. Lizzie remembered how people had suspected Baby Doe of having gained her millions through sexual favors, and she feared now that Silver would be the object of the same vicious tongues. Lizzie knew her moral character would be judged by the deeds of her daughter. A June 6 diary entry shows how daily life and divine signs intersected for Lizzie Tabor:

> *my heart was broken about Silver and the low crowd she was with Edd Brown and all so terrible & I was walking passed the church on Poplar and 7ᵗʰ Sts & after I had knelt down on the sidewalk in front of the church this lovely bright thing blew down from the air above me & landed close to the church touching the church on my left I picked it up & it looked so bright to me in my worried condition I hope it means that all this will change & things will be bright for me and that Silver will recover & from Edd Browns hypnotism he has cast over her God help her*

Again Silver is cast as the victim of Ed Brown's evil powers rather than as a sexually willing actor. On the back of this entry, Lizzie wrote about events that occurred the next day, linking them to her otherworldly experience in front of the church (the "bright thing" had, after all, dropped on her left side): "Had the worst sorrow next day. Silver went to Glenwood Springs my heart is broken Trouble at Vendome."[16] A caustic letter Lizzie had received that day, June 7, signed simply "P," gave her knowledge of Silver's where-abouts and hinted at Silver's misdeeds: "Dear Friend Mrs. H.A.W. Tabor, if you alow me to meet you where and when exept from you. I found out all about it last evening. Thinks you Know. P. I think your daughter when [*sic*] to Glenwood Sps this morning with 3:20 train. Please don't Give me away."[17] The writer's mysterious line "I found out all about it" hints at an event that changed Silver and Lizzie's lives forever.

"MY POOR UNFORTUNATE CHILD SILVER"

This letter's indirect language hinting at indiscretion, combined with my inferences from Lizzie's diary and dream accounts, convinces me that Silver discovered she was pregnant in summer 1914, perhaps as a result of her affair with Ed Brown earlier that spring. To complicate matters, Silver had been seeing other men in an attempt to get over her breakup with Ed Brown. One beau was Harrison Dewar, to whom Silver wrote a letter on June 13, 1914, filled with vague references about a pressing matter. Its con-tractual language could simply be Silver's reminder to Harrison about their pledge of monogamy—or it could be a letter full of meaning from a girl who found herself in trouble: "Dear Harrison: I feel that we should have a

clearer understanding in order that I may know what to do. I made an agree-
ment with you and am ready to keep it with pleasure if you keep your part of
it. . . . You will understand my position as a girl—that I can not afford to
reject the company of others if you do not intend to keep to your part. I
wanted you to phone me so I could arrange with you to talk this over. . . . I
am able to hold my head up now in the same old way, for all the citizens are
greeting me with the same effervescing warmth and keen respect which
assures me that they do not believe what they hear because of my past record
of purity. Will you let me know just how you stand in this matter and if you
stand by my side come to see me at once and if not tell me that I am free to
accept the attentions of others."[18] (The very existence of this letter in the
Tabor collection is curious considering Lizzie's estrangement from her
daughter.) Silver's anxiety was understated compared to her mother's
account of a spiritual visitation that she closed with a fancy swirl and the signature "Mrs. Tabor," a sign in her Dreamworld of important documentation:

> *August 30–1914 Sunday this A.M. or a little in afternoon I was lying down &*
> *all of a sudden I was half concious trying to sleep when I was nearly thrown from*
> *my bed by what seemed a terrible strong jar or as if something terrible had hap-*
> *pened like an accident & I knew that was all about Silver then came quickly*
> *another great shock not quite as strong but terrible & I thought that had to do with*
> *me I feared something fearful was to happen to my poor darling child Silver*

Then on September 3, Lizzie wrote a long explanation of that terrible por-
tentous shock. Although the brown paper Lizzie folded to form a "booklet"
on which she wrote a four-page account is filed with her "Dreams and
Visions" in the archives, on its front is written "Dream and Reality September
the 3rd and 4th 1914." "Reality" probably refers to the scene Mrs. Tabor created
when she dramatically interrupted a party Silver was hosting for several men
in a Leadville hotel room. Silver reacted by finding police and requesting
them to remove her mother. This public attention would have surely mortified Lizzie and explains the forewarning "strong jar" she had experienced.
Lizzie Tabor was convinced that her two worlds spoke to each other, and she
was attentive to this permeable barrier between dream and reality. In this
case, the reality of Silver's behavior was so unspeakable that Lizzie could not
even name this bedeviled creature who was once her daughter:

> *September the 3rd and 4th—1914 : Dream and Reality September the 3rd and*
> *4th 1914 The two shocks I had about [crossed out] & other about one Sunday*
> *August 30th 1914 have come true Last night about 11–30 I went up to ___ room*

and I found two . . . toughs drinking beer & eating cheese & crackers with _____
I ordered them out & told them if I ever saw them again I would have them
arrested they ran down stairs & out and _____with them and waited for along time
then looked out of the window and saw _____ coming with two Police men to eject
and put me out of ___rooms they looked at me so sad I was so calm & quiet
through such a frightful terrible disgrace & I spoke so lovingly of _____ & shealded
_____ so that they spoke bitter to _____ & would not permit me to endure such terrible suffering I never shed a tear _____ said take her with you they said O no
never I said I will go & they can stay with you for a while, I thought they might
help _____ weak brain & hipnotized state that Edd Brown put _____ in _____ said
take her out she has got to get out of here, they said no I went out in the night
alone O my merciful God you were so good not to let me die of agony & grief.
Two shocks shock of finding such low ruffians & tramps there & shock of being
put in the hands of Police men I fell asleep after 12 the next day to day last night
that all happened Sept 3 last night was Sept 3rd 1914 the shocks came to me last
Sunday Aug 30–1914—to day is the 4 of Sept 1914 well I fell asleep and had a
wonderful dream which our blessed Jesus blessed my poor aching heart with my
darling Honeymaid & I were riding in a buggy I think I was driving just we two
were riding slowly going to the Matchless I think along & through the mountain
roads when to our right between the mountains appeared a great and mighty and
wonderous Rainbow O with such a wide part of it in Ruby glittered light all aflame
in Ruby fire & the Ruby colored red made the sky Ruby red & O it was so bright
it dazzeled you to look at it O too glorious to look at & we saw other colors but
the wonderful Ruby color aflame dazzled all it sank between the two mountains
& at no time could we see it all we rode along slowly & all seemed peaceful &
arrived home and then I seemed to be in bed with some one I think Miss Dr Fantz
I don't just remember yet I don't think it was Honeymaid it may have been but I
dont think so while we were lying in bed Harvey was walking in the room just
came in back of the head of our bed & told him to come & stand by the side of the
bed & talk to me but he came & got right in bed on Miss Fantz side & he had a
black slouch hat on & black overcoat on in bed & we three were in bed together
he some how pushed himself in the middle near me & we three were there only a
minute & I woke up from this beautiful glorious wonderful Rainbow dream all
aflame with Gods glory. what does it mean? after my broken heart last night O
my blessed Savior I give this suffering to you my only comfort my sorrow is yours
to save her soul her soul [across top of two pages, separated by a line:] I dont
remember seeing Honeymaid after we got home after riding together along the
mountain road & after seeing Rainbow

The "Dr Fantz" in the dream who shared Lizzie's bed with Harvey was a central player in the pregnancy drama. Doctor Theresa Fantz was a Denver physician who had loaned Lizzie Tabor some money and who would play a key role in the troubles with Silver over the next months. Dr. Fantz was associated with the Florence Crittenton Home for unwed mothers and orphans near Denver, making her an ideal person for Lizzie to consult if Silver were pregnant. The dream shows both the power and the limitations of Lizzie's subconscious to shape reality. Clearly the dreaming Mindful Mother received solace from the closing rainbow-tinged images of a more docile Honeymaid who rode quietly in a buggy headed back to the cloistered safety of the Matchless. Yet when the dream ends, Lizzie feels a nagging uncertainty as to whether Silver ever returned to the mine.

Another letter veiled in circumlocution points toward Silver's pregnancy. On September 12, 1914, beloved confidant Father Guida wrote a letter to Mrs. H.A.W. Tabor about Silver's plight: "I must without delay come to tell you that *16* days ago came to my hand a very long and anxious letter of 'Honeymaid,' asking me to write and obtain your consent to a marriage to which she engaged her self six months ago, but to which, she says you *are*, I would say you *appear* to be unfavorable. Well, dear Mrs. Tabor, after reading your child's letter, which from several respects was a surprise to me—perhaps principally because it was the bearer of unexpected, although not unpleasant information; still it being a matter of very great importance in the life of young persons especially *in the circumstances in which the writer of that letter finds herself,* I thought of taking time to reflect well on the subject and to pray to Our Lord about it" (my emphasis). Father Guida continued in his letter to advocate the blessed state of marriage for Silver and her unnamed partner. While the priest's missive seems to confirm in language typical of the era that Silver was pregnant, the documentary route leading to a "buried child" bisects at this point. Since Silver was rarely in Denver or Leadville during the fall of 1914, there is no direct evidence in Lizzie's papers about her daughter's body or pregnancy. However, Silver's disembodied spirit occasionally visited her mother's Dreamworld. Lizzie lamented after transcribing a sad dream, "O my dear Savior where is she and what is the matter with her my poor poor darling child." Lizzie made a notation to herself, "Keep with Silvers Paper Spirit came to door her Voice called me."[19]

Sept. 25–1914 my birthday I am all alone alone in this world now alone my birthday where is my poor unfortunate child Silver and how is my Lily and her babies

I am alone alone here in Leadville our Savior gave His blessed Mother strength to
live He will give me strength to endure O if I could only see my poor darling chil-
dren I shall pray always pray for them and my loved ones I dreamed to day that I
was at a table with Silver many were about us at an eating table in some eating
house Silver became very angry at me about some man & she talked loud & bad
& cross to me & she left me & she went out scolding as she went I was ashamed
& sad. . . .

This dream indicates that, if Silver actually returned home to her lonely
mother, the shame might be unbearable. Could Lizzie—who was still denying in her "Dreams and Visions" that her twenty-three-year-old daughter
was sexually active—have been able to deal with the onus of an illegitimate
grandchild? The Tabors were so well known, however, it is inconceivable
that flashy Silver could reside in Glenwood Springs without someone notic-
ing her pregnancy and broadcasting the news that the wantonness of Baby
Doe continued into the next generation.

Lizzie wrote in her diary on October 11, 1914, "I commenced a Novena
to the Mother of God and St. Rita in the name of O Blessed Mothers lone-
someness for Jesus for Honeymaid's return & Lily as God wills it." The Warrior Mother did not leave all agency up to God and Saint Rita. She
corresponded with her brother Peter, whom she still disliked and distrusted
but who was the financially stable leader of the McCourt family. Lizzie
resented the fact that Pete was giving money to Silver, yet she asked him for
financial aid so that Silver would come home to her or move to the Midwest
to live a quiet life with their sister Claudia McCourt. In October Lizzie also
wrote desperately to A. M. Stevenson, a former Tabor family friend and
attorney down in Denver, asking for the enormous sum of $2,000 on
account of Silver's "health." She urged that in order to protect Silver, they
must "act quickly," and she seems to have gotten approximately $1,000 from
Stevenson, which she ordered sent to Dr. Theresa Fantz. Does this mean
that Dr. Fantz required the money for secretive housing for a young woman
"in trouble," housing that only a physician could discretely arrange? Again
a mysterious child image appears in Lizzie's diary, following a hasty account
of Silver "acting the cheapest" by doing the "tango & dancing & dressing so
terrible & acting the cheapest & lowest until it hurt my credit."[20] The entry
closes with Silver saying, "Mama I want to tell you something & knocks on
door & Mother & child in black." During fall 1914, "Dreams and Visions" of
a needy Silver regularly plagued Lizzie:

Oct 29 1914 . . . I had a Vision O so plain and strong "I was walking on the street and my Silver came quickly to me with her dear arms & hands lovingly stretched out to me so close to me and she smiled and she was dressed all in black her hat was black and small and sat down over her right eye but O my God she looked like a corpse that had been buried she looked like a living corpse a deathly grey like a dead corpse smiling her dear eyes were sunken & O my poor heart ached in agony and she was all like a battery of electricity, no light, only like electricity & I was so frightened she came so suddenly to me in that way" and then she Vanished as all visions do and to day I have suffered agony for her my poor darling pet my Honeymaid [on back:] God will give me power to live through all this agony Vision of my darling child Silver October 29–1914 Dear God cast the devil into everlasting hell, and come to us now and bring this sin and this world to an End O God in Thy dear Mercy Come quickly.

Despite the tortured fervor of Lizzie's "Dreams and Visions," if Silver were pregnant and in trouble in fall 1914, her letters home from Colorado Springs do not reveal it. She mentions being happy with the work she had acting in the film *The Greater Barrier,* in which she had a minor role. The film, which revolved around the interracial love between an Anglo college girl and an Indian man, shows Silver to be an open-faced young woman who is not obviously pregnant. In November Silver wrote to assure her mother, "I am going to move into a private house where they keep a few roomers, a very refined, strict place." But mother-daughter tension still permeated the chatty letter: "Write me right away. I do not believe you want to lower yourself by writing to me yourself."[21] Whether Lizzie did write is unknown, because Silver routinely pawned her trunks in which she probably stored her mother's letters. Only fifteen drafts of letters from Lizzie to Silver exist in the Tabor archives, in contrast to the deluge of desperate letters from Silver to her mother. This imbalance gives a disproportionate sense of Silver's demanding neediness, while her mother's own yearnings—that Silver convert from a life of sin and return to her role as devout and devoted daughter—undoubtedly burdened Silver with each plaintive letter she received. Lizzie's needs vividly appear for us to read in the Dreamworld, where she endlessly pursues, spies upon, and tries to regain the elusive Silver.

On November 24, 1914, Lizzie drafted a dramatic letter to an unnamed addressee: "Now You shall answer to me her mother and to the whole world for the daughter of H.A.W. Tabor." Although it is unclear what the addressee will answer for, Lizzie invokes the blessed name of H.A.W. Tabor,

Photo of herself that Silver Dollar Tabor inscribed "To my Dear Guardian Mac Lennan [?]" in 1903, when she was thirteen. Courtesy Colorado Historical Society, Tabor Photo Collection. Tabor, Silver Dollar. All Rights Reserved.

160

a signifier of great import. A new man's name enters the saga at this pivotal point, that of "Mac L___," or McLennan or McLinn, a name that Lizzie spelled in various ways. He was apparently a family friend, for Silver signed a photo of herself to him in 1903: "To My Dear Guardian Mac Lennan Compliments of Silver Dollar." Although Silver was thirteen at the time she signed the photograph, it is a picture of her at about age nine, bedecked in foliage and holding a cat in a pose that eerily foreshadows a highly sexualized portrait of Silver as a showgirl in the 1920s (see page 173). The 1905 Leadville city directory mentions a miner named MacLennan, so this may have been an old friend. During the 1914 year of crisis, there were also several MacLennans listed as reporters in Denver, where Silver briefly worked as a journalist, so MacLennan might be a new "friend" of Silver's. Lizzie's diary recounts that Silver and McLennan "went to see Dr. Fantz and made trouble for me God only knows what" in November. For several days, Lizzie was torn between altercations with Silver ("O she scolded me & was so unkind") and suspicions that Dr. Fantz was secretly meeting with McLennan in some sort of plot that involved Silver and the ever-vulnerable Matchless mine. Lizzie recorded in her diary, "I borrowed 25 of Dr. Fantz. . . . Dec 4 she came & stayed a little while never spoke Silvers or McLinnuns [?] name or about mine nor I never mentioned them to her or ever will again what is she up to."[22]

Documenting the events and people pivotal to Lizzie Tabor during this tumultuous time is extremely difficult, for on one sheet of paper she mixed dream and real events, although in her harried state some of the "real" events may have been constructed by her imagination. My imagination is drawn to a pregnancy. If Silver's first pregnancy had not ended in early fall 1914, she was nearly due to have a baby. If the first pregnancy had been terminated, it was possible Silver was pregnant again by late 1914 or early 1915 and in dire straits. The recipient of Lizzie's wrathful letter could be the man responsible for impregnating Silver a second time. Was the Silver-Fantz-McLennan plot that Lizzie so feared their arrangement of an abortion for Silver? Again the image of a baby appears in the Dreamworld, shared this time with confidant Father Guida and embraced by Lizzie:

> 1ˢᵗ of Dec 1914 I dreamed this day that Father Guida was with us and I took him up a few steps to a room to show him a crucifix and some woman came to call on Silver I sent word we were not at home I do not remember who was there but a naked beautiful golden curly haired fat white baby about two years old naked was with us and running about & O so happy & laughing & I had the fat lovely baby

in arms & kissing it, it was beautiful beyond discription & naked & strong its hair
was a dark golden color & so much & it was so happy. I was happy to have our
beloved Father Guida in a dream

Several lovely images of Silver also visit the Dreamworld in late 1914: Silver
as an innocent seven-year-old girl, Silver as a helpful daughter who assists
Lizzie with business papers as she used to do. Even the pleasant dream
child, however, torments her mother. When Lizzie awakes, she often pencils
a lament about the endangered absent Silver, even as she records the acts of
the Dream Daughter.

In the Dreamworld that December, Horace took Lizzie on a buggy drive,
coming dangerously close to the edge of a cliff, only to miraculously save
them. (Lizzie had recalled the date of Horace's November birthday in her
diary and calculated how many years she had been a widow.) But it seemed
no miracle could save Silver. In the middle of a sheet of December dream
accounts Lizzie recorded, "my poor darling Silver wrote me a letter from
Colorado Springs a terrible letter my heart is broken I wrote her begging
her to come home to me Dec 23—O my dear Lord send her to me I shall
die." Meanwhile Silver requested that her mother send a coat and her
revolver, a revolver Lizzie had previously neglected to mail, perhaps in fear
that her daughter was suicidal. Silver wrote to assure her mother, "Scandal
about me has not reached the Springs and I live in a very strict house which
bears a fine reputation." Another letter from Silver pleaded, "Wont you
please send me some money. . . . This condition is enough to drive any girl
to the wrong."[23] The 1914 Christmas season ended with isolated Lizzie's sad
"commentary" written on a piece of newsprint bearing the *Denver Post* headline "There Is Not Anybody in Denver Who Has Not Had Merry Christmas."
The careworn mother wrote above and below the claim: "O my Blessed
Lord this is not true I only wish it were many are with broken hearts like
poor lonely me alone alone alone Not one soul came to me to-day or last
even and where is my darling child Honeymaid God watch over her her
mind has gone God will save her for us O darling Lily & the babies."[24]

No living soul may have visited Lizzie Tabor that Christmas, but in the
Dreamworld, her late brother Stephen visited her from the grave. Silver
also appeared, but in a dark liminal space between life and death:

Xmas Eve day I dreamed that Silver and I were walking & hurrying down stairs
long flight & on the street & large rooms & Stephen was in the dream he was
main part of dream & Silver seemed as if in the dark it seemed as if Steph married

Christmas newspaper headline around which Lizzie wrote her dissenting lament. Courtesy Colorado Historical Society, Tabor Collection, FF 901. All Rights Reserved.

a dark oldish woman & she said it cost her $40 & I was telling her how we loved Stephen & what a comfort he was & how I wanted him & that I would clean the streets if I could only get him back. Dec 24–1914

Lizzie was blessed on the last day of 1914 with another dream of Stephen, writing at the end of her description:

I am so happy that dear God let me see darling Steph in a dream this last day of the year.

However, dream gave way to harsh reality. She continued:

at 12 to night I prayed alone the Old year out & the new one in for my darling children & family loved ones & for Silver and Lily to come back to me the loving devoted mother who never was cross or unkind to them in thought word or deed only loving and caring always for them & their comforts only to make them happy yet with all my undying tender love for them the devils took them away from me & I am alone alone alone in agony & a broken bleeding aching heart & brain but God in His mercy will give them back to me for God is my all Dec 31–1914 God help me your devoted child Lizzie Tabor.

The contrast between the pleasant dreams and the plaintive diary delineates the two worlds inhabited by Lizzie. Her waking hours were filled with agony and worry over Silver and over legal maneuvers aimed at retaining the Matchless mine. Her refreshing dreams involved her late kind brother Stephen McCourt more often than Horace "Papa" Tabor. But even in the Dreamworld, troubling specters and visions of Silver awakened Lizzie to the plight of her daughter and acted as a call to arms. Lizzie would need all of her powers to face the coming year, 1915.

"TWO SMALL BABIES IN WHITE SWADDLING CLOTHES"

The first dream Lizzie recorded for 1915 was a pleasant one, reminiscent of wealthier days that included her sister Tilly, who had married well-off Andrew Haben years ago in Oshkosh. Judging from notations on dream transcriptions for this time, Tilly was in such bad health that Lizzie sent her a book about Saint Rita. The Dreamworld supplied Lizzie with the peace and plenty she so lacked in reality. Often when Lizzie dreamt of food, her diary documented her want; thus the lush grapes that appear in this seemingly happy dream speak to her hunger:

Sat Jan 2–1915 I dreamed that Tabor & us were in a row boat & rowing around & another row boat was filled with this kind of large toys & I told Tabor to buy 3 sets of them for some children I don't remember who & several boats were on the water & lots of our folk & especially Haben we seemed all happy & united then Silver & I went to Tillys house & asked her where to get some fruit & Irean came to the door & showed us the store where they bought I wanted the fruit for Tilly & I had a large bunch of green ripe grapes somehow woke & received a letter from Dr Fantz with a little hope & then I got in bed again & fell asleep & dreamed again of my Tabor he was with me & all was peaceful but I do not remember what I dreamed.

The other McCourt family member in the January 1915 Dreamworld was her scheming brother Pete, toward whom Lizzie felt so much ambivalence. He still was financially assisting Silver, but Lizzie feared that her brother's money would lure away Silver just as the midwestern McCourts had "stolen" darling Lily. In one dream Lizzie confides to her dear mother that not only has Pete returned to drink, but that he eats fish on Friday. Beloved brother Stephen enters a dream with a theme that recurs often in the Dreamworld: her endangered bundle. (Newspaper accounts after Baby Doe's death mentioned the omnipresent bundle that was part of the madwoman's costume and reporters speculated that it held valuable ore.) In Lizzie's dreams, the bundle's contents are often unidentified, but in this case it contains clothes. On most occasions the bundle holds papers—and occasionally a baby.

Jan 7th [1915] I dreamed I was walking on a narrow mountain road & could hardly keep on road I was carrying a heavy big bundle of (white) clothes on outside & the ground & earth was yellow. I slid down with bundle held onto it I did not get very far & I got up and said Stephen will come and help me he will carry it the earth was clean & yellow

While the Tabor papers hold fewer dunning letters in January from Silver in Colorado Springs, Silver appears in half of the "Dreams and Visions," often in morally disquieting situations:

Jan 13–1915 I dreamed to day that Silver & I were happy together & she was having her picture painted life size full length She was dressed in a bright red satin long train dress narrow & bright lovely red slippers all very rich we were in our house cheap looking place & the artist & his sister came in & they sat down they looked & acted dishonorable & tricky she said something about 200 dollars a day & then Silver & I were walking on the street happy & I said I don't like the artist

*& his sister you must find out where he is going to charge you for painting your
picture or he will charge 15000 dollars & Silver how much did you pay him for
these little silver studs she said $600 I said take them back to him they are not
worth anything she said all right I will they were little round balls the size of 0
Today the Denver Post had a price [piece?] in it of a young girl offering her body
for sale Jan 13–1915 I am so sad*

The dream account merges seamlessly into a diary entry about a troubling
newspaper article Silver had sent her mother that probably provoked the
dream. Under the headline "Venus in Poverty Offers Her Body to Be Dissected" was the story of an anonymous Colorado Springs woman's offer to
sell her body for research to University of Colorado scientists.[25] In a turn-
about of Lizzie's habit of sending Silver articles to influence her behavior,
Silver implied that she might consider "selling her body" for money. To the
poor mother perpetually scrutinized as Baby Doe, Silver's threat of publi-
cizing her desperation must have hit the bull's eye in her heart. The letters
between mother and daughter form a Möbius loop of guilt and manipulation. In early February the tension between optimism and the ominous continues in the Dreamworld, but the diary notes are curiously silent from
January 1 to February 15. Perhaps something so threatening to the Tabor
image could only be addressed obliquely in the increasingly dark "Dreams
and Visions" transcriptions that flow into diary commentary:

*Saturday Feb 6–1915 before 8 am I had this most terrible dream I was standing
in a house talking [to] Mr. Kirkpatrick Dr Fantz's friend & he said look at that
naked man standing & walking on that porch over there I looked over at that
white porch & saw my poor darling Tabor standing there all naked & I put my
shoes on to go over to him when he came in the back door all naked holding a dead
body in his arms a headless dead body long neck with its thin arms stretched out
straight close together stiff where the head was gone and its legs were stiff & thin
& its body was bloted especially its stomache & it was washed of its blood leaving
it a pink shiny color & streaked & he was all that same color too terrible to look
on & he held it stiff a crost his arms he had washed the body & his eyes were
turned up he said O look how beautiful the arm's look see how beautiful they are
dear are they not lovely I said O my God who did it he said I did it & some one
hit her on the head for me with a (I think monkey wrench) he said but O my God
Papa who is it who is it he was looking up his head held high & said our Honeymaid I killed her. I screamed O dont you all see he is crazy he has gone mad & I
awoke I never knew such terrible agony in my life & no one on Earth ever had*

such a terrible horrible agonizing dream O my precious Saviour give me strength to live after it [sideways:] A Dream terrible

On the back of the dream narrative Lizzie wrote:

Saturday Feb 6–1915 Silver had not been to see me for more than 8 days & at 7 pm this eve she came in looking very bad & I told her my dream (on other side of this) she was shocked but I fear it had but little effect on her my poor Honeymaid & O my blessed God have mercy on my poor brother Pete & all who has caused all this sorrow give me strength to pray for their souls to be saved & bring my Honeymaid back to me dear God. . . .

Even beloved Stephen troubled Lizzie in a dream she interpreted as a warning of imminent danger:

Feb 13–1915 I dreamed of my darling brother Steph he was dressed in black slouch hat & came close to my right side & held out his hand to take some groceries from my arm & I held them away from him & his face was sad & mouth was very sad & he went back I tried to give them to him & tried to get him to come with me home but he would not I meant for him to wait until I got home for the food when I held it back. It means he wanted to warn me I would have trouble when I refused to give Silver 140.00 to day & O what terrible things happened she pinched my arm for my talking against that terrible Edd Brown & said she would do awful things to her self kill herself because I refused to give her 140.00 God help me Last I saw her 8:15 about Feb 13–1915

Shortly after this ominous dream, the crisis over Silver and a baby is teasingly inscribed on Lizzie's calendar. The calendar page from February 1915, with code on the front and a vision on the back that evolves into a diary, contains the most concrete acknowledgment of Silver's "baby." Lizzie utilized the numerical code she had devised long ago in the 1870s to obscure embarrassing words in her scrapbooks. Atop the calendar page is written "20th b1by S36v2r," which when decoded is "20th baby Silver." The calendar (see page 169) also contains code by the February 20, 1915, date: "9:30 a.m. B1by" (Baby). It is unclear whether this means that an actual baby conceived in 1914 was born, or Lizzie learned that Silver was pregnant with yet another baby, or a baby was aborted, or that Lizzie was simply recording the exact time of a code-worthy troubling vision about Silver as a baby or bearing a baby. Lizzie's code on the top of the paper acts like a banner headline that teases the border between what she wanted to keep secret and what was a scream for attention. Yet the calendar does not tell all: there is no verb between "baby" and "Silver" to reveal what happened, no object to reveal the fate of a baby. This minimalism bars interpretation by outsiders and is characteristic of a truly private diary, of writing that most people scribble throughout their lives solely for themselves.[26] The fact that Lizzie worked so hard in her other "Dreams and Visions" to explain things to an audience—and then on the critical calendar notation withdrew into prose that only she could understand—demonstrates her skill and sense of agency. The elusive or illusive "baby" will remain forever shrouded in mystery because Lizzie Tabor swathed it in impenetrable prose.

The 1915 calendar also contains a circled entry around the date of February 18 that is puzzling: "Loan Fantz paid Foster." This could be read left to right, up and down, or in a circular direction, making who paid whom unclear. "Foster" may refer to a loan obtained from a Mr. "Foster" mentioned in a vision of February 4 that Lizzie interpreted as a sign of hope for saving the Matchless mine. Or "Foster" could refer to a foster home for Silver's baby, arranged by Dr. Fantz who now needed payment. At the bottom of the calendar page is scrawled, "Silver told me she wants 15000 Silver twice Pete Phil Wallace House." Was Silver desperate for so large a sum ($150) because she needed to pay Dr. Fantz for helping her relocate to escape scandal—or for aborting that scandal? This cryptic coded calendar, combined with the Tabor correspondence, leads to questions that may never be answered: was an actual child born out of wedlock to Silver on February 20, 1915, and taken to a foster home with the assistance of Dr. Theresa Fantz? Or did the marked day and time indicate when Silver's would-be baby was aborted by Dr. Fantz? Later correspondence teases with ambiguous language: three months after the mysterious February event, Dr. Fantz drily observed in a suggestive letter to Lizzie, "Saw Silver on the street yesterday. . . . She is looking very good indeed—She of course did not recognize me. I am here simply for people's convenience when I'm of no more use they toss me aside."[27] To make the quest for a buried child even more complicated, the February calendar could indicate the date upon which Lizzie learned from Silver about the early stages of yet another pregnancy—one that later correspondence clearly documents ended in October that year in Indianapolis where Silver was working as a chorus girl. On the back of the February 1915 calendar is this combined vision-visitation:

I had a vision of Silver coming to door with a black vale over her face to hide her identity to go to have it soon 15000 another girl was there then a vision of 2 eyes

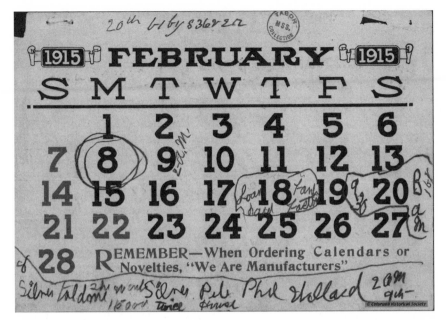

February 1915 calendar with crucial coding about Silver and a baby. Courtesy Colorado Historical Society, Tabor Collection, FF 901. All Rights Reserved.

croside purple & big of Mexican, to day she came & acted terrible & said she hated me & called me devil because I would not 15000

If this vision of veiled Silver going "to have it" refers to a live birth, my attempts to find Silver's child born in February 1915 have led nowhere. The CHS archive folder of Diary Notes following the tempestuous February date are empty; perhaps someone worried about the contents removed the telling materials. Birth records kept by the state are sealed for one hundred years. I searched the baptismal records at the Denver Catholic diocese under numerous pseudonyms Silver might have used, thinking that such a good Catholic as Lizzie would insist on having Silver's baby baptized, but I had no luck. Perhaps Father Guida performed a private baptism for this grandchild of his beloved Mrs. Tabor. The answer about Silver's child may never emerge. Ultimately, it does not matter whether an actual baby was born, for in the Dreamworld, Lizzie now often saw babies and young children who were real to her. Sometimes they are happy and laughing, sometimes Silver tries to hide them from her mother. In one intriguing dream of 1916, a two-year-old baby plays with Lizzie's left hand, a hand she had earlier depicted as devoid of a wedding ring:

Mar 28–1916 I dreamed today I was lying in bed a baby girl about 2 years old fat was playing with my fingers on my left hand. I had my hand hanging out of bed then Silver had the same baby on her lap I said I thought that was yours she loves me Silver said O no not mine I thought I must get up & cover the baby or she would get cold as she was on the floor. . . .

On occasion Lizzie and Silver together hold babies in the Dreamworld. In the account below, one baby is "new" and the other becomes Lizzie's second stillborn son. This shows the phenomenal drive within the Mindful Mother to fuse with her daughter, despite their sins. Silver and Lizzie in these dreams are joined as mothers rather than as wives, lovers, or transgressors. With their sins purged from the Dreamworld, they resemble the Virgin Mary—a mother without sexuality or knowledge of men. Whether Silver had "buried" her child in a foster home or literally buried its body, she now assisted her dreaming mother in unearthing their loss:

February 27–1919 . . . I dreamed again I was with Silver & another woman in a cheap house bare new pine floor, Silver came & handed me 2 (two) small babies in white swaddling clothes as Indians wrap up their babies & their heads had little close white hoods on she said here are your babies the dark one is your little boy who died long ago I dug him up the other is your new baby who just died I said O yes & kissed its little face & laid them both down on the lounge & Silver & the woman all danced around. . . . Now this is the second time I have dreamed lately of Silver and I digging up the grave of my baby boy who died 26 years ago. . . .

In the fluid time of the Dreamworld, a baby lost by Lizzie Doe a quarter-century earlier is freshly unearthed. Lizzie's scrapbook also attests to her ability to conjoin her two stillborn sons across the expanse of time, for she placed mementos to her two losses side-by-side. As a result, it is impossible to decipher whether the babies in the Dreamworld belong to Lizzie or Silver; sometimes their babies seem to merge:

Feb 11–1919 Tuesday I had a terrible dream I was moveing my baby boys (Tabors baby) grave, the undertaker & his wife pinned with many pins my long black vail. . . . Silver was with me talking I believed all she said about our babys grave & again I asked her & she said different I said but you told me so then she said she lied to me about babys grave—I was so sorrowful because she would lie about anything or at all, so sad & Silver looked so cold and dont care look. I fear from this above dream—death—

Silver and her baby or their babies would be regular visitors to Lizzie's Dreamworld for the next decade, until Silver's death in 1925.

Lizzie's February 1915 "Dreams and Visions" include her description of a dream Silver experienced, a sign that the Tabor twosome had reconciled enough to renew their shared spiritual experiences. But Silver continued her nightmarish descent: in September 1915 one last scandal again tarnished the Tabor name and forced her to leave Colorado. Silver, now a revue performer in Denver, was jailed after being accused by another actress of stealing a ring. The actress later discovered where she had absentmindedly hidden her own ring, but not before a *Denver Post* article had again dragged Silver and Horace Tabor's name through the wringer. Lizzie received the bad news through an old family friend down in Denver, Ollie Underwood. In her plainspoken letter accompanying the article, Underwood observed, "If they wanted to spite and worry you it would have been enough, but they might have had principal enough in them to have spared Mr. Tabor's name. . . . There were two old hen (cats) got to discussing what they saw in the paper with Geo. and I one evening and one said, 'Oh well, her parents were pretty gay before her.'"[28] Lizzie processed this hurtful information about Silver in a dream that included Horace—and yet another nameless child. After her dream Lizzie wrote a diary account that again rendered Silver innocent and tied Silver's fate to that of the mine:

Thursday Sept 30–1915 . . . I talked to Silver in a troubled way about it she was trying to get out of telling me about it & I said come in Papas room & we went I rushed ahead of her & there in a clean bed white sheets & he in a white night gown lay Papa & a child in bed with him he turned & looked at me I said stick with me when Silver comes Silver came & stood by the bed at the foot and talked & I said something I don't know what but it stopped her talking at once for what she said was untrue she was going to run away from us. . . . I did not know to day when I dreamed this dream that Silver had left Denver I had not heard from her for months but after that terrible disgrace which was put upon my poor child to get me to leave the Matchless Mine I wrote her and begged her to come home to me. . . .

In October 1915 Lizzie received an unsettling letter from Silver, who had moved to Indianapolis and was performing in a chorus line: "There is a lot of satisfaction in being a beautiful dancer and picked up by a large audience as the prettiest girl in the chorus, and called to the front to sing, but with the wine you've got to drink the dregs too, and there's a lot of dregs, my almost

fatal operation is part of the dregs." Silver wrote of being hospitalized for
"blood poisoning," which necessitated her uterus being scraped "to assure
future health."[29] Lizzie Tabor, although penniless, somehow found the money
to take a train to Indianapolis, where she made an unannounced visit to Silver.
Even while on the train, Lizzie could not escape a disquieting dream that she
merged into a diary entry written on a telegram form:

> *Oct 28–1915 I dreamed while on train of O so many snakes & a mean face &
> tonight I went to that hell hole to find & O my God what terrible treatment I
> received & could not get help from Police I am in agony for fear she is dead*

However, the death was not that of Silver but of a baby, lost by what Silver
termed a "miscarriage" when confronted by her mother. Mrs. Tabor did not
learn this news from her daughter but from a doctor in the hospital where
Silver had been treated. Was this the "baby" alluded to in the coded calendar of February 1915? If so, that would mean Silver was a chorus girl while
almost nine months pregnant, an unlikely prospect. This was probably yet
another pregnancy, the "dregs" of being the prettiest chorus girl. As all pre-
tense of her daughter's innocence and veracity finally crumbled, Lizzie
returned to the Matchless to dream repeatedly of Silver with deathly white
eyes, of Silver's dying cat, of snakes and demons. Silver had mentioned
being homesick in her letter from Indianapolis and confided that she
would come back to Leadville—if she had a private room with running
water and a guard at night to assure her safety. Silver reported troubling
dreams: "Have just awakened from another strange dream, did I mention
them to you? . . . They are so vivid I wake up with the horrors and on that
account never sleep without a dim light. The dreams are always that we are
in awful danger and we are always scared."[30] Silver's offer—that if her
mother had the funds to support her, she would return home—must have
encouraged Lizzie's frenzied motivations to revitalize the Matchless. Silver's
endangerment dreams were mirrored in Lizzie's Dreamworld. It would be
another two years before Silver was forced to confide to her codreamer
mother the reason she felt so besieged.

In 1916 Silver sent her mother letters every week, sometimes every day,
begging for money. It must have frustrated Silver to know that Lizzie had
valuable Tabor family items hidden away in trunks held at the Leadville
Catholic hospital. At one point Silver pointedly asked her mother to make
a Christmas gift of a nice topaz, which Silver wanted set in gold and sent to

Silver Dollar Tabor as a young woman. Edgar McMechen used this portrait in his book *The Tabor Story*. Courtesy Colorado Historical Society, Tabor Photo Collection. Tabor, Silver Dollar. All Rights Reserved.

Portrait of Silver Dollar Tabor as actress or dancer. Note how her makeup and eyebrows have provocatively altered her youthful features. Courtesy Colorado Historical Society, Tabor Photo Collection. Tabor, Silver Dollar. All Rights Reserved.

her. Just such a topaz was indeed found in the trunks after Mrs. Tabor's death, a mute symbol of Lizzie's bedrock resistance to Silver's bottomless needs. When Lizzie somehow found funds that she wired to her daughter, Silver castigated her slow response: "So if you let me die, suffering alone, in want without even answering my letters—you will regret it to the end of your days."[31] Silver continued to play upon Lizzie's fears of scandal: "Sometimes the end will come, as it does to all shamed women who degrade themselves when driven on by hunger."[32] Yet gaps in Silver's tormenting correspondence also filled Lizzie with worry. The remoteness of the Matchless mine meant that letters from Silver often accumulated until a kindly soul brought them to Mrs. Tabor. Likewise, Silver kept moving and used a series of names such as "Mrs. Ruth La Vode," which probably signaled to Lizzie that her daughter was cohabiting with some man. To the dreaming mother, "communication" via the Dreamworld must have seemed faster and surer. In her papers Lizzie attached her dream of Silver to a letter from Silver, showing how each world verified the other. In one dream Lizzie used a new strategy to cope with the increasingly venomous and tawdry Silver, who could no longer sustain her mother's idealization. She split her daughter into two girls: the good Honeymaid and the slatternly Silver:

> *June 8–1916 again I fell asleep & dreamed a sad dream I was in a quack Doctors office dingy & dirty doctor had a cheap face & dishonerable looking long hair & whiskers long & darkish another doctor was near Silver sat way back on a lounge the Dr said pay me first I said O no I shall not I cannot not as I have two men to pay & I would not pay you if I could first we went out of the door & the Dr got up & walked over to Silver took her hand & said say good bye to your mother she said I will but she did not & I said to Honeymaid Silver is 63v389 [living] with that Dr she said yes in the dream I thought Silver was with me & she was sitting on lounge so in the dream she must have been double it was a terrible dream & the black man started a minute & God woke me up & save me I am sad sad to day [sideways:] God save Silver*

Silver's ongoing complaints in her letters of "miscarriages" and "weak womb" problems requiring surgery (and money from her mother) no doubt fueled the host of unnamed endangered or dead children in the Dreamworld, where the story is told obliquely:

> *August 6–1916 . . . Then I saw Silver with this big baby in her arms she & Tabor were going to take it with them to the opera box & I thought the people will say*

just like her mother use to do with her & Lily, & then she handed me the baby and would not take it to the theatre. . . .

Aug 7–1916 I dreamed I had a little all white Poodle dog on my lap & its front leg was bent to its back & I did not pull it around to the front soon enough & it was dying & blood was on it & I could see its stomache swell out & see the dark red blood bulged out in the stomache through the skin it died & its face was calm & lovely & I kissed it and Silver was with us & she kissed it. I am sad over this dream.

This period of 1914–1916 is when the Mindful Mother transcribed almost one dream or vision per day, evidence of the enormous subconscious work she was performing on behalf of Silver, who permeated her sleep.

"I PROTECT"

In 1917 Lizzie was mortified to learn that Silver had now turned to a new target for her money-seeking correspondence: their old family friend A. M. Stevenson, the attorney from whom Mrs. Tabor herself had received a great deal of money that she forwarded to Dr. Fantz "for Silver's health" in 1914. Mrs. Tabor learned from Stevenson about Silver's ploy because he sent Lizzie at least two letters he had received from her errant daughter. Silver's letter of May 9, 1917, closed with unsettling familiarity, "I never answered your letter of last summer because there were things in it that I could not discuss but I appreciated your help and I am appealing to you again as I am sick and without money. Will you please, for old times sake, lend me ten dollars."[33] In his role as family friend, Stevenson may have forwarded Silver's letter to Lizzie out of concern for the Tabor reputation. In the more uncomfortable role as recipient of a blackmail letter from the notorious Silver with whom he had shared "old times," Stevenson may have forwarded the letter to Lizzie to pressure the aging mistress of the Matchless mine into interrupting Silver's demands, in order to avoid yet another scandal concerning her daughter. When Lizzie confronted her daughter about the letter, Silver wrote a nine-page rebuttal providing her version of a sordid story. Silver began her saga with a conspiratorial overture: "My Dear Mama: I am going to write you something now which I have always wanted to keep you from knowing but I am telling you now for your own good as the power of the Parasite was too strong and terrible for me and I want to protect you from it if I can. A. M. Stevenson is the vilest Parasite on earth and he has

ruined my life and tried to ruin yours so you must be protected. . . . At the
time when the Maid of Erin [a Tabor mine] case was hanging fire he ruined
me in his office." Silver described how Stevenson had tried to accost her
and finally succeeded in 1910 when he lured her to his office one Saturday:
"he told me . . . he had something to tell me that was very important. I went
and he locked me in and also all the outside doors and and [sic] struggled
with me until I was so weak that I almost fainted and then he ruined me by
force. I never intended to give in to any man until I got married but the
great, vile parasite A. M. Stevenson ruined me and my whole life there in his
office that day." Silver enclosed a letter from Stevenson, the contents of
which will never be known for Lizzie wrote on its envelope, "I burned it &
tore in fine pieces that terrible letter."[34] Silver closed with a warning about
Stevenson that connected mother, daughter, and the Matchless mine in a
bond that would haunt Lizzie to the end of her days. "Several times when I
was out on the road and sick and broke I wrote him for money and last summer he wrote and asked me to return to Denver and start proceedings to
have you adjudged insane, and a receiver appointed for the estate. If he had
done that I would have shot him dead, the beast in the jungle. I am sending
you his letter about it, it speaks for itself. . . . He will try to get you out of the
way and for God's sake protect yourself for his power is terrible."[35]

The name of Denver figure A. M. Stevenson still carried such power in the
1950s that it was eradicated by editors from the *Denver Post* newspaper series
that reporter Eva Hodges wrote as a result of her brief access to the Tabor
papers before they were again sealed for processing at the Colorado Historical Society. The name of Silver Dollar Tabor still bore such an onus of
promiscuity that, even though her tale of rape was at last made public in that
series, Eva Hodges remembers she could not disclose the name of the man
Silver claimed had ruined her.[36] Whether Silver's version of her relationship
with Stevenson was true or not, Silver's letter, which closed with a suicide
threat, rang true for her Warrior Mother. Lizzie drafted a wire to her daughter promising money and warned, "Stevenson lied about all to get mine gave
me your letter be careful hide he will try to harm you. . . . I protect."[37] Silver's
tale of ruin, repeated frequently in letters to her mother, urged Lizzie to
defend an endangered fortress comprised of Silver-Matchless-Mother. Lizzie
responded with money during the days—and with dreams at night. In her
Dreamworld a threat to one was a threat to all. Former family friends could
no longer be trusted. All those who showed interest in the Matchless mine
were potential demons. The Stevenson specter also allowed Lizzie to cope

with Silver's absence: if innocent, Silver must stay away in order to avoid the Parasite. And even if Lizzie suspected Silver was deceitful, she must stay away lest she couple with Stevenson in his desire for both her body and the mine. Clearly, enemies awaited any sign that Baby Doe Tabor had lost her mind. The safest place became the Dreamworld—or was it? While protective Lizzie could destroy evidence of her sexually manipulative daughter by burning letters, she could not eradicate doubts from her subconscious, where they waited to torture her in "Dreams and Visions." In the time period 1916–1917, neither research assistant Patty Pokigo nor I could find any happy dreams about Silver. Silver was perpetually endangered or bad.

> *Aug 24–28 1917 I dreamed to-day I was at big Rail Road Station I waited & hid & then ran around to get on the other side of train & then I saw my Darling poor sick child Silver standing forlone & sick looking in an old black round hat with brim like a small sailor hat she had on a long black cape & shabby & O so old & cheap her face was pale & drawn & O so sad*

> *Oct 16–1917 I dreamed of being with H482y713d [Honeymaid] & she acted so & leaned over a railing in the hotel & laughed & yelled & shook a beer bottle at the crowd below I scolded her & said you will never change will you & took hold of her & went down stairs together she did not answer me back & was calm & seemed not to care what I said or did she was so calm & I was heart broken & said O your poor Fathers name. Gladus Thorne was sitting on the other side of the balcony holding a baby. I was so mad & heart broken in this terrible dream and nearly died & woke up suddenly out of it & H482ys [Honeys] eyes were looking at me so sick & strange it was a powerful Vision of them. . . .*

Silver's activities in the real world were equally nightmarish. She continued to move from town to town, changing her name as often as she changed jobs, repeating in her letters to Leadville her fears about Stevenson. Nothing seemed to suit Silver, who found being a saleswoman of embroidery goods boring and the chorus line now too taxing to her health. She wrote often of suffering "female problems" and vague infections. Eventually, she wrote from a Lincoln, Nebraska, hospital about emergency surgery to remove an "overy" due to infection—which may have been venereal disease.

> *Mar 27–1916 Today this afternoon I had a Vision of Silver & I heard her voice She said "mama the Doctor said the fire would be out for about 10 days" I understood it ment she was to have an operation & all was sad with her & I was so sorrowfull & worried about her. . . .*

Silver tried to conceal the nature of her surgery from a new beau named Clair Sloninger, who came from a wealthy family and provided hope for domestic normalcy. She wrote to her mother that Clair had grown suspicious about Silver after hearing "terrible reports about me around town." Silver attributed these rumors to the long arm of Stevenson and then deflected the opprobrium onto her mother: Silver warned that Clair intended to make a trip to Denver to learn for himself about her background and was curious to meet Mrs. Tabor. Silver wrote, "Mamma, you are my only friend and I ask a favor of you. I told Clair that you were very religious and was so modest in your living that no one would know you were wealthy. If you see him, or hear from him, for my sake please let him think you are wealthy and tell him that I have never been married and try to keep from him that I was in jail there."[38] Silver included her beau's address in hopes that Lizzie Tabor would write her approval of a marriage. On top of this letter is written "Destroy this letter" in a hand that could be either Lizzie's or Silver's. Destruction of such a letter would eradicate the shame that implicated both mother and daughter in deception aimed at hiding Silver's past and normalizing her eccentric mother. It seems Clair heard enough stories circulating in Denver about the notorious Tabors to terminate his interest in Silver without ever meeting Baby Doe.

Despite numerous setbacks, the Mindful Mother continued to "reform" Silver in the Dreamworld. By 1918 even Lizzie called Silver a whore, yet she held out hope for redemption:

> Oct 7–1918 I dreamed of being with S3672r in a store she gave two terrible men her address & I got so angry with her that I said O you slut you Whore then she said in the dream "you are right mama I shall never do it again I shall always be good & pure"

After 1919, according to Silver's biographer Evelyn Furman, Silver's letters were written on better stationery and no longer dunned her mother for money. In 1923 Silver informed her mother that she had married a man named William ("Billy") Ryan, but shortly afterward she wrote of being divorced. Silver was financially comfortable enough to send her mother small presents, perhaps a sign she was being taken care of by a male companion. Still signing her letters "Your loving child" at age thirty, Silver sometimes wrote about her dreams and responded positively to ones her mother described in her letters back. Although they were physically separated, mother and daughter remained linked in the spirit world as codreamers. In some ways, Silver even began to nurture and mother Lizzie: "I am terribly worried about you as I dreamed of you the other night and I got up at 2-a.m. and went out and called Lily to see if she had heard from you. . . . Lily said she had not heard from you for a long time. Please answer right away. Your loving child Silver." On August 24, 1925, Silver closed the last letter of her life to her mother, "Please write to me as I worry so about you. I have dreamed so often of you and Papa, so often lately."[39] Two weeks later, Silver died in Chicago.

Lizzie also "dreamed so often" of Silver. She also dreamed obliquely, I suggest, of Silver's lost babies. This troubling dream of a nine-year-old girl shows how those babies, lost through adoption or abortion a decade earlier, continued to live and age in the Dreamworld:

> *Sunday Aug 22–1925 I awoke from a terrible sad dream this a.m. a little girl not over 9 years stood facing me she came quickly & she looked all dark & swolen trembling & sobbing crying in great agony some one had whipped her life almost out of her & I wondered that she was alive all bruised in her greatest agony sobbing she could hardly move & all swolen & red & very dark looking she quivered in agony O such agony they all but murdered the child she could not speak only tears fell & her whole body seemed damp with them & blood she was a crushed swolen mass of agony only alive. . . .*

Despite the pain such dreams caused Lizzie, she recorded them because she felt they were divinely sent. Even if the "Dreams and Visions" tortured the mother, they documented her vigilance during both day and night. Cut off by distance that her poverty could not overcome, separated from her daughters by their questionable moral choices, Lizzie used her dreams as a bridge to her beloved.

> *Milo Hotel May 22–1916 10 P.M.*
> *To my children*
> *Weary hearts O weary hearts*
> *Lean upon my love for thee*
> *It is a bridge that will reach out acrost*
> *Where ere thou be*
> *Place your sorrows one by one*
> *Dampened with thy tears*
> *& kiss each each message for me,*
> *lay them on your hearts*

& I can feel your sorrows
Thou we're far apart
My answer will get swiftly
ore the bridge of love.
They are so light
They are so bright
They'll pierce thy hearts
with hopes at night
& though will know my Love
My love is true
& in the dreamland hours
the bridge will bring me ore to you
& on the bridge our joys for life
will be shown & lighted by our stars
Chasing thy sorrows
Far far away
We will never be parted
Again for a day[40]

CHAPTER 6

Mining the Dreamworld

Aug 23–1921 . . . the little girl in a blue & white plaid gingham dress, who comes so often in my dreams to me, she means (The Care) (The Match-less Mine) she came close to us happy with her light bright golden hair hanging down all over her face you could not see her face but I think it ment she & mine was protected

The human urge to mine the depths of our dreams and visions is ageless. Early cave drawings depict powerful visions of the divine and the demonic for all to see and ponder. The Puritans paid careful attention to recording their dreams.[1] The Native American participants in the Ghost Dance embraced an earth-changing vision that struck fear in the hearts of their colonizers. Psychoanalysts are richly rewarded for guiding clients into the meaning of their dreams. Our dreams and visions tease us with the possibility of knowing our deepest selves. Lizzie Tabor, a devout Catholic familiar with the lives of saints who experienced visions, welcomed many of her dreams as messages from God and searched for their meaning. As Lizzie became an experienced dreamer, she gained authority concerning the recurring symbols in her Dreamworld. She also read tea leaves for useful messages about her future, conforming to the early twentieth-century American concept of pragmatic spiritualism.[2] We can never fathom the mind of Lizzie Tabor, just as we cannot know the mind of any other being or even our own innermost depths. If we draw back, however, and think of Tabor's "Dreams and Visions" as a text about dreams, albeit an eccentric and obscure one, there are many ways to interpret it.

"DIVING INTO THE WRECK"

I came to the "Dreams and Visions" of Baby Doe Tabor with modest specialized mining tools: the curiosity, experience, patience, and presuppositions of a diary scholar. I awakened to the potential of the diary as a form of life-writing well suited to women during the second wave of the feminist movement in the 1970s, when I read the seductive diaries of Anaïs Nin, which spoke intimately of being female. Nin meditated on things women such as myself felt safe discussing only in consciousness-raising groups: sexual desire, deep insecurities, and the pleasures of our bodies. In the first women's literature courses offered at the University of Iowa, I read Virginia Woolf's *A Writer's Diary*, her husband's distilled posthumous edition of the modernist author's journals. The diaries of bona fide authors such as Virginia Woolf and Fanny Burney—who themselves had only recently been admitted into the university curriculum as "great (women) writers"—were considered quasiliterary, for one could see the mind of the Artist grappling with the challenge of producing Literature. But what if the writer were not a great artist and her story not skillfully edited to seem like memoir? I had become interested in pioneer midwestern women's history and began reading a manuscript diary, which was filled with accounts of "usual work" rather than erudite meditations or sexual angst. As diary editors Mary Jane Moffat and Charlotte Painter have observed: "The form has been an important outlet for women because it is an analogue to their lives: emotional, fragmentary, interrupted, modest, not to be taken seriously, private, restricted, daily, trivial, formless, concerned with self, and as endless as their tasks."[3]

I ended up studying just such an "endless" twenty-five-hundred-page manuscript diary written over a thirty-year period by an Iowa pioneer farmwoman named Emily Hawley Gillespie for my American Studies Ph.D. research. I came to the Gillespie text with the assumption, based on my undergraduate students' brief forays into short sections of the journal, that Emily Gillespie was a Victorian heroine who endured the failure of crops and her marriage, ultimately martyring herself to the ideal of motherhood, and recording her struggles within the pages of her journal. However, my own nightlong sessions with Gillespie's manuscript upset these assumptions and showed her to be a garrulous self-righteous woman writing a defensive diary. I did not like her as a person, but I admired her compensatory text and her persistence in telling her own version of her life in what Robert Fothergill terms a "serial autobiography." I proposed that even in "ordinary" women's diaries we could uncover a form of literature achieved through their creation and manipulation of characters, plot, and their own persona. (A dozen years later, I was both chagrined and vindicated in my diary-as-literature argument when newly available Gillespie manuscripts revealed her canny agency in crafting an image of herself as martyr by subtly revising elements of her youthful diaries.)[4]

In the midst of the seemingly endless Gillespie project, I dipped my toe into the Dreamworld of Baby Doe Tabor during the trip to the Colorado State Historical Society described in the preface to this work. Somewhere within the thousands of fragments, I was certain, was the self-defending story that would be a counternarrative to the legend. Many things puzzled me: the code, the saints, the demons, the two very different sets of handwriting. Even though I could not discern an obvious narrative line within the "Dreams and Visions," Lizzie Tabor's attention to dating her accounts assured me that I was dealing with yet another form of journal, and that a "plot" would eventually emerge. I had spent years unearthing a compelling narrative, what Emily Gillespie called a "secret to be burried," from within that farmwoman's diary dealing mostly with weather and health. Everyone knew the story of Baby Doe and now surely I would be able to add to and contest it by discovering Lizzie's inner story via her "Dreams and Visions." I enlarged my concept of diaries to include the long tradition of dream chronicles kept by medieval mystics and Puritans. I also learned how these dreamers were wary of entering the Dreamworld, where human openness to the divine made one vulnerable to the demonic and to spiritual chaos. Determined to apply scholarly order to chaos, I made a closer examination of Lizzie's "Dreams and Visions," her intermittent diary, and the correspondence—all housed in separated archive containers—and I discovered their complex interaction. I again enlarged my concept of Lizzie's diary to that of an "interior journal" that integrated her waking and sleeping worlds.[5] For days on end I transcribed her "Dreams and Visions," indexing pivotal words I thought would provide a map into Lizzie's mind. Before I suggest what I found in my mining, and what I hope other experts better equipped might find within the "Dreams and Visions," I want to disclose the presuppositions I initially brought to the task. One by one I discarded them as I went deeper into the Dreamworld and searched widely for new tools more appropriate to Lizzie's labyrinthine text. I held fast to Adrienne Rich's poem, "Diving into the Wreck":

> I came to explore the wreck
> The words are purposes.
> The words are maps.
> I came to see the damage that was done
> and the treasures that prevail.
>   . . .

the thing I came for:
the wreck and not the story of the wreck.
the thing itself and not the myth.[6]

At the outset, fully immersed as I was in the Tabor legend, I expected to find a feisty sexual woman, misunderstood for her time, a defensive and angry Baby Doe. Instead I discovered a weeping woman who in her tender moments was the devout Catholic Lizzie and in her greatest trials became the Warrior Mother Mrs. H.A.W. Tabor. The saga of Baby Doe's ill-gotten marriage to millionaire Horace Tabor and her retreat to the Matchless mine predisposed me to find a dreamer obsessed with past riches and her idealized husband. What I found undermines the male-centered capitalist story of rags to riches to rags. I eventually discarded the heteronormative Horace-driven load that weighed down my pack of tools as I became attentive to recurring narrative nuggets that signaled what was important to the real Lizzie. I chose the longer process of listening to Lizzie anew, rather than trying to fit her into and against the legend of Baby Doe.

Starting at the surface level, I assumed that the writings of the famous Baby Doe were fully preserved at the Colorado State Historical Society. Then I learned that Mrs. Tabor's late-life writings had probably been removed from her cabin, and that her carefully collected papers may have been compromised several times before they were turned over to archivists for processing (see chapter 2). Theresa O'Brien stated in her Leadville memoir of Baby Doe: "The attorney who administered the estate . . . regretted having destroyed a large bundle of clippings contained in the canvas bags she had cached with the Saint Vincent's Hospital nuns."[7] I also discovered that primary documents, which my CHS research notes from 1993 indicate held crucial information, were no longer in their designated places in the Tabor archives. I was forced to admit "the damage that was done" and my dependence upon what survived of Lizzie's life's work. In discarding any notion that the surviving fragments would provide a story, denouement, closure, or answers to gnawing questions about Baby Doe, I felt the biographer historian's burden lighten. I took up the more capacious tools of the literary critic, which are adept at multiple interpretations and polyvocality.

Even the surface feature of the handwriting in the "Dreams and Visions" overturned my initial assumption that Baby Doe deteriorated from a writer of tidy rational script into a madwoman capable only of scribbled swirls. While the very last scraps show the large handwriting of an elderly woman whose eyesight and health were waning, some of the earliest "Dreams and Visions" are also recorded in scrawled writing, which I now attribute to Lizzie's quest to record an experience immediately, in imperfect "rough drafts." The hand-writing is that of a writer who existed on at least two planes, the rational and the spiritual, of a woman experimenting with "automatic writing" as it was once called. Thus the legend I had carried of a sinner's descent into madness was displaced by a more pragmatic—and poignant—one of a woman whose manual dexterity suffered from age and malnutrition.

This 13 day of Dec [1921] I have nothing to eat not a cent & no rent money God don't let me get hungry I have had very little to eat lately. Bless God forever

I thought my mining would find dream after dream of the once rich Baby Doe's past possessions. In reality I found touching animal symbols of the Tabors' wealthier past: Silver's beloved pets, Lizzie's splendid horses and carriages. Did the isolated Lizzie, stranded by poverty, most miss her physical mobility under the protection of Horace, rather than her social mobility that was circumscribed by Denver's social elite? When Lizzie was most hungry, she would dream of splendid banquets that she viewed but could not enjoy because her shabby clothes—not her morals—were unacceptable. I expected to find, especially in the early "Dreams and Visions," glowing memories of the great love story of Baby Doe for her Silver King. Instead I found poor Horace competing for Lizzie's attention with incompetent first husband, Harvey Doe, who was nonetheless an entertaining and cheerful figure in the Dreamworld with his singing and his piano playing. Lizzie did dream of Horace, but often in ambiguous situations; sometimes Horace was not a shining Silver King but, rather, a stained and earthy man:

May 29–1914 To day I dreamed that Silver & I were walking together & I helped carry her bundles they were too heavy we went to our home door & found a broken pad lock an old one Best [hired man] had put there then my Tabor was with me & he said "I thought a good safe lock was there["] & next I saw him standing naked in a white bath tub & there were yellow stains down his legs & on his bottom. This dream means evil & to night I found a miner I trusted was false & had lied to me about the Best men's trouble & what I asked him to do & I know it we have troubles [sideways in margin:] & that means dirty money

Horace also competed with Lizzie's prolific natal family in the Dreamworld. The riches Lizzie dreamt of were rarely the garish ones Horace had provided, the ones so lavishly detailed in the legend of the Tabors. Instead, in her Dreamworld Lizzie returned to the rich affection of the McCourts, who doted on her when she was young and still embraced her. The dreamer spent far more time in her natal Wisconsin home than she did in the splendid Denver mansion. As Lizzie's dreams grew more troubling, their settings became darker: unidentified boardinghouse rooms and houses with steep mysterious staircases she felt compelled to ascend, for Lizzie was attentive to these explorations and what they would reveal.

After 1914 Horace receded even farther into the background, displaced by the true love story I did not expect to find dominating the papers of Baby Doe: the consuming, painful mother-love of Lizzie for Silver. Lizzie's decade-long obsession with Silver, from 1914 to 1924, overshadows the story of millionaire Horace and his Baby. Horace is dethroned as the scraps of paper reveal a woman-centered mother-daughter love story with ageless antecedents: Demeter and Persephone, Naomi and daughter-in-law Ruth. Whether the Dreamworld dominance of Silver continued during the ten years in which Lizzie outlived her daughter may never be ascertained, for there are few papers dated after 1925 in the collection. However, mothers know deep in their hearts that Lizzie's love continued after Silver's death, despite the lack of documentary evidence. In fact it might have been easier for Lizzie to dream of an idealized daughter once Silver's dunning letters about miscarriages and men stopped.

I did find in the dreams the anger and defensiveness I had expected— but they were not weapons wielded on behalf of past wrongs done to Baby Doe. They were the armaments Lizzie employed in her primary role within the Dreamworld: a mother fighting on behalf of the urgent real-world needs of her daughters. There were many enemies to confront: scheming brothers, former family friends, creditors and dishonest mine leasees, licentious men who hypnotized Silver, the devil himself. Central to the defense of the Dreamworld is the ever endangered, ever promising Matchless mine. According to the legend of Baby Doe, the mine symbolizes both the mad hopes of the gold-digging wanton that the Tabor wealth will return and also, eventually, the mad widow's faithfulness to Horace's deathbed wish. However, Lizzie's writings insist that the Matchless meant far more to her than money: it stood for a mother's hope. Buried deep within her papers, part vision and part interpretative memoir, is a mother's lament that reveals the Matchless was a symbol of the return of her wandering daughters, not her wealth. It shows Lizzie's realization that she had unwittingly made a choice—as cruel as Sophie's Choice—between her daughters and her mine (which was also her only home), when her McCourt kin first wooed her eldest child, Lily, to Chicago to escape her mother's poverty and the stigma of the Tabor scandals. In 1915 it appeared that McCourt siblings Peter and Claudia might do the same with Silver, who was rebelling under her mother's moralistic surveillance:

> *Sept 27 [1915] at 10 to 8 P.M. I heard like the sound of a message wire ring so long as if coming from far. Pete has been trying for over a year to get Silver to go to Chicago & live with Claud he had in fact tried it for years & offered me 100 dollars a month if I would go & turn the Matchless mine to him Now he has got Silver there & he & Claud took my darling child Lily & they have robbed me of both my children if I could have realized they could accomplish the devilish crime I would have given the Matchless to them gladly gladly All I wanted was my poor orphant darling children my own babies*

In Lizzie's mind, she had unwittingly preserved her rights to the Matchless by giving up her rights to her girls. She was guilty of bad bargaining, not bad mothering. Having paid so dearly for the mine, of course Lizzie would hold onto it until her dying day. In her Dreamworld, Lizzie battled all threats on behalf of both her mine and her "babies," repeatedly stating her hope that once she got the Matchless to produce a livable income, surely Silver would return. The driving force behind this consuming vigilance over the Matchless was not fidelity to dead Horace but action on behalf of her very alive daughters. Indignation and worry fueled Lizzie's obsessive concern about the Matchless in both the Dreamworld and the real world, where she repeatedly wrote diary entries about shadowy men following her to the mine.

The final notion I originally brought to the papers of Baby Doe was the expectation that, although this formerly notorious woman might appear penitent in her madwoman's clothes to her onlookers, she would reveal herself in her private writings to be merely "performing" the abject, in mockery of a judgmental world. I thought that surely her rags and crucifix were yet another costume flouting convention, like the lavish white wedding gown she wore as a divorcée at her Catholic marriage ceremony to Horace. I found instead the earnest voice of a devout Catholic, who I believe dressed as a religious pilgrim or mystic, not a penitent. She dressed as one who converted bankruptcy into a purposeful vow of poverty and in so doing drew attention to her calling via her clothing, just as nuns once did in their habits. And just as people assisted nuns with acts of modest devotion, some in

Leadville brought food to their local religious recluse in her cloistered cabin. O'Brien recalled, "Baby Doe also was a mystic. . . . She was senile and proud at eighty-one years of age."[8] In her reclusive world, Lizzie suffered horrifying specters of devils, as one would expect of a penitent sinner. But she more often received lovely dreams from God that confirmed His love for her. While these wonderful dreams gave her a sense of power, the devilish figures tortured her in ways she was incapable of escaping. I was compelled to pay attention to Lizzie's suffering as well as her resistance, just as Lizzie did when recording awful images of filth, bugs, and Silver's yellow dying eyes. As I peeled away layers of legend, I encountered an uncompromising Dreamworld scribe, whom I followed into vivid surrealist scenes that sometimes permeated my own nights. For me, the way out of the Dreamworld and into a modicum of understanding has been to look at Lizzie Tabor's writing as an intensely complex autobiographical text, an "out-law genre," to use Caren Kaplan's term.[9] I intimately know how this text affected me as a reader. Using the tools from several disciplines, I can illuminate ways in which it may have served Lizzie as its writer.

SEARCHING FOR FIDELITY

Lizzie Tabor clearly found the workings of her subconscious mind interesting and attempted many times to interpret her dreams. After her record of a particularly vivid dream of sailing with her family in a boat on the beautiful ocean, she wrote on November 17, 1921:

> Then God gave me the interpretation—that Stephen sailing with Mother and Silver—Stephen in dreams or Visions always means safety in Mine & all our affairs & life & success a little girl means the Mine—and Mother a warning of sorrow—so Steph with them and it getting dusk means our relief will be a little longer coming. . . .

If psychologists were to "analyze" Lizzie Tabor based on her "Dreams and Visions," they would come to completely different conclusions depending on their perspectives. In the most elementary terms, the Freudian-based school of psychoanalysis argues that dreams represent our deepest repressions while Jungian analytic psychology sees dreams as positive dramas in a process that moves us toward psychological integration.[10] In essence, for Freud dreams were symptoms of pathology whereas for Jung they were cre-

ative and healthy. Thus Silver Tabor, the dominant figure in the most active
years of Lizzie's dreaming, would symbolize contrasting things to these ana-
lysts. From the Freudian perspective, the sinful Silver could symbolize Lizzie
herself and the repressed sexuality of her own past. Silver's sexual misadventures, that her mother was doomed to view in tormenting unbidden
nightmares, would represent Lizzie's own sexuality. Lizzie Tabor was, after
all, a Victorian woman who was very uncomfortable whenever she dreamed
erotically about her own body. On the rare occasions in which Lizzie
appeared in a sexual dream, she was worried and disgusted.

> *March 18–1916 . . . I fell asleep & dreamed a nasty terrible dream of L1b4r and*
> *3 L5stf56 [code for Tabor and I Lustful] This dream seems to have always meant*
> *sadness*

From a Jungian analytical psychology perspective, on the other hand, Silver
might be Lizzie's coping strategy toward her own past as a misunderstood
woman, a past in which she unwillingly starred as the hypersexual Baby Doe
who seduced Horace Tabor away from his first wife. In one dream, Silver
plans to take her baby in the company of Papa Tabor to the Opera House,
"just as her mother used to"—but decides against it. Thus the dreaming
mother protects Silver from the gawking crowds eager to spot Baby Doe
that she once faced. In another dream, Silver and Horace slip away from
the sixty-seven-year-old Lizzie, just as Baby Doe and Horace long ago had
eluded Augusta:

> *. . . Silent and tall Silver said "Papa and I have arranged for you to live in a*
> *house—and we are going to some where" I was hurt and I did not speak I wanted*
> *to hear a little longer the plans. [November 18, 1921]*

Rather than interpret Silver as a symbol of either Lizzie's sexual or her
suffering shadow self, what if we credit Lizzie's own interpretation of Silver's
purpose in her dreams? If we give up the notion of psychoanalyzing a dead
woman and instead listen to her as an actor in her own life, we can arrive at
what Donna Haraway calls "situated knowledge"—which means "we give up
mastery but keep searching for fidelity."[11] Lizzie based her actions on her
certainty that the spirit of Silver, not some Freudian symbol of her own sexuality, visited her in the Dreamworld and that these dreams were relevant to
her present and future, not her past. After describing particularly horrific
nightmares about Silver, Lizzie would write her own urgent commentaries:

"I must save her," or "O Blessed Jesus let me get to her." These dreams motivated the Mindful Mother to send money, write letters, travel to Indianapolis, and pray endlessly on behalf of Silver.

There is a field of functional dream analysis that allows us to focus on how
the "Dreams and Visions" served Lizzie Tabor in utilitarian ways. For example, how did Lizzie "process" Silver within the deep mine of her own psyche
in order to serve her own needs as a mother? My following analysis of six
ways in which Lizzie Tabor dealt with her Silver in the Dreamworld seems
orderly, but its framework is imposed by my intellect in search of a compre-
hensible text. Lizzie's Dreamworld was far from tidy. In one night she could
"see" Silver as an innocent child who then metamorphosed—with the irrational fluidity we know from our own dreamworlds—into a slattern. However, if we turn our attention away from the fascinating Silver, and toward the
ways in which the dreams functioned for her mother, we can begin to understand the superhuman dream work undertaken by Lizzie Tabor.

PROCESSING SILVER

The seemingly simplest dreams are those in which Lizzie *relives* experiences
when Silver was young and unproblematic. As Silver matured and her reputation became sullied, how soothing it must have been to recall the pure
youthful girl in the Dreamworld. A particularly provocative dream from
March 1917 features Silver surrounded by curls and flowers, much as Lily
was in the famous Thomas Nast childhood drawing used for the cover of
Harper's Bazar. However, Silver is dancing with a group of "girls," probably
Lizzie's response to a recent letter from Silver boasting that she was the prettiest girl in the Indianapolis chorus. The dream functions to transform the
adult sexualized dancing Silver back into the innocent dancing child. Then
a baby enters the dream—a mysterious baby who perhaps is the one Silver
"lost" in 1915, or the one she would "miscarry" in November 1917. Yet all is
"happy" in this idealized world of Silver's past in which perhaps two lost
babies accompany Silver—or perhaps Silver herself reverts into baby form:

> *Mar 9–1917 I dreamed my darling Silver came dancing towards me with a whole
> string of other girls following afer her all dancing she leading them she was beauti-
> ful gay & laughing one leg thrown high & dancing & she seemed to be all curls &
> flowers. Then I dreamed of buying pearl beads & I put a long string of some kind
> of big white beads around my neck. Then I dreamed of being at Matchless Mine*

snow all over & Mother was there & others & a large man dark whiskers was
holding & carrying about a baby & the baby was bald-headed I think we were
laughing & all happy I was telling that the baby said is that bald head its bottom
so it may have been two babys & one bald-headed all was friendly & happy

Unhappily for Lizzie, most of the events she relived in the Dreamworld regarding Silver were suggestive. The dream below blends McCourt family disapproval of Silver, as embodied by Lizzie's brother Phil, with mortifying incidents reminiscent of Silver's wild 1914 Leadville party, the one that the irate Mrs. Tabor had invaded. The condition of Silver's eyes—bright or darkly dull—predicts in the Dreamworld whether the "relived" dream experience is good or bad. Although the dream is painful, its ending shows how it functions for Lizzie: she gives her grief to God, to lighten the "mother load" of concern over Silver:

June 2–1915 I dreamed this terrible thing I was walking on a Denver St Phil was
standing on the edge of the sidewalk several people were standing near him as I
passed he jeered at me & said "your daughter your daughter" & sneered at me.
. . . Then I . . . saw my poor darling child Silver all bent over drest in light with
a white cloth tied over her head her face was O so white & her eyes were the
blackest & she was so drunk she was unconscious she was talking to trying to to
some men that stood in a door way she was looking so hard at me O I thought I
would die of grief in this terrible dream. . . . I gave it to God when I woke up.

A second way that Lizzie copes with Silver in the Dreamworld is to *reunite* with her in a variety of settings, ranging from the McCourt family home in Wisconsin to cheap hotel rooms. Codreamers in their happier days, Lizzie and Silver are usually cast in these dreams as coactors who cooperate. But there is an undertone of anxiety because the mother is unable to control Silver's actions. Silver slips away like quicksilver, seems to hold secrets, and talks to "dark" unsavory companions, despite her mother's disapproval. Yet there are striking moments when Silver and her mother share experiences such as digging up dead babies (see chapter 5) or preparing for what is revealed to be a dual wedding:

Sept 15–1921 I dreamed my darling Sister Nealie was fitting a grand rich white
brocaded wedding dress on me a princess dress all pure white long old fashioned
wedding train & full skirt low neck. . . . It fit me tight & made my figure more
beautiful than any had ever seen. . . . Silver sat in a chair looking on I sat close
to her & I was watching myself being fitted. . . . Silver & I sat together (strange)

and my Silver was also going to be married also, & I was going to marry Judge
Pendry. . . .

Always attentive to the meaning of her dreams, Lizzie wrote on the bottom
of this seemingly benign account, "Sept 15 Silver wrote me from Chicago
that she was going to get married & she asked me to go & live with her O my
poor darling my heart is broken for her I received her letter Sept 17." The
fact that Lizzie "knew" in her Dreamworld of Silver's wedding plans before
Silver's letter arrived must have motivated her to delve into the exterior
rather than interior meaning of every dream.

A third way in which Lizzie processed her troubles with Silver in the
Dreamworld was to *recast* her anxieties onto animal figures, a strategy
acknowledged by almost all dream theories. For example, Lizzie's vivid May
1914 vision of Silver being bloodied and probably raped on the grounds of
the Matchless mine (see chapter 5) is immediately followed by an account
of an ominous vision of Silver's childhood pet:

> *The next day I had a vision of her black cat Lamie [?] he was lying on his side &*
> *holding out his 4 legs and paws to me to play with me & that wonderful beautiful*
> *yellow eye (his dying eye) look at me so lovingly. These visions must mean some-*
> *thing terrible for my poor Honeymaid. . . .*

In the turbulent period in which Lizzie first learned of her daughter's sexual promiscuity, her animal dreams were usually about past pets, symbols of
(lost) innocence. In 1916 Silver kisses a bloated—perhaps pregnant—poodle that dies in her mother's lap. By 1921 the association of Silver with sen-
sually evil animals was inevitable:

> *July 15–1921 I dreamed a sad & terrible dream of my darling child Silver—she*
> *was sitting down she had I think white wrapper on and she looked sad and on her*
> *knee sat a small long black snake with its body standed (part of it) straight up &*
> *its terrible head up high the snake was sticking out its terrible tongue and (O my*
> *God save her) for she was putting out her finger and touching that snakes tongue*
> *every time he stuck it out & that was all the time quickly it was the devil & the*
> *snake showed it was the devil My heart was broken I should die of grief to see my*
> *precious child touching a snakes tongue & it sitting up on her lap. O she is in trou-*
> *ble O Blessed God let me get to her. . . .*

Despite the fact that Silver repeatedly touches the snake's tongue (a horrible image to any Christian familiar with Eve's fall and obvious to any post-

Freudian), Lizzie interprets her dream as a call to arms for Silver "in trouble." She does not admit that Silver reached out to touch trouble.

The predominant dream work the Warrior Mother undertook night after night was to *rescue* Silver. The most recurrent "plot" in the Dreamworld is Lizzie's attempt to rescue her valuables—Silver, the mysterious bundle, nameless babies, the Matchless mine, and ultimately the very souls of her daughters and herself. The usual result, however, is Lizzie's ultimate powerlessness. She hides from evil men lurking in shadows but can never be certain she has escaped them. She repeatedly sees Silver as endangered but cannot assist her. Lizzie is the Cassandra figure who anticipates disaster but is unheeded, a role in the Dreamworld that mirrored her condition in the real world: shunned, penniless, mad. The dream of agency below is striking in its rarity and startling in the degree of aggression Lizzie demonstrates toward the snakelike figure of Ed Brown, the young man Lizzie "saw" raping Silver a year earlier in a vision. However, in the line that ends the vivid account, Lizzie "rescues" Silver from complicity with evil Ed by rendering her quietly dressed in white, albeit a nightgown.

> *June 18–1915 . . . I dreamed we were in a house & Silver & several other smaller than Silver girls or folks were hiding Edd Brown from me. I tried several times to get hold of him but he got away & finely I got him he came walking to me thin & weak looking I grabbed him pulled him down stairs out in the yard & got hold of his throat & held it it was so thin & little & it had no bones or mussels in it on skin & wind pipe I held on his throat & he was so scared he did not struggle or move but a death white came over his face & around his mouth & I lessened my grip, thought he was going to die of fright, but I kept a good hold on his throat anyway & he looked terrible & I held him near the white picket fence & asked him if he raped he said yes, he did & said yes to all the questions I asked him . . . I woke up then. When I got Edd Brown out of Silver's room I dreamed she was in a white night dress & did not then try to get him away she was quiet standing up looking at us. . . .*

The lack of a definitive pronoun before the line "did not then try to get him away" leaves unanswered for us whether it was Lizzie who did not try to get Ed farther away, because her white-clad innocent daughter was now safe, or whether it was sinful Silver who did not assist Lizzie in getting Ed away. Did Silver not try to hide Ed away because she was innocent—or guilty? The ambiguity of Silver's position no doubt stimulated the myriad dreams of her as endangered, for Lizzie had to fend off not only predatory men but her daughter's own nature.

The most poignant dreams are those in which Lizzie *releases* Silver to her doom. Many of these dreams feature departures (Silver leaving in a black carriage, Silver disappearing) that I believe symbolize her moral departure. These recurrent images functioned perhaps to inure Lizzie to the inevitable split between mother and daughter when Silver matured into womanhood. But Lizzie's dreams are so agonizing they seem to foretell a more permanent separation—Silver's death. In these dreams of release, Lizzie suffers as the agonized and helpless onlooker, rather than the savior:

> *May 1st—1922 I dreamed of being with my darling Child Silver She was in a sort of white all snowy white cheap gown & She looked pale & white & weak & was worried in trouble some child was with us She Silver came up to me and She kissed me in the mouth, said "mama kiss me good bye I am going forever away" & she started to go down a long flight of broad light colored stairs all clean & bright she then had a long hose in her hand & was at the top of the stairs & out of the hose was pouring water on some rats that was coming up after her I said something to her & she said I like snakes better it made me sad that she liked snakes. . . .*

Although Lizzie might release Silver, she never rejects her daughter in the Dreamworld or in the real world. The bedrock of Lizzie's mother-love was unshakable. This mother-love enabled Lizzie to have phenomenal dreams in which she *resurrects* Silver as a Dream Child. In 1915 Lizzie could still dream of her daughter as being amenable to religious salvation:

> *March 12–1915 To day I dreamed that I went with several through our new cathedral & that my child Silver was with me & when she came to St Rita statue she fell on her knees and said "O this will make me think & change my thought["] & she prayed*

By 1922, however, greater resurrection was required, one that included Horace's presence, in order to counter all the information concerning poverty, pregnancies, and love affairs that Lizzie received in Silver's letters.

> *Easter Sunday April 16–1922—I dreamed Jesus Blessed me to ease my sorrow. I saw my darling Silver come she had on a table the most wonderful, most beautiful Marvelous Magnificent snowy Pure White Marble Statue a Bust of her Father H.A.W. Tabor—her darling papa. . . . She had made all by herself it was her Masterpiece hers alone, she stood close to the Statue her hand resting on it she*

was in a long blue & white large plaid gingham apron which she wore while mak-
ing the wonderful Statue—O Bless Jesus our Divine Saviour

The plaid gingham costume worn by Silver resembles the gingham dress of
Lizzie's beloved Matchless Mine Girl, the recurrent figure who was very welcome in the Dreamworld as a good omen. This little girl may also have been a
stand-in for Lily and Silver, who grieved Lizzie by no longer living at the Matchless. If in Lizzie's tortured mind she had unwittingly traded away her daughters
in order to preserve the Matchless, conjuring up this substitute resident
Dream Child brought solace to the mother that her real-life, complicated, and
compromised daughters could not. This girl would stay youthful and pure, forever cavorting in gingham on the grounds of the Matchless mine.

Lizzie might be deemed mad to both release and resurrect Silver in such
contradictory dreams. Yet I see this as a survival strategy in which the
resilient mother "divided" Silver into two beings: the sinful one who must
depart (representing her dead departed daughter) and the redeemed one
who came to codream, as they had done together at the Matchless long ago:

September 17–1920 O, our Lord Jesus Christ our Saviour Let me see the most
wonderfull blessing to-day Silver and I were close together both looking up for
God had us look up and we saw the great white clouds in the sky part in a round
ring and all the rest of the Sky remained covered with the big white clouds and in
the open place where the clouds had parted & formed a large round space in the
round place was the richest lightest blue sky O such a rich light blue color and that
while blue sky was sparkling with the brightest golden Stars of all sizes . . . such
granure I can not at all describe O that Heavenly Sight for us to behold. Jesus had
some short time ago let me see a Vision of the figure No 17— & I had been wait-
ing for this 17 of Sept to come not knowing what to expect. It is to-day & this
glory God Jesus has blessed us with

My Silver is in Chicago to-day I am here in Room 103 Vendome Hotel Leadville
Colo—but God had her with me to behold this glory to tell us her & our suffer-
ings would soon be healed. . . . Mrs. H.A.W. Tabor

This Dreamworld acknowledgment of dual Silvers—one "close together"
with Lizzie and the other "in Chicago"—could explain why, five years later,
Mrs. Tabor publicly insisted, despite stark evidence to the contrary, that Silver had not died in Chicago in 1925. Perhaps the Sinning Silver was
deceased, but the Resurrected Silver continued to live on in her dreaming
mother's heart.

DREAM WORK

Although the legend depicts Baby Doe as driven deservedly mad by her tor-
turous dreams, my research suggests that Lizzie was undertaking useful
psyche-healing work via her dreams, work much like that outlined by Carl
Jung in his voluminous writings. With only a general knowledge of Jungian
psychology, I find convincing connections between the symbols in Lizzie's
Dreamworld and Jung's interpretations. Jung wrote, "To me, dreams are a
part of nature, which harbors no intention to deceive, but expresses something as best it can."[12] Lizzie welcomed pleasant dreams, which she felt came
from God, yet she also recorded devilish dreams because she was eager to
decipher what they were expressing to her. Jung perceived dreams as the psyche's way of problem-solving; Lizzie used her dreams to address unsolvable
problems. While Jung's archetypes have been convincingly critiqued by feminist scholars as masculist, some are appropriate for Lizzie Tabor, who was
only twenty years older than Jung and thus was influenced by cultural icons
he used in defining his "universal" archetypes. For example, Jung's figure of
the Hero, expanded through the insights of feminist archetypal theory,
could include the heroic Warrior Mother so prevalent in Lizzie's Dreamworld. Psychologist and educator Jeanette Renouf, who kindly read several
"Dreams and Visions," shared her interpretation of Dreamworld actors: "My
way with dreams is that we dream in symbols and since the dream is created
in the dreamer every part of it is a part of the dreamer. Perhaps, when Silver
appears in a dream I would not see it as Silver but symbolizing a part of Baby
Doe. Not so much guilt at her past but an effort of the unconscious to somehow reconcile the life experiences of Baby Doe. Her efforts to cope on her
own, first deserted as a pregnant young bride and, secondly, as a poverty-
stricken widow with two young children. There was very little guidance for
how to do this and she probably did the best she could with what she had;
her looks and later the Matchless Mine. Whatever she did it was socially
unacceptable. The dreams are perhaps the unconscious' way of sorting it all
out—but it is Baby Doe's unconscious, therefore the real people who appear
are only symbols of parts of Baby Doe."[13]

Lizzie was also familiar with the archetypal quest pattern of descent into
the underworld and rebirth so integral to the figure of Jesus Christ. As a
Catholic, she believed that a woman could undertake this quest, as had the
Virgin Mary, who witnessed her Son's death yet faithfully awaited His resurrection and now sat at His right hand in heaven.

Saturday Blessed Virgins day March 28–1925 God gave me a wonderful long dream to-day—I dreamed I was with God all during His Crucifixion I can not explain any of it it was terrible & a dark mass of people in a sollid dark big crowd but seemed close to God & with Him O Blessed suffering—Divine Jesus Christ we adore Worship Thee

Four months after this dream, Lizzie would join the Blessed Virgin Mary as a grieving mother who outlived her beloved child.

Lizzie also incorporated the Pure Child, a major Jungian symbol of rebirth, into her dreams through the figures of the little Matchless Mine Girl and other smiling babies. Throughout my exploration of the Dreamworld, I have interpreted most babies as symbols of Lizzie's or her daughters' children. However, Lizzie also understood a baby could be symbolic of good things, not a buried child. Harvey Doe also reenters the Dreamworld (Lizzie had been corresponding with the Wisconsin Does in her quest for mining funds). Note how Lizzie selects which items from her dream to accept as portents, and which to contest:

Dec 20–1921 . . . Then I dreamed Harvey Doe sat in the room with me & on his lap he had a fat baby—the Baby cried & I went over & took it off his lap & laid it down on my lap & lifted up its dress and I tried to spank it with my hand. . . . (I never slapped any thing in my life and I hated to dream I did) I think the dream means that I will have protection at the mine because Harvey held the Baby—& the Baby or a child has always meant the Matchless Mine in dreams or Visions. . . .

Another useful Jungian concept of dream functionality is that of synchronicity, the "meaningful coincidence of outer event and inner image."[14] Lizzie used the mystical and religious language of omens and signs to express her belief in her dreams' unfailing predictive synchronicity. As she withdrew from the real world and her peers died, she grew more reliant on her dreams as "confidants" who could warn her of danger.

The most vexing, persistent figures in the Dreamworld are the devilish men and demons who haunt and harass Lizzie. One explanation for Lizzie's obsessive dreams and visions of lurking dark men comes from Jungian Calvin S. Hall, who studied women's dreams and dream diaries. Hall posited that in their aggressive dreams, women took the role of victims—usually victims of men. Perceiving herself as constantly the victim of unscrupulous men in the real world and in the Dreamworld, Lizzie may have been processing aggressive emotions for which there was no acceptable outlet for a woman born in 1854. The dark and evil part within each of us, which Jung called the Shadow self that should not be repressed, could be played by Silver in the Dreamworld, although Lizzie did not see her functioning in that way. In dreams that disgusted Lizzie, an unbidden shadowy, sexual Lizzie occasionally appeared kissing Horace or kissing other men while Horace looked on.

Even this superficial brush-stroke portrait of Lizzie Tabor as Jungian dreamer shows what great agency and interpretative work she brought to her task in her roles as heroic woman warrior, victim or aggressor, quest follower, problem solver, and seer. Jungian analysis relies on a chronological series of dreams so that the intent of an individual's personal symbols emerges. How fortunate that Lizzie Tabor left behind a rich lode of "Dreams and Visions" awaiting such analysis. How frustrating that the "Dreams and Visions" from the last decade of her life are practically nonexistent.

In traditional Freudian dream interpretation, the devils and demons who tortured Lizzie mirror the evil within this infamous woman sinner's heart, while for Jung they might symbolize enemies whose intent the dreamer needed to process. Clearly some of the devils in the Dreamworld stand for actual figures, such as creditors or the series of men who futilely leased mining rights to the Matchless from Mrs. Tabor. Going deeper into the Dreamworld, I interpret the consistent darkness of her demons as mirrors of the racial anxieties of her era. Horace Tabor had employed and exploited recent immigrants in his mining heyday and was a victorious strikebreaker. Did the menacing dark figures, especially the few identified in the "Dreams and Visions" as "Mexican" and "Chinese" by Lizzie, symbolize her recognition that the wealth of the Matchless and its rich sister mines was in truth the result of the labor by dark men and therefore not legitimately hers? This would help explain her constant worry over ownership of the mine in the Dreamworld, where her conscience may have questioned her rights. Or perhaps the devils symbolized Lizzie's own dark role as a disdained Irish woman. As Davis Roediger has documented, immigrant Irish workers were associated with abject racial "others" in nineteenth-century America.[15] Thus the demons who threatened Lizzie could represent the illegitimacy of her role as the Irish wife of a mining millionaire, a short-lived position lost so long ago that it must have itself seemed only a dream. Other devils point to demons from the past that Lizzie could not bring herself to name. The devils could simultaneously symbolize fears of dark people and a darker secret, deeper within Lizzie's soul that pointed to unnameable evil:

incest. Early in my research on Lizzie Tabor's writing, I turned to the analysis of women's dreams conducted by Janet Jacobs in her heartbreaking study, *Victimized Daughters*, because certain descriptions of Horace and Silver in bed together, sometimes with a baby, troubled me. I could not tell if my suspicions of a licentious Horace, suspicions fueled by recent studies documenting how child sexual abuse was rampant, were leading me to overinterpret Lizzie's dreams—or if she was trying to tell something she could not speak:

> *July 10–1921 I dreamed a terrible dream about our darling Tabor (it is a warning of sorrow) I was lying in a big clean bed all white bed clothes with him he was 1b5s289 h37 s26f [abusing him self] terribly and I feared it would mark the ch36d [child] that he had just put the s22d [seed] in for I was very sad & sorrowful for him to do so & it was so strange for him to do it. . . .*

If, as Jacobs argues, dreams are a coded way of telling us something, then this code-within-a-code is a double mask. In Jacobs's interviews with women who had been sexually abused by their fathers, many of them as children under the age of eight, Jacobs uncovered manifestations of fear-filled sleep disorders and dreams of a faceless demonic figure. Only through analysis would the women realize that certain features of this dark figure, such as his hands, were identical to those of their abuser. Jacobs found that for particularly religious women, this figure appeared as the devil. "Among the survivors in this study, nearly half the respondents exhibited symptoms of post traumatic stress disorder in which religious symbols of evil were internalized as representative of the abuser, suggesting that the trauma of incest may result in the 'demonization' of the perpetrator."[16] When I carefully scrutinized Lizzie's dreams about her own father, I found fears of his judgment and desire for his safety, but no devils. However, Lizzie did write about one provocative scene with her father:

> *Nov 24–1919 I dreamed of being in a clean white bed & my Father came & sat down by the bed & was so nice & pleasant but he did not look like Pa he looked like that old devil of A.M. Stevenson. Then he & my Mother went to bed. . . .*

Lizzie dreamt of Horace (Papa Tabor, as Lizzie often called him) several times accompanied by young children in bed. Was Lizzie seeing herself as a baby in bed with Horace because he called his much-younger wife his baby? Could Horace have been a sexual abuser of the very young Lily and Silver? Perhaps he was just an affectionate man who fondled his daughters, a familiarity that some of the women in Jacobs's study nonetheless considered unwelcome and sexually traumatic. Sexual abuse can leave girls with the specter of an "evil other" lurking within themselves that can manifest itself in promiscuity. As Silver became promiscuous, perhaps Lizzie unconsciously laid the blame ("the seed") on Horace, a man she knew to have been highly sexual, even if young Silver did not consciously understand or even remember her father's physical affection. Deceased Horace, idealized in the real world by mother and daughter, perhaps metamorphosed into a sexual and secret-holding figure in the twilight Dreamworld.

> *April 19–1917 I had a Vision or dream of Tabor our darling to-day he came to me carrieng Silver in his arms she was a baby he came over to me & I was lying down he picked me up off the floor with his right hand still holding Silver in his left arm he was taking us to put us both in bed with him when he came to get me he said come to me I said O Papa I cant I am sick so he picked me up & carried us both he looked dark & Silver looked dark & I looked dark all seemed rather dark*

Traditional religious interpretation of the host of devils haunting Lizzie Tabor instead turns the dark mirror toward the dreamer, not the daddy, as the sinner. Catholic theologian and colleague Robert Burns read the collection of 270 "Dreams and Visions" I had transcribed verbatim, and he found Lizzie a fearful woman full of guilt who could not find peace. He drew a parallel between Lizzie's attacks by devils and Silver's attacks by bad men as coming from the same source: the drive to blame sources outside oneself for one's own evil nature.[17] Burns pointed to the following dream as symbolic of Lizzie's deep-set guilt:

> *June 6–1929 after I went to bed to night . . . as soon as I lay down to sleep I had just put out the light & lay down when I saw the biggest & most terrible terrible face & head of a man with the biggest most horrible terrifying eyes glaring close to me at me & the head & face was moving close to me not a foot from me O it was terrible it was the devil coming to attract me but I quickly held my crucifix close to him he vanished & [rest of account is torn off. Sideways is written:] he was a terrible devil*

To me this graphic account provides an alternative interpretation, one that ultimately emphasizes Lizzie's ability, with the aid of her beloved crucifix, to repel the terrible devil and prove her religious fidelity rather than her guilt. The struggles of holy pilgrims to rebuff the attractions of the devil form a major theme in Christian writing. Christ Himself was tempted by the devil, who first played upon His hunger in the desert (how hungry Mrs. Tabor must have been) and then offered Him all the kingdoms of the world if He would forsake God. The writings of religious mystics are filled with temptations resisted with the help of God. Saint Catherine of Siena, who like Lizzie Tabor suffered from sexual visions such as naked people coupling, chastised people seeking her help: "Alas, every day I am tormented by evil spirits; do you think I want anybody else's?"[18] Julian of Norwich wrote a dream account in her Long Text that is far more articulate than Lizzie's but expresses a similar struggle against the devil: "And as soon as I fell asleep, it seemed to me that the devil set himself at my throat, thrusting his face, like that of a young man, long and strangely lean, close to mine. I never saw anything like him; his colour was red, like a newly baked tile, with black spots like freckles, uglier than a tile. His hair was red as rust, not cut short in front, with side-locks hanging at his temples. He grinned at me with a vicious look, showing me white teeth so big that it all seemed the uglier to me. His body and his hands were misshapen, but he held me by the throat with his paws, and wanted to stop my breath and kill me, but he could not."[19]

Lizzie's urgent 1929 account is one of the rare writings from late in her life and shows her still valiantly resisting the forces of terrible evil. Compared to Julian's, Lizzie's descriptive language is repetitive, which I have argued in my diary scholarship is not a sign of a text's marginal literacy but of its authenticity. She does not paint a vivid word portrait of the devil, a product of many years reflection, as Julian does. Instead, Lizzie scribbled her rough sketch in the night on paper whose rough edges show that someone tore off the rest of the narrative. Did Lizzie self-censor a dream account that upon rereading she found too explicit? Did Edgar McMechan rip off the paper while reading it in his home, because of disgust or because it mentioned some powerful person? Do the tormenting devils indicate that the aging Mrs. Tabor was succumbing to madness, where former sins of her flesh now tormented her in the shape of devils? Or was the devout dreamer experiencing the numinous world of a religious mystic, in which she was repeatedly tempted and yet was able to overcome the devil?

FINDING A MYSTIC IN THE ROUGH

The tradition of female mysticism that Catholic Lizzie would have known provided another literary legacy in which she could define herself. Mysticism was one of the few ways in which women could be empowered in the

Catholic Church, an option that would appeal to a devout and isolated widow. If Lizzie considered herself a visionary or mystic, recording her "Dreams and Visions" would be her God-given duty. Lizzie's late-life circumstances paralleled those of many medieval female mystics, as outlined by Carol Flinders: "Turbulence, in any event, and sorrow of a great many kinds, commonly pervade the mystic's life from beginning to end: ill health, overwork and exhaustion, political opposition, alienation from friends or loved ones, spiritual aridity."[20] Mystics often came from humble backgrounds and could be former sinners, although explicit descriptions of those sins—with the exception of marginalized Margery Kempe—were left to canonized men such as Augustine and Francis. (Flinders notes that Theresa of Avila tried to write of her youthful sins, but her advisors edited them out.) Lizzie Tabor, familiar with the lives of the saints, knew that carnal women could be converted by God into spiritual models. Even arch sinner Mary Magdalene was embraced by Christ and then became a model of contemplative solitude, retreating to a cave after Christ's ascension. Likewise, twice-married sinner Lizzie Tabor had been reembraced by a few priests, as evidenced in their friendly correspondence with her. Even though Baby Doe had been publicly rebuked in 1883 by the Catholic priest duped into marrying two divorced people and would be therefore banned from the sacraments, her diary from the 1920s indicates that she made Confession and received the Holy Communion in Leadville. Andrew Scrimgeour, dean of Denver's Regis College, explained this paradoxical acceptance of the notorious Baby Doe as the church's tradition of "informal pastoral sensitivity," which acted as a bridge between official policy and a sinner's needs.[21] And on a stormy night in 1914 Lizzie recorded in her diary that she had baptized a drunk lying in the gutter lest he die unsaved. This was not a woman who felt severed from her church:

> *Oct—12–1914 Just about 7 PM in ally I Baptized a man who fell drunk acrost my path he fell a well dressed man in light cloths cane about 60 or 65 years old he fell back of Milo Hotel near stable door Baptised him with the water that lay in middle of ally. . . . I went to confession after that to West 6 Ave church where St Jerods statue is. . . .*[22]

As a woman given a second chance to prove her religiosity, Lizzie was particularly drawn to the figure of Saint Rita, who was canonized in 1900, the very year of Baby Doe's involuntary "conversion" into widowhood. Lizzie prayed to Saint Rita and sent Lily information about her. Saint Rita's hagiography in many ways parallels the life of Baby Doe. Rita of Cascia, Italy (1380–1457), was known as "the reluctant wife" who wished to become a

nun but instead acceded to her parents' wishes by marrying an abusive man
with whom she had two sons. Her husband was murdered, and the widow
then bore the additional grief of her two sons' deaths. Rita, now a middle-
aged widow, sought to join the Augustinian Nuns of Saint Mary Magdalene
but was refused three times because she clearly was not pure. She persisted
and became a nun renowned for her devotion to prayer. Perhaps Lizzie saw
in Saint Rita a role model of a woman who, despite marriage and two sons,
was able to dedicate the remainder her life to God. As early as 1912 young
Silver had explained her mother's religious goal in a letter to Father Guida:
"it now looks as if God is going to give her a chance to serve Him Him [*sic*]
in this life."[23] Saint Rita was also known as a supplicant's last resort, the
"Saint of impossible cases." Among Lizzie's "Dreams and Visions" is a diary
entry:

> *Blessed Saint Rita*
> *Wonderful St Rita*
>
> *Feb—18–1915 God* _Jesu made us_ *a Loan on the Matchless Mine Leadville all its*
> *great wealth will be used for charity and for the glory of our Savior. Mrs. H.A.W.*
> *Tabor*

Despite this brief ecstatic prayer, what Lizzie prayed for surely was impossible—the return of her mine's riches so that her daughters would come
home to join her forever in religious devotion. Several times Lizzie also
mentioned Saint Catherine of Siena, an Italian visionary who sought solitude and recruited her nieces into religious service. People who were familiar with Catherine's sweet voice were awed by a second powerful voice that
emerged when she spoke of God. Lizzie once dreamed of Silver in association with Catherine, but if Lizzie hoped that Silver would accept a religious
life, the outcome was ominous:

> *May 26–1915 I dreamed today that Silver had 3 of my grand rings 2 diamonds and*
> *a very bright ruby all about the same size 1–1/2 carret she put them all on her wed-*
> *ding finger a diamond each side of the ruby like the one God gave St Katherine of*
> *Sienna I don't know how large her jewels were & Silver was a little girl running,*
> *about 11 to 13 years she would take them off and put them on & then she tied the*
> *three together with a white twine & gave them to me to take care of for her. . . .*

I was encouraged to pursue the idea of Lizzie Tabor as a mystic by British
theologian Gerardo Wood, an Oxford-trained scholar of medieval mysticism who kindly read selected "Dreams and Visions." Wood pointed out

that, in her role as the Good Widow, Lizzie adopted many of the habits of medieval mystics: she was virtually cloistered, dressed in rags, attended religious services daily, and often had so little to eat that she experienced what she perceived as divine illuminations. Medieval nuns seeking visions knew that starvation was one route out of their bodies and into a numinous state; some became so extreme in their asceticism that they were chided by their superiors for becoming too weak even to serve God. Lizzie attributed her most glorious dreams to the power of God in her "prologues" to her accounts, which matches Wood's definition of mysticism as a "consciousness of experience of uncreated grace as a revelation of self disclosure from God."[24] "Uncreated grace" is the perfect term to describe this combination within Lizzie of both the passivity of a nineteenth-century female sinner and the assertiveness of a religious widow that justified her pursuit as an aspiring mystic. Lizzie could find both meaning and solace in what Flinders calls, "the mystical premise itself, the positing of an inner world that is 'more real' than the one around us, one that will receive us and strengthen us once we find our way into it."[25]

When I asked Professor Burns, at that time head of religious studies at my university, to read the "Dreams and Visions" as potential mysticism, he rejected the idea. He observed, "The writings of the mystics *flow*. This is not mystical writing." However, I suggest that the "madwoman in the cabin" did experience mystical visitations but lacked the infrastructure to make her prose "flow"—access to education, the encouragement of priests, the service of scribes to "improve" her writing. A graphomaniac with rudimentary education, limited vocabulary, no mentoring, and anxieties about an audience after Father Guida and Silver were no longer there to appreciate and encourage her dreams, Lizzie was doomed to be a mystic-in-the-rough, what Flinders calls a "paramystic." Lizzie's "Dreams and Visions" are "rough drafts," prototypes of Julian of Norwich's early "short form" descriptions of her "Shewings" that were twenty years later developed into a Long Form that "flowed." Lizzie left records of several miracles she felt were performed on her behalf, demonstrating her confidence in a personal relationship with God. Although youthful Silver wrote enthusiastically to Father Guida about her mother's miraculous escapes from accident and illness, neither mother nor daughter claimed Lizzie could perform miracles. She was extraordinarily devout but clearly did not consider herself a potential saint. However, the very fact that Lizzie wrote about visions, a far more risky and interactive religious manifestation than dreams, again shows how devoted she was to her calling. Flinders defines mysticism as the experiential discovery that meaning is within the self, via prayer and meditation. The sheer volume of Lizzie's writing shows how deeply she cultivated—and needed—this meaning. I requested that diocese archivists scan the papers of both Father Guida of Denver, who knew of Mrs. Tabor's dreams, and Father Horgan of Leadville, who was her last religious confidant, to find if they mentioned the "Dreams and Visions," but they located nothing and the papers are not open to the public. We are left with only Lizzie's word, her validation of her spiritual life that she authenticated page by laborious page.

THE MARVELOUS REAL

Lizzie's mystical world, in which she could commune with spirits and receive omens, echoes that of the literary tradition today called "magical realism." An early term for magical realism suggested by Cuban Alejo Carpentier, "lo real maravilloso americano" (the American marvelous reality), contains religious echoes that are muted when the term "magical" is employed, with its connotations of trickery and the fantastic.[26] At first glance, the placement of a ranting mining-camp woman in the company of such literary giants as Gabriel García Márquez, Toni Morrison, and Leslie Marmon Silko seems itself crazy. But the perception that an alternative universe exists, one that resists the hegemonic "rational" world, ties Lizzie to marvelous realism as a prototypal link in a long lineage of mystical writers. For example, Lizzie's belief that she was visited and guided by the dead in the Dreamworld is in cadence with Toni Morrison's insistence that Beloved could haunt her mother from her uneasy grave. Marvelous realism acknowledges the permeable membrane between the living and the dead, harking back to earlier Catholic traditions that Lizzie found so comforting: "the natural and daily presence of the dying and the dead among the living, the popular belief in an intermediate space between death and the definitive conclusion of life—in sum, a death that is neither a complete separation nor a total annihilation."[27]

> *August 5–1925 I dreamed a long bad dream of being in our home with darling brother Stephen now in Heaven and that he was displeased with me and that he was going to leave us forever and my heart was broken and I begged and implored him to stay and he refused I thought I would die with grief. . . .*

Like the marvelous realists, Lizzie was writing against the grain, against the powerful men in a capitalist society who had defiled her daughter, threatened her mine, and discarded the aging widowed Baby Doe like useless tailings. Marvelous realism and mysticism both resist the Western patriarchal perception of the world as "controlled, atomistic and one-dimensional," claiming instead that it is "chaotic, holistic and multi-dimensional."[28] Today's marvelous realism emerges from previously colonized peoples who push the boundaries of neocolonialist language to evoke preconquest concepts of the universe. Writing from the margins, postcolonials use "ex-centric" discourse to write against the dominant society about a different space, one that is steeped in the marvelous. It is a universe in which mythic time displaces linear time, in which life and death coexist on the same plane, where the living converse with the deceased, where imagination is encouraged. We see in the "Dreams and Visions" evidence of what Adrienne Rich calls "the damage that was done and the treasures that prevail" in Lizzie's torturously long, repetitive, chantlike phrases. As postcolonial scholar Kum Kum Sangari puts it: "The long sentence is an index of the *fecundity* of the repressed, of the barely begun and unfinished—*not uncertain*—stories simmering beneath the strident sounds and tight enclosure of dictatorship, and so gestures toward unopened possibilities. From within the loops and whorls of narrative bursts the recognition that the stories people tell will never finish, will strain and break through the controlling constraints of grammar. The speech of the many unnamed storytellers gels, coheres, contradicts, overlaps, and is retold."[29]

It may seem odd to depict Baby Doe—who grew up comfortably in Oshkosh and later enjoyed a decade as the wife of millionaire Horace Tabor—as a "colonized" subject. Yet, despite all the claims in the legend of Baby Doe's irresistible sexual power, which displaced poor Augusta Tabor (the only one in the love triangle to die wealthy), Lizzie became the abject. The abject is that figure onto whom we project all we fear, desire, and foresee within ourselves. Thus the back-to-rags Baby Doe saga is a hegemonic tale that draws its power through repetition of unexamined assumptions about morality and female sexuality. Hegemonic tales in essence colonize the consciousness, by using particular characters to reinforce dominant values that keep the powerless in their prescribed place. Women are the variously colonized subjects of patriarchy; the level of their oppression operates within a complex system of race, class, and politics. Thus women in powerful classes can assist in the project of colonizing other women. Objectified by the male gaze and colonized by female opprobrium, Lizzie found solace, sustenance, and voice through her subversive Dreamworld text. As Sidonie

Smith and Julia Watson observe: "To enter into language is to press back against total inscription in domination structures. . . . the autobiographical speaker can resist the processes of negation. Deploying autobiographical practices that go against the grain, she may constitute an 'I' that becomes a place of creative and, by implication, political intervention."[30] Subversive stories emerge in folk narrative and other devalued verbal forms such as fragments, which break the silence and challenge the assumption that there is a single agreed-upon hegemonic tale.[31]

Another way in which the "Dreams and Visions" functioned to free Lizzie Tabor's voice as an abject woman can be illuminated using the tools of second-wave feminist theory, particularly the field of semiotics. French feminist thinkers such as Julia Kristeva have argued that traditional language traps woman in a patriarchal prison in which she is always the "other." Because she must use language that is man-made, woman's speech can be flawed. For example, Carol Flinders argues that medieval women mystics used the only linguistic imagery available to them—Christ as romantic lover—because it was understandable to the larger culture and therefore safe. Because woman lives on the margins of power, the way she speaks and writes are demeaned. In Lizzie Tabor's era, a proper woman's name, much less her words, appeared in public only at her birth, marriage, and death. Baby Doe, however, had been a very public woman, dominating news stories written by men—in which she never spoke. If such an anomalous woman actually gave herself permission to write, she would struggle with traditional words in her compulsion to express herself in the very same language that had vilified her for decades. Her voice might sound like the mad "laugh of the Medusa," a figure embraced by Hélène Cixous to personify woman's alienation from language. And in dressing like a madwoman, aged Mrs. Tabor gained attention to her needs and very existence. It seems plausible that she would also write like a madwoman, given the perspective of French feminism: "Women, for Kristeva, also speak and write as 'hysterics,' as outsiders to male-dominated discourse. . . . Their semiotic style is likely to involve repetitive, spasmodic separations from the dominating discourse, which, more often, they are forced to imitate."[32] Lizzie Tabor strains to use— and reuse—words in an effort to describe what is for her indescribable—her numinous visitations:

> *Wednesday April 23–1919—this a.m. I had the strongest Vision, I saw a woman in light colored clothes O so quickly walking straight from my bedroom door. . . . I could only see her form in whitish clothes the skirt was very full all old fashion,*

she rushed up to me & she held a large white hand over my forehead a few inches
from and over my head and I screamed out Mother O my Mother Mother Mother
as she was quickly going the same way she came & I saw her go out the door & I
could see something still white over my head a longish white like a paper. Every-
one in the house could have heard me scream Mother.

The debate about woman's place in man's language heatedly continues in America's culture wars. Seeking access to a more authentic expression, second-wave feminists resuscitated and embraced earlier marginalized words such as "curandera" and "crone," or created new words such as "gynocentric," which emerged out of academic feminism. New words were also invented by patriarchal society, such as "femiNazis," to discipline these women. Third-wave feminists, particularly women of color, have demonstrated how unconventional hybrid language emerging from the United States–Mexico borderlands richly expresses previously muted experiences and perspectives of those who literally and figuratively inhabit two worlds. No longer dreaming of a common language, writers such as Gloria Anzaldúa use uncommon language that repels those who do not take the time or put in the energy to learn it. Others, like bell hooks, tell of code-switching, which allows them to inhabit both the world of academia and their home communities. Lizzie's oscillation between lucid business correspondence and stream-of-consciousness "Dreams and Visions" shows how she manipulated words to serve her needs. Her negotiation between discourses also keeps us off-balance. Ultimately we cannot learn Lizzie's language. The intertexual connections between the "Dreams and Visions" and other outrageous verbal acts—whether we call them mysticism, marvelous realism, postcolonialism, or feminism—suggest that, throughout history, there exists a subterranean mine of subversive writing. The disruptive potential of nonconforming writers such as Lizzie is vast and dangerous, "an account of the world as seen from the margins, an account which can expose the falseness of the view from the top and can transform the margins as well as the center."[33] I suggest that if we were literate enough in the many oral and written tongues of the dispossessed of the world, truly multiglossic, we would find connections that unseat the notion of a linear, unified "Western man."

THE MATCHLESS MEMOIR

If we return from the depths of the mine of "Dreams and Visions," to the surface, having surveyed its pockets with suggestive methodological tools, we can view Lizzie's text in its most capacious role: that of life-writing. I made the case early in my career as a diary scholar that women's journals contain more authentic versions of life than do the traditional linear autobiographies of famous men. I argued, "After we reassess our ideas of what constitutes legitimate autobiographical design, we can appreciate the nearer truth that exists in diaries. I liken reading a diary to watching a young child at play. If you can catch her in a private moment, you come close to hearing her real voice; once she knows you are listening, however, that voice becomes adulterated."[34] My claim that one could identify "truth" or a singular "real voice" proved both naive and arrogant once I encountered the "Dreams and Visions." Felicitously, postmodern theories emerged to contest the simplistic notions of stable identity just at the time I was entering Lizzie's Dreamworld. This paradigm shift allowed for—and searched for—disorder, border crossings, fissures, and transgressions, providing me with more tools. I now envision Lizzie as a resistive postmodern life-writer rather than as a madwoman to be dismissed.

When the elderly Mrs. Tabor confided to a visitor that the boxes of her important writings crowding her cabin contained her memoirs, she was staking a claim for herself as an author. The memoir in the 1930s was considered a highly personal, less formal type of writing than autobiography, the prestigious form usually reserved for elderly noteworthy men. *The Autobiography of Benjamin Franklin* was a staple of many schoolrooms as a model of American ingenuity and the success of Enlightenment man. Mrs. Tabor, in contrast, was signaling that hers was not a classic autobiography, but a memoir written from her perspective on the margins of society. The term "memoir" also allowed her to diverge from expectations of the linear chronology of standard autobiography and to give a more impressionistic view of her life. However, when does the "impressionistic" become "incomprehensibility"? The principal players in the "Dreams and Visions"—Silver and Horace—are confusingly contradictory by conventional narrative standards. Viewed through a postmodern lens, however, they are richly enigmatic and open-ended, lifelike. In Lizzie's text one character such as "the devil" signifies a creditor, a seducer, a laborer, even the Evil One himself. Likewise, the babies in the Dreamworld might be those unearthed from Silver's graveyard of "miscarriages," or the very opposite, a sign of hope for the future fertility of her beloved Matchless mine.

Nov 30–1920 at No. 6 shaft [of the Matchless mine] bucket-full of children it looked like a bouqet of flowers going down 6 & when it got down the baby got

frozhen [sic] & cryied & they brought baby right up & all the rest of children
stayed down it looked lovely like a boquet of bright flowers

Lizzie's dominant persona in her "Dreams and Visions" is defined rela-
tionally, as mother, daughter, or wife, rather than sensationally, as the scandalous individual Baby Doe. Lizzie's absolute exclusion of Baby Doe from
the Dreamworld undermines all other narratives, displacing the hypersexual caricature with a concerned family woman. The varied relationships
Lizzie undertook in her life are played out simultaneously in the Dreamworld, a surreal reflection of the multiple roles women assume in a single
day. The characters in the Dreamworld call out to Lizzie using a litany of
names she bore: "Mother" to Silver, "Baby" to Horace, "Lizzie" to departed
brother Stephen, "Mrs. H.A.W. Tabor" to enemies. Given this context, it is
striking that the religious figures such as the Virgin Mary and Jesus who rescue Lizzie from devils never address her by any name. This could signify
Lizzie's humble acknowledgment that she was unworthy of direct address
by the divine. Or perhaps she was so attentive to her God that He need not
call out to her; she was always awaiting Him in her cloistered cabin.

Some of Lizzie's symbols are easy to decipher. The snakes, devils, and
leering men are evil, while Stephen and little Matchless Mine Girl are aus-
picious. Sister Nealie, who died in childbirth, usually represents the sad burden of woman's lot. Other symbols recur with teasing regularity and
multiple meanings, such as "the little bundle."

June 3–1918 I dreamed Silver & I had a room in the Clarendon hotel & the man
Mr. Mattivi [?] locked us out our baby & my bundle were in the room Silver
rushed to the open window & cried fire fire lots of people were in the street, none
would come up to help us. . . . I said he has stolen the baby & bundle. I suf-
fered—terrible in this awful dream.

At the time of Mrs. Tabor's death, much was written about the "little bundle"
that she carried everywhere throughout her final years. Journalists speculated that she hid ore samples, silver, or money in the bag that formed an
integral part of her costume. Given her obsessive care for the Matchless
mine, others surmised that she stored contracts or mining stock in that bag.
Lizzie repeatedly dreamed of losing, hiding, or rescuing her beloved bundle, a bundle often resembling a baby. I see the bundle as signifying Lizzie's
many threatened possessions—her mine, her daughters, the babies of her
daughters, along with the literal bundles of papers she hoped would become

her memoirs. The labor she put into writing and accumulating her personal papers surely made her dread relinquishing that bundle, in which resided her cherished "Dreams and Visions." Lizzie's nightmares were prescient, for her final bundles of papers were ultimately stolen from the cabin.

The narrative complexity of the "Dreams and Visions" suits their subject matter, for while we tell stories and autobiography in a coherent form, dreams dance to a lifelike tune all their own. As Louis Mink observed: "Stories are not lived but told. Life has no beginnings, middles or ends; there are meetings, but the start of an affair belongs to the story we tell ourselves later, and there are partings, but final partings only in the story. There are hopes, plans, battles and ideas, but only in retrospective stories are hopes unfulfilled, plans miscarried, and battles decisive, and ideas seminal. . . . We do not dream or remember in narrative, I think, but tell stories which weave together the separate images of recollection."[35] When one first awakens from a particularly vivid dream, the mind races like Lizzie's prose, repeating the strongest images, trailing off without resolution, fragmenting. When we begin to tell our dream to a listener, however, it becomes coherent in order to fulfill expectations of more narrative clarity.

Ultimately, Lizzie lost her beloved earthly listeners. Alone in her cabin, she rambled on. Her prolific writing eventually found a doggedly tolerant reader and listener in me. Throughout this book, I have asked you to become the audience for tiny samplings of the "Dreams and Visions." But there are limits to what we can know about what Lizzie Tabor was writing and thinking during the last ten years of her life. Some of the limits were set by Lizzie herself, because she burnt letters from enemies like A. M. Stevenson, effectively silencing them. Other limits are set by Lizzie's code, which sometimes highlights her secrets but at intense times is indecipherable. Diary scholar Jennifer Sinor characterizes this truly private writing: "The reader stands outside the action, the people and events that move through the diary, and outside a form of writing that is often illegible, out of order, coded, and crossed out. We are not being invited in."[36] Lizzie's obsessive writing seems to signal her hope for an audience, but perhaps she was still searching for a soul mate among her contemporaries as her ultimate reader and biographer, and not for us. Even for a postmodern scholar like myself, who embraces the idea of the unknowable and the ambiguous, Lizzie's strategies to protect her privacy are frustrating. We are invited into the Dreamworld mine only down to a certain level, while Lizzie's deepest core remains inviolable.

VEXING QUESTIONS

There are vexing questions that my years of exploration and probing are unable to answer. First, I wonder about the deeper symbolic meaning of Lizzie's "Dreams and Visions" as a map into her mind. I am not equipped by training to do this mining, but my sampling of various dream theories convinces me that there are various interpretations available for Lizzie's text, rather than one route to a single verity. This is why I suggested several ways in which the dreams functioned for Lizzie rather than any one perspective, which would analyze her in order to disrobe her to yet another generation. I hope the "Dreams and Visions" I have selected for this book will intrigue others to explore the psychological terrain that Lizzie recorded.

Second, I wonder if the Lizzie I have grown to know over the past decade is a more authentic creation than the mythic Baby Doe. Like each Tabor biographer, I have brought *my* Lizzie to this book. My selection of which "Dreams and Visions" excerpts to include tells more about my purposes and values than they do about Lizzie's. I chose accessible dream accounts that forwarded my narrative of how the passive caricature of Baby Doe, the abject, evolved into a Warrior Mother. Ours is a collaborative text. While I am the one who selected her writings, it was Lizzie as the speaking subject who changed my initial assumptions about what I would find. It was she who compelled me to listen to the mother's lament, through the sheer volume and vehemence of her prose. I still oscillate between my deference to unsolvable mysteries within the "Dreams and Visions" and my scholarly determination to interpret this unwieldy text. The dozens of question marks concerning Silver's baby or babies show that I have no documented answers, only speculation fueled by fragmentary writings. In other cases, I have selected the dream to insert into my text that reinforces a certain image of Lizzie. In the huge body of "Dreams and Visions" there are absolute opposites and contradictions, which give me as the dream-miner great power over which story is brought to the surface. For example, when I searched for a relevant dream about babies to use in chapter 3, where I analyzed Lizzie's plight as a deserted and pregnant Mrs. Harvey Doe, I selected this excerpt, for its ambiguity and possible allusion to stillbirth:

> *Wed March 15–1922 . . . in a few moments I saw several Visions—I saw all so white & clear a young babys head & face with a small piece of white cloth in its open mouth. . . .*

However, I could have selected this more damning dream that implies guilt and bad mothering, perhaps even infanticide:

> *May 27–1921—I dreamed I had a little baby in long white dress as big as a doll & two babys round all [?] face they seemed about as big as a saucer & dressed so fancy just round babys, a woman came & she stood in door-way & took up one of the round babys she said she has killed this one & she kissed it several times. . . .*

In crafting a narrative empathetic to Lizzie I may be guilty of what Rona Kaufman calls "hyperperformance." Kaufman observes that "hyperperformance occurs when a reader assumes so much authority in reading that she disregards the text, trammeling right over it. She rearranges, ignores, and makes demands, forcing the text to fit into her predetermined space. A halted performance, on the other hand, happens when the reader garners so little authority that she brings no influence to bear upon her reading. The reader is overwhelmed by the voices of others."[37] Lizzie created such a variety of voices in the "Dreams and Visions" that they do overwhelm her reader and require some kind of order. I decided first to use Lizzie's fragments to illuminate and complicate the Baby Doe legend, then to gradually introduce more prose and perspectives from the Dreamworld in each chapter. This gradually led to an immersion in the Dreamworld that focused on Silver. Yet even this intense sampling of the "Dreams and Visions" was mediated through my chronological integration of outside events in order to pair them with Lizzie's numinous experiences. A brief series of "Dreams and Visions," as they were written by Lizzie, appears in the epilogue, untouched by editing. Is this the "text" Lizzie intended for posterity—or one compromised by the disorder within Lizzie's mind and cabin, by thieves, by moralists?

A third question piques me, as it has previous biographers of Baby Doe: was she organically mad? Early on in my research, when I learned from Lizzie's diary that Leadville had cut off her water and she was probably drinking from pools near her mine, I suspected she was delusional because of lead poisoning. Or her behavior could be the manifestation of mental illness, according to psychologist James Wood, who was kind enough to review my work on Lizzie's dreams found in my *Colorado Heritage* article. He wrote me, "I keep wondering if Baby Doe was truly 'mad.' Not at all clear. There are hints in the article, but none are entirely clear. . . . Going to bed very, very late (can be associated with bipolar disorder, but can also be due to a myriad of other factors). Seeing devils or angels (can be psychopathological, but not necessarily). Gross denial of reality (Silver's death—but some fairly normal people deal with unbearable facts by denying them. Also, out of pride, some people won't admit what they know at heart to be true). Social withdrawal (sometimes a symptom). Litigiousness (sometimes a symptom). Eccentricity (sometimes a symptom)."[38] Professor Wood suggested that the best source of information for pursuing a hypothesis of mental illness would be to accumulate incidental details from Lizzie's later life; her state of physical health—no doubt affected by her malnutrition, isolation, and age—would influence her mental health. He also described as potentially useful the method of content analysis, as pioneered by Calvin Hall, for understanding the "Dreams and Visions." My rudimentary content analysis (as laid out in the previous chapter, on Silver) shows that this is both a promising tool for mining the Dreamworld and a limited one, because of the censored and compromised nature of the archival "remains."

Wood suggested intriguing starting diagnoses that may interest experts in psychology. "*Bipolar disorder or cyclothymic disorder.* This would be a prime diagnosis to rule out. For example, what was she like, that she attracted Horace so strongly? Some cyclothymic people are so full of energy and verve that they are *very* attractive. (By the way, I wonder about Horace too. The way that he and Baby Doe went so overboard suggests—just a hint—that he might have had some manic tendencies himself.) There are many, many examples of bipolar individuals who amassed great fortunes—their energy and optimism can sometimes be a great asset. But the fortunes can be unstable if they get too grandiose." This psychological hypothesis radically revises the legend of Baby Doe: what if Horace were attracted to "Baby's" personality rather than her plump and sexually pleasing body? Some of Tabor's milder male biographers painted Baby Doe as a good-natured woman who understood her desirable female role as a stimulant to Horace's egotistical schemes. What if Horace Tabor is revised per Wood's suggestion into a bipolar speculator rather than the archetypal western dreamer? Wood continues, "if either Elizabeth or Horace had bipolar disorder, we'd expect to see the disorder in some of their relatives. Anything known about their ancestors? I wonder too about Silver. Was she simply alcoholic and promiscuous, or was there bipolar disorder operating there? Alcoholism and promiscuity can be the result of bipolar disorder. Was Silver a bit grandiose, I wonder?"

Wood provided ideas about other potential causes for Lizzie's behavior and visions. "Some form of dementia in the later years of Elizabeth's life (in other words, there's a possibility that Baby Doe was normal up until age 65 or 70, but then developed vascular dementia or a slow form of Alzheimer's that made her seem very eccentric.)" Again, this organic theory for Lizzie Tabor's mental deterioration undermines the moral dramatic narrative that attributes a series of "punishments" visited upon sinner Baby Doe as the cause of her demise. Wood also included substance abuse (alcohol or opiate drugs available at the time) or poisoning (fumes from the cabin stove or something in the water) as possible factors affecting Lizzie's mental state. He closed with, "Schizotypal personality disorder (this is a mild form of schizophrenia.) Schizotypal people are often very likeable and bright, but they tend to be reclusive, have magical thinking—like a belief they are visited by spirits—and sometimes rambling in their thoughts. They also may have 'illusions'—Elizabeth's description about how she could feel Horace with her, after he was dead, sounds like an illusion."

Wood's hypotheses about the madness of Baby Doe bring to the western legend a new range of questions. In her later years, how often did Lizzie find herself on the brink of starvation, which resulted in torrents of visions? Could her starvation have been at times self-imposed by fasting in order to bring on hallucinations that the madwoman thought were sent by God? If Widow Tabor was descending into senile dementia, why did the Leadville community stare at her as she grew stranger and let her live alone? (O'Brien recalled her as "senile and proud," not a good prospect for supervised group living.) On a more abstract level, the entire legend of the Tabors—one of irrational risk-taking, incredible luck, inevitable failure—is bipolar in its cycle of manic profligacy followed by depressive poverty. This legend speaks to the ongoing speculative American character, reflected in stock market gambles that place irrational hope on unprecedented future riches, only to inevitably crumble in down cycles, leaving egotistical Taborlike CEOs with their trophy houses (and trophy wives) as flotsam. The fascinating question of Lizzie's mental soundness can probably never be resolved. It is ultimately immaterial for me as a reader, for I am intrigued by her text, no matter how it was generated. Lizzie joins a legion of other half-cracked authors—Dickinson, Poe, Kafka, Woolf, Plath—whose torments form a brilliant literary legacy.

The mystery that most haunts me is this: how did the story of Lizzie Tabor as a writer and dreamer end? The striking paucity of "Dreams and Visions" and correspondence in the Tabor archives for the last decade of Lizzie's life, from 1925 to 1935, suggests that Lizzie fell uncharacteristically silent. This drought might be explained by the loss of understanding listeners; Father John Guida died in 1919 and her fellow dreamer Silver in 1925. Despite

Widow Tabor's insistence to the outside world that Silver's scandalous death was a case of mistaken identity, the few "Dreams and Visions" that exist after 1925 do not focus on Silver. This striking disappearance of Silver from the Dreamworld in which she was the star actor indicates to me that, at her core, Lizzie acknowledged Silver's death. If a major motive for Lizzie's life-writing was to leave a legacy to aspiring author Silver, Lizzie might have become so disheartened after Silver's death that she fell almost silent. However, the few extant "Dreams and Visions" from 1925–1935 show Lizzie's characteristic passion, so it is possible that this compulsive recorder of the spirit world searched for another audience, perhaps distant Lily.

In 1932 Lizzie may have found a surrogate daughter and recipient for her "Dreams and Visions" in her new nearby neighbor and eager listener Sue Bonnie. Bonnie's short account of their relationship, "Our Lives Together," recalled Mrs. Tabor saying, "Song bird you are like my 3rd daughter."[39] Or if Lizzie perceived a loftier audience for her "Dreams and Visions," whether it be God or future sympathizers, she would persist in her writing. Lizzie's poignant, fervid, and almost unreadable account of an ominous vision of war from 1932, when fascism was gaining power in Europe, indicates to me that Mrs. Tabor stayed faithful to her "important writing." Her penmanship is huge and forms a scrawled frame in the only space available to her on the typed form letter she used for her transcription:

> Dec 12–1932 Night of Visuns . . . I saw Vision of thousands of soldiers & men & horses men on then great troupes marching from north to south on East side after they passed. . . . There is to be a War so much Vision

The dearth of surviving "Dreams and Visions" from the last decade is more likely a silencing, not from within Lizzie Tabor herself but from outside, by treasure hunters. The fact that few diary scraps and correspondence from 1925–1935 exist supports the scenario of pilfering intruders taking any paperwork they could find. Confident that Lizzie wrote until the bitter end, I wonder what became of Dream Child Silver. Silver was probably never completely silenced in the Dreamworld, where such an inconsequential thing as death could not separate mother and daughter. After all, Lizzie had continued to record tender dreams of her stillborn sons decades after their deaths. A *Denver Post* article from March 24, 1935, shortly after the death of Baby Doe, described scribbled dream accounts about Silver on a 1935 calendar found in the cabin. It included this passage from what it called Mrs. Tabor's "calendar-diary": "Silver Dollar and big red, gold horse, Oh so big. As big as four or five horses."

Large multidirectional hybrid account of August 1925 visions and mine negoti-
ations, approximately 17 x 20 inches. Note how Lizzie's # mark at very bottom
left-hand corner guides reader to another # in the center of the page where the
narrative continues. Courtesy Colorado Historical Society, Tabor Collection, FF
1028. All Rights Reserved.

If Lizzie was still writing about Silver in 1935, perhaps she was not so much
a madwoman. Perhaps she was more a woman willingly engaged in a cha-
rade recounted by Sue Bonnie. There was a kindly Mrs. Perkins of Leadville
who sent a monthly check to Mrs. Tabor and put Silver Dollar's name on it.

According to Bonnie, Mrs. Tabor had a reputation for rejecting charity and food parcels left at the Matchless, but she eagerly took the checks "from Silver." Bonnie wrote: "One day when I got up there [the Matchless] Mrs Tabor came running to me and she said Look I got a check from Silver Dollar and letter."[40] Mrs. Perkins's act of exceptional sensitivity could fuel Lizzie's need that was far greater than hunger—the need to believe that Silver still lived and cared. I believe Lizzie dreamed on, attaining her highest accomplishment by conquering death in the Dreamworld, even though this meant she was deemed the madwoman in the cabin.

While the diary scholar in me understands that the most authentic life-writing can stop midsentence, as a reader I long for Lizzie's pronouncement that it is finished. I want to hear that at long last Lizzie found peace in her Dreamworld. One of her last accounts describes a lush "glorious vision" of foliage, perhaps an indication she was drifting in and out of consciousness, within view of the branches she had draped near her Sacred Heart picture in the cabin, perhaps reminding her of the bowers that draped her Washington, D.C., wedding site. But the last vision transcription in the Tabor collection haunts me with the plaguing question of whether the devils ultimately triumphed as Lizzie weakened.

> *Dec 15–1932 after I went to bed to night O the most frightful devil of a man terrible—Big head & face & big devil eyes all as big as a dozen or more mens heads & faces came & terrified me so I had to keep a lamp burning all night O such a terrible devil came—devils are appearing to [me] every night—& O such a lot of them*

Yet I do not weep for Lizzie, for in this final account the old recluse describes her efforts to resist madness and spiritual darkness on a cold December night by lighting her precious lamp. I believe that she retained to the end her most precious possession, her matchless *mind*.

> *Thank God for dreams, when nothing else is left,*
> *When the sick soul, all stricken with its pain,*
> *Knowing itself forevermore bereft,*
> *Finds waiting hopeless, and all watching vain;*
> *. . .*
> *Thank God, thank God, for dreams!*[41]

In Her Own Words

"Dreams and Visions"

The last photo taken of Baby Doe, still the object of the gaze as Dick Wilmoth looks down upon her diminutive figure, is as enigmatic as her single surviving midlife portrait. The story of the picture's origin is that Wilmoth and a friend had given Baby Doe a ride up to her cabin during a snowstorm. In return, Wilmoth asked to have a picture taken. Widow Tabor tilts her head in a welcoming way, yet she clutches her omnipresent crucifix, a weapon she often used against devil figures, holding it between the camera's eye and herself. Is this a witchlike madwoman or a gaunt widow whose piercing eyes confirm that she held "God in my heart"?

Below are two sets of "Dreams and Visions" uninterrupted by my voice, except to indicate the type of writing and paper used by Lizzie for each account. The first "Dreams and Visions" deal with particularly strong visitations from the divine or devils. Originally I had planned to include only God-sent images the paramystic described, but this would misrepresent the Dreamworld and efface the tremendous work Lizzie did in fending off evil spirits. The second short series of "Dreams and Visions" is an unedited chronological sampling, to give a sense of how the mundane, mystical, and muddled intermixed for Lizzie. Madwoman or mystic? Perhaps Lizzie herself did not know for sure.

"O THAT HEAVENLY SIGHT"

On a small piece of good paper in fine handwriting that gives no indication of the year:

Last known photograph (1933) of Baby Doe Tabor, with Dick Wilmoth outside her cabin. She continued to live there two more years before her death. Courtesy Colorado Historical Society, Tabor Photo Collection. Tabor, Baby Doe. All Rights Reserved.

May 27–28—29–30 I think it was 28 or 29—I was in my room & it was dark in the evening I jumped up quickly to turn on the light & I run in to the iron bed post it had a sharp lump of iron fancy sticking out of cheap bedsted I run in to it with my left eye it struck my eye full & only my eye it was about as big as my eye ball I thought it had knocked my eye out I felt my eye & thought it was gone the pain was terrible I put my face down on the bed in suffering, when I could look at it I lighted the light & it looked enflamed & pained I bathed it & tied it up in a towel the next morning it was all well & strong God Jesus our Blessed Lord saved my eye in His great mercy it was not even sore or discolored not a bit black a true miricle Mrs. H.A.W. Tabor [on other side:] My eye a miricale[1]

On a large piece of paper, written horizontally in large handwriting. On the bottom is a drawing of the Virgin Mary with "Vision" written next to the illustration. This vision account is shown on page 144.

March 6 1909 Monday night after 12 I had gone to bed & I saw a small vision of the blessed Virgin she was sitting at a Piano her hands & arms stretched out as if playing her hair was down her back dressed in a white soft clinging dress & a wonderful Halo of light around her head then a few forms of Angels came floating down she was tall & light

On regular paper in medium handwriting:

This a.m. March 7–1913 I dreamed Mother Silver & I think Steph & Claudia and some more were standing talking to me their backs were to the opening of our house & I was facing the opening & I was looking out on a very light wide path leading from our house it had light colored & lacy looking trees on either side of this path, I said O look look see some one coming & they turned & we saw Our dear Savior Jesus clad in a light robe of pale lavender walking up the path towards us tall and something around the top of his head as the crown of thorns were but I could not see what it was His arms was extended full length over His beautiful Head His arms & hands straight up high pointing to Heaven & we all looked at Him coming & I thought it meant some one was going to die O it was the most beautiful I ever saw He was slight and very tall [on other side:] My dream about our Savior March 7–1913 It must have been a Vision dream [inverted on other side:] March 7–1913 this A.M I dreamed that my mother Silver & I think Claud not sure mabey some one else was with me we were standing (I think also Steph) out on a light road leading to our house

On the bottom half of regular paper in dark semi-scrawled handwriting:

Aug 9–1913 we slept the first night after coming back to Leadville in the cabin & the devil attacted me & tried to pull me out of bed by taking hold of both ankles trying to pull me over the foot of the bed—this was not a dream it was real I said Jesus and was saved

On stationery from Leadville's Vendome hotel in neat handwriting:

September 17–1920 O our Lord Jesus Christ our Saviour Let me see the most wonderful blessing today Silver and I were close together—both looking up for God had us look up and we saw the great white clouds in the sky part in a round ring and all the rest of the sky remained covered with the big white clouds and in the open place where the clouds had parted & formed a large round space in the round—place—was the richest lightest blue—sky O such a rich light blue color and that whole blue sky was sparkling with the brightest golden Stars of all sizes they were so thick that they were piled on top of each other little & big shining sparkling Stars shining down on us & flashing out their sparkling glory nothing ever sent out such sparkling bright lights the glourious blue was covered with the golden Stars & we could look far back in the rich light-blue Sky and see Stars way deep in the & thru the blue each Star sparkled & all around the round blue place the white clouds for a reath & the rest of the Heavens was covered thick with the white clouds. The blue was a very light blue and we never saw that color before [over] and it was the richest color blue ever seen outside of Heaven, and of a very light shade you could almost see the golden Stars thru it, such grandure I cannot at all describe O that Heavenly Sight for us to behold. Jesus had some short time ago let me see a Vision of the figure No 17—& I had been waiting for this 17 of Sept to come not knowing what to expect It is today & this glory God Jesus has blessed us with

My Silver is in Chicago to day I am here in Room 103 Vendome Hotel leadville Colo—but God had her with me to behold this glory to tell us her & our sufferings would soon be healed

Early this 17 day of September 1920
Mrs. H.A.W. Tabor

Written sideways on regular paper, with a drawing captioned "I only wish I could draw it as fine as it was":

Thursday Feb 17–1921 In my tea-can—after I had finished drinking tea It was like a lovely Angel—watching and protecting the little girl climbing mountain a little girl always means the Matchless Mine in my dreams—&c—this means we will have a hard time but Jesus sends His Angel and it will be protected

First of several accounts that fill two pages of lined paper in fine handwriting:

July 25–1921—While I was praying between 3 & 4 a.m. I saw a large Cross with Jesus nailed to it more than life-size and in colors the flesh color and all and His feet and hands and the thornes all as they were both His feet one the side of the other and the spikes one in each foot and the blood on each foot where the spikes were and the blood in each of His Hands, this Vision was different & I seemed to see it in my mind all the other Visions I could see for a long time and watch them look away & then back the Visions still there.

The handwritten text on the drawing reads:

I only wish I could draw it as fine as it was

Thursday Feb 17 – 1921
In my tea-can – after I
had finished drinking tea
It was like a lonely Angel –
watching and protecting the –
little girl climbing Mountian
a little girl always means the –
Matchless mine in my dreams –
4C – this means one will have a
hard time But – Jesus sends His Angel and
it will be protected

Drawing and description of vision Lizzie saw in her tea-can February 17, 1921. See Epilogue for text. Below the drawing of an angel hovering over a figure of the Matchless Mine Girl in her gingham is written, "I only wish I could draw it as fine as it was." Stan Oliner located this crucial drawing in the Tabor Collection. Courtesy Colorado Historical Society, Tabor Collection, FF 1048. All Rights Reserved.

Well-written with title, heading, or rough draft at beginning:

Aug 15–1921—Jesus our Lord and Saviour The Ever Living God

Aug 15–1921 I had a glorious dream to-day of Jesus Christ The Everliving God Talking to me 4 times (four times) I was so so happy,—I told Him I only wanted Hill [sic] Will to be done to us and me—O all was so peaceful so happy far too glorious for me to be blessed so by our Saviour

Mrs. Elizabeth B. Tabor
Mrs. H.A.W. Tabor

One account in a long succession of "Dreams and Visions" written on regular paper in fine handwriting:

Nov—18–1921 . . . I made a thankgiving in Church this eve, Tonight as I was praying God showed me all the Sky where the Blessed Virgin Mary appeared in her assention—the sky was all rippled and moveing in waves in a big circle around the spot in the sky of grey so large a circle biger than blocks and all moving in towards the middle of circle in mottled forms & little waves all in colors of grey. God has shown me this same apperation at least 3 different nights while I was praying, & the moon looked strange for a moment, the mottled Sky was for 3 times different nights in succesion & the 18 I saw while praying after 3 A.M. Purple on the Sky. (Sorrow)

Written on the back of Vendome Hotel stationery, in neat handwriting that runs in slightly slanted lines. Sideways is written "May 17–1922 I was in throes of devil":

Wednesday May 17–1922 I awoke after 2 A.M. A.M. today I instantly was in the terrible throes of the devil he was trying to kill me O what agony I suffered and I all alone I writhed in agony O such horrors such agony—Instantly at the very instant I tried to say aloud the Blessed Name Of Jesus but the devil would not let me speak I every second had the Name of Jesus trying to speak Jesus alout—I was lying down on my back in our Catholic Church in front of the Alter-Rail my head was up against the Communion-Rail—my feet towards the Church door, where God had taken my Spirit to endure this terrible agony—I struggled every second to say Jesus but the devil held fast on to me twisting me & in agony I suffered then I felt something like Ice-cold over me and I smiled—and thought Jesus is putting me in a condition He is going to Show me some of His Heaven—the devil increased his torture and my head would bump against the Communion Rail and

*O how he twisted me I was suffering agony, try to speak the Blessed Name—
Jesus which would drive the devil into hell instantly The name of Jesus was said
aloud—but every second of this long struggle of agony I was trying to say Jesus—
then all in an instant I heard my voice speak aloud—Jesus Jesus and that second
I was free from the devil and at once God brought my Spirit back to my room in
this Vendome Hotel in Leadville May 17–1922. It is a long time since our Blessed
Saviour let the devil put me in his throes—he used to put me in this agony some
and up to 2 or 3 years ago—then—Jesus would not let him—I was surprised to
be in the throes of the devil today—I think Jesus told the devil he could torture
once more—so he would see I would only be with Jesus our Divine Saviour forever and only try to speak the Sweetest Name Jesus—I think now our troubles
will soon be ended and I can have my darling children soon again. Silver often saw
me in the throes of devil.*

On a piece of advertising paper, in large scrawled handwriting:

*I went to bed this 23 night about 10 P.M. March 23–1925 & O—& instantly
O such a lot of black snakes came close to my face & terrible faces in the Name
of Jesus who has come in the flesh drove them away after a long time*

*24 as soon as I got into bed the black snakes devils & faces came I drove them
away with Jesus Christ has come in the flesh & with the name of Blessed Mary
Mother & Virgin—Early in morning this 25 A.M. dreamed of Black man &
God saved me—I also dreamed of Jesus & that devil Laksa [?]*

On a torn scrap of paper, in large scrawled handwriting:

*Saturday Blessed Virgins day March 28–1925 God gave me a wonderful long
dream today—I dreamed was with God all during His Crucifixion I cannot
explain any of it it was terrible & a dark mass of people in a soiled dark big crowd
but I seemed close to God & with Him O Blessed suffering Divine Jesus Christ
we adore Worship Thee*

"I SAW"

The following short series of transcriptions comes from "Dreams and
Visions" of 1925, all written by Lizzie in pencil. Note her determination to
accurately ascribe dates for her entries and how she negotiates between the
Dreamworld and the real world. People approaching her cabin made her
anxious, and the water company operator infuriated her. I hear her at this

point in her life as a mad woman, angry at those trying to cheat her out of her mine and her cabin.

Written on a cut-off corner of mining assayer's accounting sheet:

Aug 2 1925 The star over the cloudy night hover [however?] not another star & could only see the outlines of full moon

Written on a small ivory envelope, unfolded to form a sheet:

Sunday Aug 2–1925. This AM I saw several strong Visions 1st I saw a small thin stream of light colored smoke rise up out from under a new pine floor it was a little over a foot high & thin not big around as if in engine house which has no floor

Written on the same sheet of assayer's paper:

Aug 3–1925 came with Lunch [or a proper name, perhaps Tony Lazonchich, who was working for Mrs. Tabor at the time] I screamed in sorrow Mother a Voice answered brought ——[engine? enzyme?] & start work & slashed house Aug 3

Written on a cut piece of assayer paper:

Aug 3 1925 I dreamed all night that Tony started after sulphites 2 dreams about starting No 6

Written on a piece of assayer paper:

Aug 4–1925 see other people also the car was old & cheap had many dreams lots of folk I can not remember I am not well to-day

Written on a piece of assayer paper:

Aug 4–1925 Darling Sister Nealies Birthday she is in Heaven her sad life was the most terrible her death an agony she died a saint I saw a strong Vision today of automobiel on the road of Matchless Mine (over) believe no's 5 & 6 shafts oppasit of cabin all stopped there & a little girl about 4 or 5 years got out of it no one else in & came walking to my cabin she was clothed in darkish callico & no hat & very poor & shabby & the car was old cheap

Written on both sides of a cut piece of nice stationery:

Aug 5 1925 I dreamed a long bad dream of being in our home with darling brother Stephen now in Heaven and that he was displeased with me and that he was going to leave us forever and my heart was broken and I begged and implored him to stay and he refused I thought I would die with grief for I was in great agony over it all night; he looked so handsome well & strong & O how I loved him & coaxed him to stay with us forever he would not stay I awoke with a broken heart & am sad all day God save him for us he is so dear

Written on a small assayer card:

Sat Aug 8–1925 I saw a bright yellow gold light at my left up high about as large as a dime while I was praying my rosery

Written on an unfolded envelope:

Sunday 9 Aug—1925 I saw a Vision of a woman in a new bright royal blue callico dress full old fashion skirt new callico & stiff so bright a blue not light blue she had a little girl the little girl always means Matchless Mine in Visions or dreams to me) she held the little girl by the childs right hand & they were both in my door of my cabin near Boiler that the devilish men of Leadville burnt and No 6 shaft. I dreamed also to day many & big dreams but I can not remember them Aug 9–1925

Written on a small unfolded envelope:

Monday Aug 10–1925 After I went to bed I saw terrible devil faces & bannished them in the Divine name of Jesus I fell asleep & had very sad & troubled dreams of Tony Lazonchich not starting after sulphures & that the engine was not right then I dreamed 2 dreams of my darling Silver being terrible to me & she said to another woman & I that there were no sulphites in Matchless mine—& 2 men came in Vision or dream one was friendly other an Enemy. That devil Sharp [?] of the water Co turned on the water for us to drink & charged 2— months double to the price to any else he is a devil we have an Electric Engine Aug 10–1925

Written on the top half of a mining assayer form:

Aug 11–1925 I had bad dreams of folks trying to keep Tony Lazonchich [?] from starting after sulphides Following him & me all over terrible when I woke I saw a Vision of a thin man carry in something like thin looking piece of lump as wood to No 6 trussel from Dunkin side of the dump

Written on a cut piece of lined paper:

Aug 12 1925 I saw Visions of 2 men in black slough hats awful in the dark peaking & sneeking around No 6 Engine house & after I went to bed at night saw another on trussel am of Aug 13

Written on an unfolded envelope:

> *Aug Wednesday Aug—12–1925 Jesus our Divine Savior gave me a glorious dream this A.M. He sent Tabor & brother Stephen to me both so young strong & well & handsome & so prosperous fine & we were so happy & gay & I think Silver was with us in a lovely home & Tabor Stephen & I had lots of (seemed) small rought bright things & different colors of Value—& I was in by stars & all happiness & prosperity and Peace*

In this manner, Lizzie Tabor dreamed on and recorded her experiences as best she could for ten more years.

Notes

PREFACE

1. The "Dreams and Visions" written by Elizabeth ("Lizzie") B. McCourt Tabor are part of the enormous Horace A. W. Tabor archive collection housed at the Colorado Historical Society in Denver. They are located, in chronological order, in MSS 614, box 11, file folders 922–1037. When a fragment is undated, filed in with the "Diary Notes," or not in its expected folder, I indicate its file folder (FF) location in an endnote. The Colorado Historical Society (CHS) was originally called the State Historical Society of Colorado (SHSC) until its name was changed in the mid-1970s. For the sake of clarity, I use CHS throughout.

2. Bancroft, *Silver Queen*, 4.

3. Elizabeth B. McCourt Tabor Diary, FF 906.

4. From 1981 to 1987, I had minimal time to devote to the Tabor papers. My major research project during this time involved bringing an Iowa pioneer woman's thirty-year-long diary into print, arguing that it was what Robert Fothergill in *Private Chronicles* calls "serial autobiography." I painstakingly edited the twenty-five-hundred-page manuscript diaries of Emily Hawley Gillespie, which overwhelmingly focused on her farm work, into a compelling story (see Lensink, *"A Secret to Be Burried"*). This research gave me confidence that I could do the same with the fragmented Baby Doe writings, to which I turned in earnest in 1990.

5. Undated Diary Notes, FF 919.

6. Issues of what is "legitimate" autobiographical writing can be found in the essays of Suzanne Bunkers and Caren Kaplan. A discussion of the limitations of current interpretive methods for addressing unconventional life writing can be found in Jennifer Sinor's remarkable book, *The Extraordinary Work of Ordinary Writing*.

7. Emily Dickinson, Poem 435, in *Complete Poems*, 209.

8. Gilbert and Gubar, *Madwoman in the Attic*, 78.

CHAPTER 1

1. The epigraph is from Mrs. H.A.W. Tabor to Mr. and Mrs. Wallace, 24 November 1932, FF 792.

2. Karsner, *Silver Dollar*, 347.

3. Fothergill, *Private Chronicles*, 82.

4. Richard Slotkin, *Regeneration through Violence*, 3. Slotkin provides a convincing analysis of one such myth of American exceptionalism and its ongoing legacy.

5. The suspect biographers include Bancroft, Burke, Hall, Karsner, and Vernon. Iversen and Smith, on the other hand, are responsible biographers.

6. Karsner, *Silver Dollar*, 147.

7. Bancroft, *Silver Queen*, 13.

8. Burke, *Legend of Baby Doe*, 12. Bancroft, however, was the first to dub Elizabeth "the Belle of Oshkosh." Bancroft, *Silver Queen*, 12.

9. Burke, *Legend of Baby Doe*, 12.

10. Karsner, *Silver Dollar*, 140.

11. Burke, *Legend of Baby Doe*, 27, 33.

12. Ibid., 37.

13. See Smith, *Horace Tabor*, 72–75.

14. Burke, *Legend of Baby Doe*, 44, 46, 46–47, 39.

15. Iversen, *Molly Brown*, 83.

16. Hall, *Two Lives*, 45.

17. Augusta may also have become sexually unavailable to her husband, as evidenced by the fact that she bore only one child.

18. Karsner, *Silver Dollar*, 152.

19. Hall, *Two Lives*, 106.

20. Burke, *Legend of Baby Doe*, 92.

21. My conversations in the 1990s with CHS curator of books and manuscripts (now retired) Stan Oliner, touched several times on items that CHS staff believe were removed from the Tabor papers prior to their processing. See also the typescript narrative for a CHS 1982 exhibit called "The Horace A. W. Tabor Collection," by CHS historian David Halaas.

22. Burke, *Legend of Baby Doe*, 85.

23. Hall, *Two Lives*, 98.

24. Smith, *Horace Tabor*, 211, 217.

25. Burke, *Legend of Baby Doe*, 101–102.

26. Ibid., 103.

27. Smith, *Horace Tabor*, 224.

28. Karsner, *Silver Dollar*, 216.

29. CHS exhibit typescript.

30. Smith, *Horace Tabor*, 229.

31. Ibid., 232–33.

32. Hall, *Two Lives*, 156; McMechen, *The Tabor Story*, 20.

33. Smith, *Horace Tabor*, 229.

34. Hall, *Two Lives*, 164.

35. Smith, *Horace Tabor*, 246.

36. Ibid., 237.

37. Burke, *Legend of Baby Doe*, 131.

38. Hall, *Two Lives*, 181.

39. Ibid., 183, 192.

40. Karsner, *Silver Dollar*, 243.

41. Burke, *Legend of Baby Doe*, 160, 161.

42. Smith, *Horace Tabor*, 278.

43. Burke, *Legend of Baby Doe*, 169.

44. Smith, *Horace Tabor*, 246, 294.

45. Bancroft, *Silver Queen*, 64.

46. Smith, *Horace Tabor*, 301.

47. Hall, *Two Lives*, 204, 202.

48. Burke, *Legend of Baby Doe*, 181, 166.

49. Karsner, *Silver Dollar*, 288.

50. Burke, *Legend of Baby Doe*, 183.

51. Karsner, *Silver Dollar*, 291.

52. Burke, *Legend of Baby Doe*, 190, 193.

53. Tabor, *Star of Blood*, 69, in Furman, *Silver Dollar Tabor*, 219. Silver Dollar Tabor's novel has long been out of print, but a facsimile is included in Evelyn Furman's biography, pages 145–224. The novel is also available at the Stephen A. Hart Library, CHS.

54. Hall, *Two Lives*, 220.

55. Karsner, *Silver Dollar*, 305, 336.

56. Burke, *Legend of Baby Doe*, 208.

57. Karsner, *Silver Dollar*, 314, 337.

58. Ibid., 298.

59. Burke, *Legend of Baby Doe*, 198, 182, 199.

60. Ibid., 219.

61. Ibid., 216.

CHAPTER 2

1. Slotkin, *Regeneration through Violence*, 4.

2. Ellis Scrapbook, 96. Newspaper coverage following the death of Baby Doe Tabor was collected into a scrapbook by Clara Layton Ellis and presented to the Colorado Historical Society in the 1950s. Most clippings contain no date or page information, but the microfilmed scrapbook available in the Tabor Collection, FF 1439, reel 2. My endnotes indicate the page in the scrapbook on which the clippings are located.

3. *Denver Post*, March 8, 1935, 2.

4. Ellis Scrapbook, 21.

5. *Denver Post*, March 8, 1935, 3.

6. Ellis Scrapbook, 53, 112.

7. Ibid., 124.

8. Ibid., 61.

9. Quoted in Stoddard, *Saints and Shrews*, 4 .

10. *Denver Post*, March 9, 1935, 3.

11. Quoted in ibid., March 14, 1935.

12. Ibid., March 26, 1935.

13. McMechen, *The Tabor Story*, 41.

14. *Denver Post*, March 27, 1935, 6.

15. George W. Casey, Stickley Insurance & Agency Co., to CHS board of directors president Ernest Morris, 27 March 1935, Tabor Collection, box 12, FF 1075-8.

16. McMechen, *The Tabor Story*, 35.

17. Maria Davis McGrath to Judge Evans, 5 April 1935, Colorado State Archives. Given the uneasy relationship between families and their diary-writing relatives (see Bunkers, "Whose Diary Is It, Anyway?"), Willard McCourt may have immediately destroyed his sister's papers, once he realized their content.

18. Ellis Scrapbook, 116.

19. Ibid., 45, 3, 2, 7.

20. Ibid., 22.

21. Earnest Morris to Edgar C. McMechen, 29 March 1935, Tabor Collection, box 12, FF 1075–10. While it is still common policy to seal private papers of a sensitive nature when they are first placed in repositories, a period of time is usually designated after which access to the papers is granted (e.g., twenty-five years). No record of such a deadline for the Tabor papers exists.

22. "Silver Queen: Baby Doe Tabor's Life Story as Told to Sue Bonnie," *True Story* 37.6 (January 1938): 31, 33. The Tabor story appeared in a five-month serial. CHS holds the first four volumes of the series in the Tabor Collection, box 16, FF 1369.

23. Caroline Bancroft to William Rapp, 25 February 1937, Bancroft Papers, box 17, FF 14. Caroline Bancroft's papers are held in the Denver Public Library Western History archives, MSS WH1089.

24. Sue Bonnie's handwritten account, "Our Lives Together," resides in Denver Public Library Western History Collection as part of the Bancroft Papers, MSS WH1089; also in WH 398 M75–1662.

25. Riley, "Sin, Gin, and Jasmine," 41.

26. Castle, *Golden Fury*, 234.

27. Bancroft, *Silver Queen*, 7.

28. Ellis Scrapbook, 189.

29. McMechen Collection, CHS, Mss. 742, Scrapbook, 58.

30. Smith, *Horace Tabor*, 250.

31. Riley, "Sin, Gin, and Jasmine," 41.

32. Caroline Bancroft to William Rapp, 25 February 1937, Bancroft Papers, box 17, FF 14.

33. *Denver Post*, October 19, 1953, 3.

34. *Denver Post*, October 2, 1955, section 8, 1.

35. *Colorado Magazine* 13.1 (January 1936): 15, 16.

36. *Silver Dollar*, First National Pictures, producer David Chudnow, 1932.

37. The museum is currently owned by the National Mining Hall of Fame.

38. *Denver Post*, July 16, 1953, 32.

39. Moore, *The Ballad of Baby Doe*, 2.

40. Sprague, *Colorado*, 101.

41. Moore, *The Ballad of Baby Doe*, 2.

42. Ibid., 23.

43. Diary notes, FF 898.

44. Sills, *Bubbles: A Self-Portrait*, 85.

45. Blooding, *Douglas Moore's "The Ballad of Baby Doe,"* 49.

46. Duane A. Smith, conversation, January 5, 2000. In 2001 Smith, with John Moriarity, published *The Ballad of Baby Doe: I Shall Walk beside My Love*, which provides the complicated back-story of the opera's origins as well as its impressive lineage of Central City productions.

47. McKee, "You've Come a Long Way, Baby Doe," 27.

48. *New York Times*, January 10, 2001.

49. Ralph Blumenthal, "Beverly Sills: You've Come a Long Way, Baby Doe," *New York Times*, March 24, 2001, 24.

50. Hall indicated that the Butler memoir was housed at the Denver Public Library, but it is now missing from the Western History archives. *Two Lives*, 228.

51. Hall, *Two Lives*, 210.

52. See Karsner, *Silver Dollar*, 268, 283.

53. Furman, *Silver Dollar Tabor*, 106, 107.

54. Moynihan, *Augusta Tabor*, xiii, 6.

55. *Rocky Mountain News*, May 8, 1994, 74A.

56. *Denver Post*, May 29, 1914.

57. This good fun keeps the tale of Baby Doe alive, but at a cost. Ironically, it was a female graduate student from Limerick's campus, the University of Colorado, who at the 2005 Western History meetings asked me what research I was conducting. When I said "the life-writings of Baby Doe Tabor," her immediate response was, "Oh. That buffoon."

58. *Publishers Weekly*, July 24, 1995, 46; *New York Times Review of Books*, September 17, 1995.

59. Undated diary note, FF 910.

60. Iversen, *Molly Brown*, xxiii; Minich, *The Letters of Silver Dollar*, foreword.

61. Filmmaker David Wright quoted in Christine Smith, "Baby Doe's Tale now on Tape," *Denver Post*, August 4, 2000. His video Web site is www.Babydoetabor.com.

62. Conversation with Dennis Gallagher, February 25, 2000.

63. Diary, April 1, 1937, Caroline Bancroft Papers, container 15, FF 6. In 1939 CHS received a letter from Sue Bonnie, the woman who had sold Caroline

Bancroft the right to use her name for the *True Story* series. Bonnie was offering to sell several personal items she had retained of Mrs. Tabor's to the museum. She ended, "I am in need of a little money and what would you give for them." CHS historian LeRoy H. Hafen responded with a polite note stating there were no appropriations for such items. He added, "We already have about all we have room for anyway." Sue Bonnie to Colorado State History Museum, July 18, 1939; unsigned letter from Historian and Curator to Miss Sue Bonnie, 22 July 1939, CHS archives.

64. Tom Noel, conversation, February 26, 2000.

CHAPTER 3

1. The term "baby" also is used affectionately by the Amparo family for a young daughter and sister in *The Squatter and the Don*, published in 1888 by María Amparo Ruiz de Burton.

2. Oshkosh Tabor biographer Jim Metz located the 1915 letter from Ida Doe and shared it with me. It is located in FF 710–8.

3. Petrik, *No Step Backward*, 98–100, uses a U.S. government report on divorce that shows one out of three marriages failing in Helena between 1865 and 1870.

4. Ibid., 98.

5. Karsner, *Silver Dollar*, 143, 147.

6. Bancroft, *Silver Queen*, 30.

7. Scrapbook, FF 1438, reel 1, III-72. The code was 1 = a, 2 = e, 3 = i, and so on, for vowels. Consonants were more irregularly coded, with 6 = l, 7 = m (with some vexing exceptions). See page 80 for a detail of this scrapbook page.

8. Jake Sands, letter of 1880, Tabor Papers, box 1, FF 2 (Love Letters).

9. See Gunther Peck, "Manly Gambles."

10. Smith, *Horace Tabor*, 308; Hall, *Two Lives*, 106.

11. Karsner, *Silver Dollar*, 197.

12. Moore, *The Ballad of Baby Doe*, 22; Sprague, *Colorado*, 101; Burke, *Legend of Baby Doe*, 50; Vernon, *All for Love*, 81; Bancroft, *Silver Queen*, 37.

13. Burke, *Legend of Baby Doe*, 84.

14. See also Susan Lee Johnson's book, *Roaring Camp*.

15. Ellis Scrapbook, 15.

16. See Daniel Scott Smith's early work with birthrate records in his case study of Hingham, Massachusetts. His argument for what he terms "domestic feminism"—the power over childbearing that educated Victorian women could obtain if they bore their husbands a son—is persuasive.

17. Moore, *The Ballad of Baby Doe*, 10.

18. McKee, "You've Come a Long Way, Baby Doe," 43.

19. Ellis Scrapbook, 1; Hall, *Two Lives*, 41; Vernon, *All for Love*, 72.

20. Hall, *Two Lives*, 40–41; Tompkins, *West of Everything*, 55.

21. Euripides, *Medea*, 30.

22. Hall, *Two Lives*, 16; Moynihan, 47

23. Bancroft, *Silver Queen*, 6, 5.

24. Caroline Bancroft to Alice Knude, Sec. to Marvin Creager, *Milwaukee Journal*, 18 April 1953 (typescript from Stan Oliner, provenance unknown); *Denver Post*, October 7, 1954, Ellis Scrapbook, 235; Bancroft, *Silver Queen*, 80.

25. Riley, "Sin, Gin, and Jasmine"; Iverson, *Molly Brown*, xv.

26. Caroline Bancroft Papers, box 31, FF 64.

27. Ibid., FF 63.

28. Margaret F. Fanning, letter to author, April 20, 2000.

29. McMechen, *The Tabor Story*, 5; *Colorado Magazine* 13.1 (January 1936): 16–17.

30. Rosen, *Popcorn Venus*, 247.

31. Ibid., 339.

32. Hall, *Two Lives*, 157, 242.

33. Father John Guida to Mrs. Senator Tabor, no date, 1897, FF 140; Rev. James O'Mally, no addressee, 12 March 1883, Scrapbook VI-190.

34. Donald H. Menzel to Mr. Edward Blair (regional CHS curator), 25 April 1973. CHS Biographical Vertical File "Tabor, Baby Doe."

35. Burke, *Legend of Baby Doe*, 136, 85.

36. Vernon, *All for Love*, 64, 211, 111.

37. They are Kristen Iversen, whose working title of her novel is *Night Owls like Us*; Donna Stein, whose award-winning manuscript is entitled *Fortune*; and Hélène Reynolds.

38. Karsner, *Silver Dollar*, 227.

39. Smith, *Horace Tabor*, 228.

40. Scrapbook XI—199. Lizzie preserved twenty-five pages of newspaper coverage about the Bush suit.

41. Williams, *Legendary Women of the West*, 113.

42. Stone, *Men to Match My Mountains*, 408.

43. Karsner, *Silver Dollar*, 283.

44. Ellis Scrapbook, 26.

45. Ibid., 122.

CHAPTER 4

1. The quotation used in the subtitle is from Emily Dickinson, Poem 435, *Complete Poems*, 209.

2. Flinn, "The Deaths of Camp," 82, 64.

3. O'Brien, *Bitter Days*, 5.

4. Furman, *Silver Dollar Tabor*, 93.

5. Silver Tabor to Beloved Father Guida, 21 February 1912, FF 1160.

6. *Denver Post*, November 29, 1903, 6.

7. Ibid., July 19, 1928, 1, 18 (both quotes from page 1).

8. Kristen Iversen's study of Molly Brown analyzes depictions of this Irish-woman. David Roediger's *The Wages of Whiteness* provides a history of anti-Irish attitudes and laws in the nineteenth century.

9. Iversen, *Molly Brown*, 54; *Denver Post*, July 19, 1928, 1, 18.

10. Iversen, *Molly Brown*, xviii.

11. Burke, *Legend of Baby Doe*, 186.

12. Hall, *Two Lives*, 210.

13. Furman, *Silver Dollar Tabor*, 95.

14. Ibid., 104, 106, 106.

15. Ibid., 104–105.

16. Diary notes, April–June 1911, FF 897; Furman, *Silver Dollar Tabor*, 107.

17. Furman, *Silver Dollar Tabor*, 222.

18. Vernon, *All for Love*, 170.

19. *Chicago Daily News*, September 19, 1925, sent to the author by Kristen Iversen.

20. Hall, *Two Lives*, 223.

21. *Rocky Mountain News*, March 13, 1934.

22. The words between the two carets (^) were interlined.

23. *Denver Post*, March 24, 1935.

24. "Much Madness is divinest Sense" is from Emily Dickinson, Poem 435.

25. Descartes cited in Foucault, *Madness and Civilization*, 108; O'Brien, *Bitter Days*, 5.

26. Foucault, *Madness and Civilization*, 281.

27. When he was CHS curator of manuscripts, Stan Oliner located this June 26, 1938, letter in the archives of the Sisters of Charity, Leavenworth, Kansas.

28. Hendee cited from *Rocky Mountain Life Magazine*, Ellis Scrapbook, 169.

29. Foucault, *Discipline and Punish*, 187.

30. Letter from Mrs. Clarence Boerner, Tabor Collection, box 12, FF 1078–10.

31. Karsner, *Silver Dollar*, 344, 345, 348.

32. O'Brien, *Bitter Days*, 7.

33. Ellis Scrapbook, 94.

34. Burke, *Legend of Baby Doe*, 181.

35. Diary, FF 906. (When I read this passage aloud to an amused Denver Public Library desk clerk during a 2000 visit to their Western History collection, a patron who overheard me responded, "Horace Tabor as father of Colorado? No way. The earliest miners could be called the fathers, or the Utes! Not Horace Tabor, that latecomer.")

36. Leckie, *Elizabeth Bacon Custer and the Making of a Myth*, 199.

37. Ibid., 236, 312, 199.

38. Ibid., xiii.

39. *Jackie: Behind the Myth*, PBS-WNET-1999.

40. *Arizona Daily Star*, May 27, 1995.

41. *National Enquirer*, May 10, 1994.

CHAPTER 5

1. The epigraph is from Diary, May 21, 1919, FF 906.

2. Many editions of *The Book of Margery Kempe* exist, and "this creature" is used throughout but first appears on page 19 of the *Norton Anthology*. Poetry and the autobiographical letter by Sor Juana that provoked a bishop into silencing her can be found in *A Sor Juana Anthology*. Dickinson is cited from Poem 1129, *Complete Poems*, 506–507.

3. *Denver Post*, March 27, 1935, 6.

4. See Jacobs, *Victimized Daughters*.

5. Sinor, *Extraordinary Work of Ordinary Writing*.

6. Woolf, *Room of One's Own*, 43–44.

7. Fothergill, *Private Chronicles*, 82.

8. Silver to Aunt, 28 June 1908, FF 1159. See Bunkers and Temple, "Mothers, Daughters and Diaries" for a case-study analysis of how mothers inscribe ideology onto their children via their diaries. Diary, July 14, 1908, FF 896.

9. Horace Tabor had associated David Moffat with the failure of his beloved Little Pittsburg mine. The Henriett and Maid of Erin mines were once Tabor holdings (Smith, *Horace Tabor*, 183).

10. Furman, *Silver Dollar Tabor*, 113.

11. Burke, *Legend of Baby Doe*, 192.

12. Father Guida to Silver, 14 April, 1913, FF 679-2.

13. Silver to Mother, n.d., FF 1159.

14. Silver to Mother, 17 March 1914, FF 1161.

15. Silver to Mother, 20 April 1914, FF 1161; Diary, April 23, 1914, FF 899.

16. Diary, June 6, 1914, FF 899.

17. P to Mrs. H.A.W. Tabor, 7 June 1914, FF 695-8.

18. Furman, *Silver Dollar Tabor*, 250.

19. Father Guida to Mrs. H.A.W. Tabor, 12 September 1914, FF 697; "Dreams and Visions" fragment dated September 22 or 23, 1914, FF 993.

20. Draft of letter to A. M. Stevenson, 21 September 1914, FF 699–7; Diary, October [day erased] 1914, FF 899.

21. *The Greater Barrier* is one of three short films collected on videotape as *Silent Movies of the Pikes Peak Region*. Silver to Mother, 8 November 1914, FF 1163.

22. Draft of letter to unknown recipient, 24 November, 1914, FF 1195; Diary, November 27, 1914, FF 900.

23. Diary, December 17, 1914, FF 935; Silver to Dear Mother, n.d., marked by BDT "received 11 November 1914," FF 1164; Silver to Mother, 17 December, 1914, FF 1164.

24. Diary, December 1914, FF 901. See also page 163.

25. Silver to Mother, 8 January 1915, FF 1165.

26. See Lynn Z. Bloom's essay "I Write for Myself and Strangers," on characteristics of truly private diaries, and Jennifer Sinor's *The Extraordinary Work of Ordinary Writing*, for an analysis of "ordinary writing."

27. Theresa Fantz to Mrs. Tabor, 28 May 1915, FF 710-2.

28. Furman, *Silver Dollar Tabor*, 271.

29. Silver to Mother, 14 October 1915, FF 1166.

30. Silver to Mother, 15 October 1915, ibid.

31. Silver to Mother, 24 February 1916, FF 1167.

32. Silver to Mother, 5 April 1916, ibid.

33. A. M. Stevenson to Mrs. Tabor, 9 May 1917, FF 1215.

34. This envelope, which had been in FF 1174, was missing when I looked for it during my March 2001 research trip. Like the diary entries following the dramatic February 1915 calendar, it has disappeared.

35. Silver Tabor to Mother, 21 May 1917, FF 1174.

36. Audiotape of interview of Eva Hodges conducted by Stan Oliner in 2002.

37. Draft to "Miss Ruth La Vode," [Silver] 23 May 1917, FF 1196.

38. Furman, *Silver Dollar Tabor*, 282.

39. Silver to Mama, 16 September 1918, FF 1181; Silver to My Dear Mamma, 24 August 1925, FF 1193.

40. Written by Lizzie as prose on a telegraph form, lyrical formatting mine, FF 903.

CHAPTER 6

1. See Mechal Sobel's essay "The Revolution in Selves" on various ways cultures have perceived the import of dreams.

2. I am most familiar with this brand of spiritualism and mysticism in the life of writer Mary Hunter Austin as described in her autobiography, *Earth Horizon*.

3. Moffat and Painter, *Revelations*, 5.

4. See Temple essay, "Emily Dickinson's Country Kin."

5. See Temple essay, "Fragments as Diary."

6. Rich, *Diving into the Wreck*, 22.

7. O'Brien, *Bitter Days*, 6.

8. Ibid.

9. See Kaplan, "Resisting Autobiography."

10. Lauter and Rupprecht, *Feminist Archetypal Theory*, was very useful for this comparison of approaches to dreams.

11. Haraway, "Situated Knowledges," 593–94.

12. Lauter, *Feminist Archetypal Theory*, 192.

13. Jeanette Renouf, letter to the author, April 27, 2000.

14. Lauter, *Feminist Archetypal Theory*, 196.

15. See Roediger, *The Wages of Whiteness*.

16. Jacobs, *Victimized Daughters*, 38.

17. Conversation with Robert Burns, December 9, 1999. All subsequent quotations are from this conversation.

18. Flinders, *Enduring Grace*, 104.

19. Ibid., 99.

20. Ibid., 222.

21. Phone interview with Andrew Scrimgeour, February 21, 2000.

22. Diary, October 12, 1914, FF 900.

23. Silver Dollar Tabor, letter to Beloved Father Guida, 21 February 1912, FF 1160.

24. Conversation with Gerardo Wood, June 19, 1999.

25. Flinders, *Enduring Grace*, 11.

26. See Carpentier, "On the Marvelous Real in America."

27. Sangari, "Politics of the Possible," 233.

28. Flinders, *Enduring Grace*, 83–84.

29. Sangari, "Politics of the Possible," 226.

30. Smith and Watson, *De/Colonizing the Subject*, xix.

31. See Ewick and Silbey essay, "Subversive Stories and Hegemonic Tales."

32. Jones, "Writing the Body," 363.

33. Smith and Watson, *De/Colonizing the Subject*, xx.

34. Lensink, *"A Secret to Be Burried,"* 384.

35. Ewick and Silbey, "Subversive Stories," 212.

36. Sinor, *Extraordinary Work of Ordinary Writing*, 87.

37. Kaufman quoted in ibid., 99.

38. James Wood, email to author, March 25, 2002. All subsequent quotations are from this email.

39. Bonnie, "Our Lives Together," 14.

40. Ibid., 16–17.

41. Scrapbook III-13 and -14. Poem is on the page in which Lizzie commemorated her first son's birth and death.

EPILOGUE

1. FF 916, which indicates that archivists considered this an early piece of writing, although Lizzie does not indicate the year in which it was written.

Bibliography

Austin, Mary Hunter. *Earth Horizon.* 1932. Reprint. Albuquerque: University of New Mexico Press, 1991.

"'Ballad of Baby Doe': He Fell for Her Bait, and Then She Fell for Him." *New York Times*, April 10, 2001.

Bancroft, Caroline. *Augusta Tabor: Her Side of the Scandal.* Boulder: Johnson Publishing, 1955.

———. *Gulch of Gold: A History of Central City, Colorado.* 1958. Reprint. Boulder: Johnson Books, 2004.

———. *Silver Queen: The Fabulous Story of Baby Doe Tabor.* 1950. 17th printing. Boulder: Johnson Publishing, 1984.

Blooding, Randie Lee. *Douglas Moore's "The Ballad of Baby Doe": An Investigation of Its Historical Accuracy and the Feasibility of a Historical Production in the Tabor Opera House.* Masters thesis, Ohio State University, 1980.

Bloom, Lynn Z. "'I Write for Myself and Strangers': Private Diaries as Public Documents." In *Inscribing the Daily: Critical Essays on Women's Diaries*, ed. Suzanne L. Bunkers and Cynthia A. Huff, 23–37. Amherst: University of Massachusetts Press, 1996.

Blumenthal, Ralph. "Beverly Sills: You've Come a Long Way, Baby Doe," *NYT* March 24, 2001. <www.nytimes.com/2001/03/24/arts/24SILL.html>.

Bonnie, Sue. "Our Lives Together." Denver Public Library, n.d. MSS WH398 M75-1662.

Bunkers, Suzanne. "Illegitimacy and Intercultural Life Writing." *a/b: Auto/Biography Studies* 12.2 (Fall 1997): 188–202.

———. "Whose Diary Is It, Anyway? Issues of Agency, Authority, Ownership." *a/b: Autobiography Studies* 71.1 (Summer 2002): 11–27.

Bunkers, Suzanne, and Judy Nolte Temple. "Mothers, Daughters, and Diaries: Literacy, Relationship, and Cultural Context." In *Nineteenth-Century Women Learn to Write: Past Cultures and Practices of Literacy*, ed. Catherine Hobbs, 197–216. Amherst: University of Massachusetts Press, 1995.

Burke, John. *The Legend of Baby Doe: The Life and Times of the Silver Queen of the West.* 1974. Reprint. Lincoln: University of Nebraska Press, 1989.

Carpentier, Alejo. "On the Marvelous Real in America." In *Magical Realism: Theory, History, Community*, ed. Lois Parkinson Zamora and Wendy B. Faris, 75–88. Durham: Duke University Press, 1995.

Castle, Marian. *Golden Fury*. New York: William Morrow, 1949.

Convery, William J. *Pride of the Rockies: The Life of John Kernan Mullen*. Niwot: University Press of Colorado, 2000.

Dickinson, Emily. *The Complete Poems of Emily Dickinson*. Edited by Thomas H. Johnson. Boston: Little, Brown, 1960.

Ellis, Clara Layton. *Scrapbook*. Tabor Collection (614), FF 1439. Microfilm reel 2. Denver: SHSC. Donated October 14, 1954.

Euripides. *Medea and Other Plays*. London: Penguin, 1963.

Ewick, Patrick, and Susan S. Silbey. "Subversive Stories and Hegemonic Tales: Toward a Sociology of Narrative." *Law and Society Review* 29.2 (1995): 197–221.

Ferretti, Lodovico. *Saint Catherine of Siena*. Translated by Sonia di Centa. Siena: Edizioni Cantagalli, 2001.

Fink, Augusta. *I-Mary: A Biography of Mary Austin*. Tucson: University of Arizona Press, 1983.

Flinders, Carol Lee. *Enduring Grace: Living Portraits of Seven Women Mystics*. San Francisco: Harper, 1993.

Flinn, Caryl. "The Deaths of Camp." *Camera Obscura* 35 (May 1995): 53–84.

Fothergill, Robert. *Private Chronicles: A Study of English Diaries*. London: Oxford University Press, 1974.

Foucault, Michel. *Discipline and Punish: The Birth of the Prison*. New York: Pantheon, 1977.

———. *Madness and Civilization: A History of Insanity in the Age of Reason*. New York: Pantheon, 1965.

Friedan, Betty. *The Feminine Mystique*. New York: Norton, 1963.

Furman, Evelyn E. Livingston. *Silver Dollar Tabor: The Leaf in the Storm*. Aurora, Colo.: National Writers Press, 1982.

Gelles, Edith B. *Portia: The World of Abigail Adams*. Bloomington: Indiana University Press, 1992.

Gilbert, Sandra M., and Susan Gubar, eds. *The Madwoman in the Attic: The Woman Writer and the Nineteenth-Century Literary Imagination*. New Haven: Yale University Press, 1979.

The Greater Barrier. In *Silent Movies of the Pikes Peak Region*. Lakewood, Colo.: Post Modern, 1999.

Hall, Gordon Langley. *The Two Lives of Baby Doe*. Philadelphia: Macre Smith, 1962.

Hampsten, Elizabeth. *"Read This Only to Yourself": The Private Writings of Midwestern Women, 1880–1910*. Bloomington: Indiana University Press, 1982.

Haraway, Donna. "Situated Knowledges: The Science Question in Feminism and the Privilege of Partial Perspective." *Feminist Studies* 14.3 (Fall 1988): 575–99.

Hopcke, Robert H. *A Guided Tour of the Collected Works of C. G. Jung.* Boston: Shambhala, 1989.

Horner, Matina S. "Toward an Understanding of Achievement-Based Conflicts in Women." In *And Jill Came Tumbling After: Sexism in American Education,* ed. Judith Stacey, Susan Bereaud, and Joan Daniels, 43–63. New York: Dell Publishing, 1974.

Iversen, Kristen. *Molly Brown: Unraveling the Myth.* Boulder: Johnson Books, 1999.

Jackson, Paul. Review of *The Ballad of Baby Doe. Opera News* 21.2 (November 5, 1956): 12–13.

Jacobs, Janet Liebman. *Victimized Daughters: Incest and the Development of the Female Self.* New York: Routledge, 1994.

Johnson, Susan Lee. *Roaring Camp: The Social World of the California Gold Rush.* New York: W. W. Norton, 2000.

Jones, Ann Rosalind. "Writing the Body: Toward an Understanding of l'Ecriture Féminine." In *The New Feminist Criticism,* ed. Elaine Showalter, 361–77. New York: Pantheon, 1985.

Juhasz, Suzanne. "'Some Deep Old Desk or Capacious Hold-All': Form and Women's Autobiography." *College English* 6 (February 1988): 663–68.

Kaplan, Caren. "Resisting Autobiography: Out-Law Genres and Transnational Feminist Subjects." In Smith and Watson, *De/Colonizing the Subject,* 113–38.

Karsner, David. *Silver Dollar.* 1932. 13th ed. New York: Crown Publishers, 1947.

Kempe, Margery. "The Book of Margery Kempe." In *Norton Anthology of Literature by Women: The Traditions in English,* ed. Sandra M. Gilbert and Susan Gubar, 19–23. 2nd ed. New York: W. W. Norton, 1996.

Lauter, Estella, and Carol Schreier Rupprecht, eds. *Feminist Archetypal Theory: Interdisciplinary Re-Visions of Jungian Thought.* Knoxville: University of Tennessee Press, 1985.

Leckie, Shirley A. *Elizabeth Bacon Custer and the Making of a Myth.* Norman: University of Oklahoma Press, 1993.

Lensink, Judy Nolte. *"A Secret to Be Burried": The Diary and Life of Emily Hawley Gillespie, 1858–1888.* Iowa City: University of Iowa Press, 1989.

Lorde, Audre. *Zami: A New Spelling of My Name.* Watertown: Persephone Press, 1982.

MacLane, Mary. *Tender Darkness: A Mary MacLane Anthology.* Edited by Elisabeth Pruitt. Belmont, Calif.: Abernathy and Brown, 1993.

McKee, David. "You've Come a Long Way, Baby Doe." *Opera News* 61.3 (January 11, 1997): 27, 43, 51.

McMechen, Edgar C. "The Tabor Collections." *Colorado Magazine* 13.1 (January 1936): 14–19.

———. *The Tabor Story.* Denver: SHSC, 1951.

Minich, Jan. *The Letters of Silver Dollar.* Salt Lake City: City Art, 2002.

Moffat, Mary Jane, and Charlotte Painter, eds. *Revelations: Diaries of Women.* New York: Random House, 1974.

Moore, Douglas. *The Ballad of Baby Doe.* New York: Chappell, 1957.

Morris, Edmund. *Dutch: A Memoir of Ronald Reagan.* New York: Random House, 1999.

Morrison, Toni, and Claudia Brodsky Lacour, eds. *Birth of a Nation'hood: Gaze, Script and Spectacle in the O. J. Simpson Case.* New York: Pantheon Books, 1997.

Moynihan, Betty. *Augusta Tabor: A Pioneering Woman.* Evergreen, Colo.: Cordillera Press, 1988.

Noel, Thomas J. *Colorado Catholicism and the Archdiocese of Denver, 1857–1989.* Niwot: University Press of Colorado, 1989.

O'Brien, Theresa. *The Bitter Days of Baby Doe Tabor.* [S.l: s.n.], 1963.

Parkhill, Forbes. *The Wildest of the West.* New York: Henry Holt, 1951.

Peck, Gunther. "Manly Gambles: The Politics of Risk on the Comstock Lode, 1860–1880." In *Across the Great Divide: Cultures of Manhood in the American West,* ed. Matthew Basso, Laura McCall, and Dee Garceau, 73–96. New York: Routledge, 2001.

Petrik, Paula. *No Step Backward: Women and Family on the Rocky Mountain Mining Frontier, Helena, Montana 1865–1900.* Helena: Montana Historical Society Press, 1987.

Rich, Adrienne. *Diving into the Wreck.* New York: W. W. Norton, 1973.

Riley, Marilyn Griggs. "Sin, Gin, and Jasmine: The Controversial Career of Caroline Bancroft." *Colorado Heritage* (Spring 2002): 31–46.

Roediger, David R. *The Wages of Whiteness: Race and the Making of the American Working Class.* New York: Verso, 2000.

Rosen, Marjorie. *Popcorn Venus: Women, Movies, and the American Dream.* New York: Coward, McCann, and Geoghegan, 1973.

Sangari, Kum Kum. "The Politics of the Possible." In *The Nature and Context of Minority Discourse,* ed. Abdul R. Jan Mohmaed and David Lloyd, 216–45. New York: Oxford University Press, 1990.

Secrest, Clarke. *Hell's Belles: Denver's Brides of the Multitudes.* Aurora: Hindsight Historical Publications, 1996.

Sills, Beverly. *Bubbles: A Self-Portrait.* Indianapolis: Bobbs-Merrill, 1976.

Silver Dollar. First National Pictures. Produced by David Chudnow, 1932.

Sinor, Jennifer. *The Extraordinary Work of Ordinary Writing: Annie Ray's Diary.* Iowa City: University of Iowa Press, 2002.

Slotkin, Richard. *Regeneration through Violence.* Middletown: Wesleyan University Press, 1973.

Smith, Daniel Scott. "Family Limitation, Sexual Control, and Domestic Feminism in Victorian America." In *Clio's Consciousness Raised: New Perspectives on the History of Women,* ed. Mary Hartman and Lois W. Banner, 119–36. New York: Harper Colophon, 1974.

Smith, Duane A. *Horace Tabor: His Life and the Legend.* Niwot: University Press of Colorado, 1989.

Smith, Duane A., with John Moriarty. *The Ballad of Baby Doe: I Shall Walk beside My Love.* Boulder: University Press of Colorado, 2001.

Smith, Sidonie, and Julia Watson, eds. *De/Colonizing the Subject: The Politics of Gender in Women's Autobiography*. Minneapolis: University of Minnesota Press, 1992.

Sobel, Mechal. "The Revolution in Selves: Black and White Inner Aliens." In *Through a Glass Darkly: Reflections on Personal Identity in Early America*, ed. Ronald Hoffman, Mechal Sobel, and Fredrika J. Teute, 163–205. Chapel Hill: University of North Carolina Press, 1997.

A Sor Juana Anthology. Translated by Alan S. Trueblood. Cambridge: Harvard University Press, 1988.

Sprague, Marshall. *Colorado: A Bicentennial History*. New York: W. W. Norton, 1976.

Stineman, Esther Lanigan. *Mary Austin: Song of a Maverick*. New Haven: Yale University Press, 1989.

Stoddard, Karen M. *Saints and Shrews: Women and Aging in American Popular Film*. Westport: Greenwood Press, 1983.

Stone, Irving. *Men to Match My Mountains: The Opening of the Far West, 1840–1900*. Garden City: Doubleday, 1956.

Tabor, Silver. *Star of Blood*. Denver: Tabor, 1912.

Temple, Judy Nolte. "The Demons of Elizabeth Tabor: Mining 'Dreams and Visions' from the Matchless." *Colorado Heritage* (Winter 2001): 3–21.

———. "Emily Dickinson's Country Kin: Variorum Diarist Emily Hawley Gillespie." *a/b: Auto/Biography Studies* 17.2 (Summer 2002): 81–100.

———. "Fragments as Diary: Theoretical Implications of the *Dreams and Visions* of 'Baby Doe' Tabor." In *Inscribing the Daily: Critical Essays on Women's Diaries*, ed. Suzanne L. Bunkers and Cynthia A. Huff, 72–85. Amherst: University of Massachusetts Press, 1996.

Temple, Judy Nolte, ed. *Open Spaces, City Places: Contemporary Writers on the Changing Southwest*. Tucson: University of Arizona Press, 1994.

Tompkins, Jane. *Sensational Designs: The Cultural Work of American Fiction, 1790–1860*. New York: Oxford University Press, 1985.

———. *West of Everything: The Inner Lives of Westerns*. New York: Oxford University Press, 1992.

Vernon, John. *All for Love: Baby Doe and Silver Dollar*. New York: Simon and Schuster, 1995.

Wallace, Robert. "The Frontier's Fabulous Women." *Life Magazine* 46.19 (May 11, 1959): 66–76, 79–80, 83–84, 86.

Williams, Brad. *Legendary Women of the West*. New York: David McKay, 1978.

Winchester, Simon. *The Professor and the Madman: A Tale of Insanity and the Making of the "Oxford English Dictionary."* New York: HarperCollins, 1998.

Woolf, Virginia. *A Room of One's Own*. New York: Harcourt Brace and World, 1929. Reprint, 1959.

Index

Abelard and Heloise, 111
"Abigail Industry, The" (Geddes), 74
Academic feminism, 208
Adams, Abigail, 74
Adams, John Quincy, 74
All for Love: Baby Doe and Silver Dollar (Vernon), 68, 98–99
Alternative communities, 147
Androcentric stories/culture, 65, 105
Annie Get Your Gun, 94
Anti-Irish attitudes: and laws, 236n8; lore, 113
Anti-Mormon sentiment, 84
Anti-Semitism, 82
Anzaldúa, Gloria, 208
Arthur, Chester A., 20
Atkins, (Mr.), 110
Augusta Tabor: Pioneering Woman (Moynihan), 66, 88
Austin, Mary, 127
Autobiography of Benjamin Franklin, The (Franklin), 209
Automatic writing, 185

Baby Doe. *See* Tabor, Elizabeth Bonduel (McCourt) Doe, "Baby Doe"
"Baby Doe's Secret Love Code" (Bancroft, C.), 55
Baby symbolism, 161–62, 167; in Dreamworld, 151, 169–71; implications of, 209; mysterious,

190; stillbirth, 212; of two small babies, 164–65
Bad Mother: Baby Doe's documents refute role of, 120; deconstruction of Baby Doe image as, 117; Medea as, 109
"Bad Mother begets Bad Daughter" theme, 69
Ballad of Baby Doe, The (1956 opera), 60–62, 63, 83, 86, 94
Bancroft, Caroline: book on Baby Doe (1950), 6; on Augusta Pierce, 91; Baby Doe as an innocent, 79; on Baby Doe code, 81; background of, 50; battle with Edgar C. McMechen, 52–55; bequeathed Tabor items to Denver Public Library, 71; biographer's interpretations of, 91; bought Bonnie name rights, 50; deathbed edict source, 64; defender of Baby Doe, 128; on Doe divorce, 78–79; on H.A.W. Tabor, 84; later days of, 128; legal battle over rights, 61; Molly Brown biography by, 114; personal involvement with Baby Doe, 90; personal life of, 92; publishes pamphlet version, 52; supports Leadville Museum, 59; wary of lawsuits, 79; workpapers of, 93; wrote first legend as Bonnie, 50–51

Bancroft, George, 91

Bancroft, Hubert Howe, 54

Beauty: myth, 102; as power source, 49

Belle of Oshkosh, 8

Biographers: of Baby Doe, 230n5; roles adopted by, 55; views of, 74

Bipolar disorders, 214

Blessed Virgin, 116

Blooding, Randie Lee, 62, 76

Boehmer, (Mrs.), 141

Boerner, Clarence, 129

Bonnie, Sue: additional documents for sale, 233–34n63; befriends Baby Doe, 38; on Mrs. Perkins's charity, 218; sold name rights to Caroline Bancroft, 50; as surrogate daughter to Baby Doe, 216

Boots and Saddles (Custer, E.), 134

Brown, Ed "Edd," 151, 152, 153

Brown, J. J., 114

Brown, Margaret Tobin ("Unsinkable Molly Brown," "Mrs. J. J. Brown"): aided Baby Doe, 71; on Baby Doe, 112–13; Baby Doe visits, 123; C. Bancroft biography of, 91; death of, 114; earns respect through heroic action, 113; house of, 71, 115; mythic biographies of, 114; social activism of, 91; stereotypes of, 69

Brown, Mrs. J. J. *See* Brown, Margaret Tobin

Bryan, William Jennings, 26–27

Burke, John, 97–98; on Augusta Pierce, 86; on Baby Doe conversion in mining frontier, 132; on "Denver matriarchy," 98; on H.A.W. Tabor, 84; on Silver Dollar, 115, 122; writes *The Legend of Baby Doe*, 65

Burney, Fanny, 182

Burns, Robert, 200, 204

Bush, Mrs. William, 22

Bush, William, 14, 23, 101

Butler, Henry, 38, 64

Calamity Jane, 94

Callas, Maria, 137

Calvary Cemetery, 57

Carpentier, Alejo, 205

Castle, Marian, 51–52

Catherine of Siena, Saint, 201, 203

Catholic Church: Baby Doe relationship with, 96; baptizes H.A.W. Tabor, 30; charity from H.A.W. Tabor, 101; christening feud, 24; deception of in wedding, 21, 95, 187; mysticism in, 201–202; view of Tabor marriage, 96

Catholic faith, 118, 196. *See also* Tabor, Elizabeth Bonduel (McCourt) Doe

Central City, Colo., 8, 9

Central City Opera, 60

Chappelle, P. L., 20

Chicago Daily News, 121, 122

Chicago Tribune, 36, 121

Child sexual abuse, 199

Chronicle, 13

Chronicles of the Builders (Bancroft, H. H.), 54

Church of the Annunciation, 32, 42

Cinderella myth, 102

City of Ladies (Pizan), 147

Cixous, Hélène: and "laugh of the Medusa," 207

Code: C. Bancroft on, 55, 81; codes-within-codes, 144, 199; deciphering, 144, 234n7; *Denver Post* reporting on, 55; Eva Hodges on, 55; page showing, 145; pivotal people in, 142; as private writing, 211; Baby Doe's use of, 10, 140, 183

Code-switching, 126, 208

Colorado Heritage, 67

Colorado Historical Society (CHS): 1935 Tabor exhibit, 56; collection purging, 101; as estate administrator, 45; Tabor exhibits, 57

Colorado History Museum: mural with Baby Doe portrait, 72; Tabor Association buys Baby Doe belongings for, 47; Tabor exhibits, 67

Colorado Magazine (now *Colorado Heritage*), 56, 67

Commodification, 40

Compensatory diarists, 6, 147, 182

Content analysis, 214

Conversion: of beauteous object to pitiable abject, 105; of beauty into the crone, 105; to Good Widow, 123–24; of sinner to penitent, 105; sinner's involuntary, 103; of social interloper into madwoman, 105; through true love, 103; of Wanton into the Good Widow, 105

Convery, William J., 123

Croesus of the Rockies (Tabor, H.A.W.), 13

Crucifix, aid of, 200–201

Cruz, Sor Juana Inés de la, 141

Curse of the Tabor family, 59–60, 103

Custer, Elizabeth Bacon ("Libbie Custer"): adopts role of Victorian widow, 133; compared to Queen Victoria, 135; compared with Baby Doe, 139; death of, 135

Custer, George Armstrong, 134, 135

Cyclothymic disorders, 214

Daniels, Bebe, 58–59

"Dare-Devil, The" (poem), 150

"Dawn of Sorrow" (poem), 62, 119; "sad and living grave" vision, 119

Deathbed edict, of Horace Tabor, 30, 67; claim based on, 103; source of, 64

Debts, 129

Dementia, 214–15

Demons, 183; primitive pictures of, 142, 144

Denver, Colo.: Baby Doe returns to Denver as Mrs. H.A.W. Tabor, 22; Doe couple's honeymoon in, 8; social norms in, 15–16; Tabor Denver home, 25; *Washington Evening Star* on, 19

Denver Post, 40; 1954 series on Baby Doe, 51, 94; reports Baby Doe's code, 55; on Baby Doe memoirs, 141; on Baby Doe's birth centennial, 91; Baby Doe writes in

response to, 111–12; C. Bancroft article on Baby Doe code, 81; C. Bancroft worked for, 54; devil visions pictured, 131; on dismembering Baby Doe estate, 46–47; Hodges' reporting on Baby Doe, 63; Isabella diamond story, 67; on Matchless mine, 46; on Matchless Mine cabin rebuild, 59; Molly Brown on Baby Doe, 114, 123; praises H.A.W. Tabor, 41; protects Stevenson name from public, 176; questions Molly Brown on Baby Doe costume, 112–13; reports on Baby Doe dream accounts, 216; reports death of McMechen, 53; reports on Baby Doe mementos, 45; reports Silver Dollar's cause of death, 121; on Silver Dollar accused of theft, 171

Denver Public Library, 35

Denver Republican, 23

Denver society: Baby Doe Merry Widow fears, 109; caused Baby Doe papers sealed, 49; ostracizes Molly Brown, 113; on Tabor divorce, 23–24

Denver Thirty Six, 22, 52

Denver Times, 34

Descartes, René, 125

Devils: and demons in Freudian interpretation, 198; in dreams, 196; implications of, 209; in throes of, 223

Dewar, Harrison, 154–55

Diaries: as form of life-writing, 182; ideological inscription via, 237n8; as interior journal, 183

Diary-as-literature, 182

Dickinson, Emily, 141

Discipline and Punish (Foucault), 95, 128

Dismembering: of Baby Doe, 43; of Jacqueline Kennedy, 138

Divine illuminations, 204

"Diving into the Wreck" (poem), 183–84

Divorce: causes, 77; frequency, 234n3; scandal, 19

Documents: additional for sale, 233–34n63; Baby Doe's filing

Documents (*continued*)
system, 146; battle over, 52–53;
cleansing of, 230n21, 232n17;
"copied and filed" notation, 146;
destroyed, 184; disintegrated by
archivists, 147; McMechen denies
access to, 53; missing, 71; sealing
of, 52, 62, 232n21; Silver
Dollar/Baby Doe letters, 159;
stolen/destroyed, 146; storage of, 4
Doe, Harvey, Jr., 8; Baby Doe divorces,
11; Baby Doe remarries in
Dreamworld, 77; as day laborer, 10;
in Dreamworld, 185, 197;
estrangement and divorce of, 77;
versus H.A.W. Tabor, in
Dreamworld, 185; as mine
operator, 9; postdivorce life of, 11
Doe, Ida, 77
Doe Heads Web site, 69
Domestic feminism, 86, 234n16
Domination structures, 207
Doty, Florence Naylor, 93
Double standard, 55, 98
Dreamer as sinner, 200
Dreams: to address unsolvable
problems, 196; of agency, 193–94;
aggressive, 197; animal dreams,
192; chronicles, 183; as confidants,
197; as deepest repressions, 188;
from God, 188, 196; importance
of, 181; versus memories, 99; as
messages from God, 181; as
positive drama, 188
Dreamworld: alternative community
within, 147; anxieties recast in,
192; babies in, 169–71; Baby Doe
and Silver Dollar reunite in, 191;
Baby Doe releases Silver Dollar,
194; Baby Doe resurrects Silver
Dollar as Dream Child, 194–95;
baby symbolism in, 151; brother
Stephen as good omen in, 150;
dual Silvers in, 195; exclusion of
Baby Doe from, 210; H.A.W. Tabor
in, 185; left side versus right side
symbolism in, 153; map of, 147;
Matchless Mine Girl in, 142, 151,
195; Matchless Mine in, 186;
Matchless Mine symbolism in, 151;
Maxcy Tabor in, 89; members of,
147–48, 150; nature of, 147–48;
Saint Rita in, 151; settings to, 186;
Silver Dollar's lost babies in, 179;
symbols in, 181; untouchable foods
vision, 124
"Durango divorce," 19
Dutch: A Memoir of Ronald Reagan
(Morris, Edmund), 74

Empire magazine, 55
Evans, John, 46
Evil spirits, 219
Exploitation, 98

Fantz, Theresa: Baby Doe pays, 158;
helps with Silver Dollar "problem,"
157; Silver Dollar pregnancy/baby,
168
Fatal Attraction, 90
Female mysticism, 201
Female power/sexuality: assumptions
about, 226; Baby Doe's, 90, 100;
Burke's fantasies on, 65; fear of
women's success, 92; in the Tabor
legend, 49; writers' views on, 7, 99
The Feminine Mystique (Friedan), 94
Feminist archetypal theory, 196
Fertility control and Catholic faith, 118
Field, Eugene: on H.A.W. Tabor, 12–13;
on Tabor divorce, 23
First-person narrative, 98
Flinders, Carol, 202, 204, 205, 207
Flinn, Caryl, 108
Florence (Catholic nun), 128
Florence Crittenton Home, 157
Folk narrative, subversive stories in,
207
Foretelling the future, 145, 149, 191–92
Fothergill, Robert, 6, 182
Foucault, Michel, 95, 127, 128
Fourth of July (mine), 8
Fowler, Gene, 114
French feminism, 207
Freudian school, 188
Friedan, Betty, 94

"Frontier's Fabulous Women, The" (*Life Magazine* article), 94
Functional dream analysis, 190
Furman, Evelyn: on Lily's move to the Midwest, 116–17; purchases Leadville Tabor Opera House, 59; receives offers to buy Baby Doe items, 71; on Silver Dollar's financial improvement, 178; wrote Silver Dollar book from Silver's letters, 65–66

Garbo, Greta, 108
Gelles, Edith, 74
Gender: conventions of in public discourse, 112; dynamics, assumptions about, 90; fables, 69; gap, 93; in westerns, 87; of widows, 108
Gershwin, George, 63
Giants in the Earth (opera), 60
Gilbert, Sandra M., 127
Gillespie, Emily Hawley, 182
Gilman, Charlotte Perkins, 127
Gold diggers, 91, 137
Golden Fury, The (Castle), 51–52, 94
Golden Widow, 52
Gold mines, 8; boom, 9
Gold standard, 27
Good Mother, 116
Good Widow: and Baby Doe's habits of medieval mystics, 204; conversion to, 123–24; societal expectations of, 136
Graphomania, 147
Great Barrier, The (film), 159
Great Depression, 41
Gubar, Susan, 127
Guida, Joseph: advises Baby Doe of Silver Dollar's proposal, 157; archives of, 205; Baby Doe letters to, 96; charity from H.A.W. Tabor, 102; codreamer accounts sent to, 150; death of, 215; enters Baby Doe's life, 24; Silver Dollar corresponds with, 110, 203

Haben, Andrew, 165
Haben, Tilly (McCourt), 165

Hafen, LeRoy H., 233–34n63
Hall, Calvin S., 197, 214
Hall, George Langley, 63–64, 83, 87, 122; "The Greek Tragedy," 64, 95
Hallas, David, 65
Handwriting, two types of, 141–42, 183
Haraway, Donna, 189
Harper's Bazar, 24, 190
Harrison, Benjamin, 27
Hawthorne, Nathaniel, 74
Hegemonic tales, 206
Hell's Belles (Secrest), 100
Hendee, Dorothy, 128
Hero, the (Jungian figure), 196
Hodges, Eva: on Baby Doe code, 55; protects Stevenson name from public, 176; writes *Denver Post* series, 63
Honeymaid. *See* Tabor, Rose Mary Silver Dollar Echo
hooks, bell, 208
Horace Tabor: His Life and the Legend (Smith, D. A.), 64, 101
Horgan (Catholic priest), 205
Horner, Matina, 92
Houston, Robert, 68
Hush, Hush, Sweet Charlotte, 95
Hutchinson, Anne, 109
Hyperperformance (Kaufman, R.), 213

Idealized mothers, 90
Idealized self, 90
If I Did It (Simpson, O.J.), 75
Incest, 199
Infanticide, 213
Infidelity and Mormons/Mormonism, 21
Institutional racism, 75
Irish workers, 198
Isabella diamond, 20, 32, 67
Iversen, Kristen: on C. Bancroft, 91; critiques Silver Dollar's cause of death, 121; on adapting the legend to suit current tastes, 59–60; on Molly Brown, 115; on Molly Brown and Baby Doe, 113; women-centered approach of, 68–69

Jacobs, Janet, 144, 199
Janeway, Elizabeth, 42–43
Johnson, Susan Lee, 77
Julian of Norwich, 201
Jung, Carl, 196; Jungian school, 188, 196–98

Kansas Territory, 11
Karsner, David: on Doe divorce, 78–79; on H.A.W. Tabor, 83; visits Baby Doe at Matchless mine, 130; writes first Baby Doe book, 4
Kaufman, Rona, 213
Keenan (Catholic priest), 96
Kempe, Margery, 141, 202
Kennedy, Jacqueline Bouvier. *See* Onassis, Jacqueline Lee (Bouvier) Kennedy
Kennedy, John Fitzgerald, 139
Kennedy, John Fitzgerald, Jr. ("John-John"), 139
Kennedy, Robert, 137, 139
King, Coretta Scott, 137
King, Martin Luther, Jr., 137
Kinsey report, 95
Kristeva, Julia, 207

Labor disputes, 15
Last, Elizabeth Bonduel "Lily" (Tabor)(: acknowledges Silver Dollar's death, 36; birth of, 24; on cover of *Harper's Bazar*, 24, 26; denies Baby Doe her mother, 39, 42; marriage to first cousin, 66; marries John Last, 36; mine cabin life, 32; moves to Denver, 33; moves to the Midwest, 116–17; moves to Wisconsin, 32; presence of in Dreamworld, 118; reprints of on cover of *Harper's Bazar*, 49; writes to Baby Doe of her marriage and child, 117
Last, John "Jack" (nephew of Baby Doe), 36, 117
Last, Nealie (McCourt) (sister of Baby Doe), 117–18
Latouche, John, 62
Lead poisoning, 124

Leadville, Colo., 12, 13; Catholic hospital in, 43–44
Leadville Herald, 55
Leadville Museum, 59
Leadville Tabor Opera House, 59
Leckie, Shirley: biographer of Libbie Custer, 133–34; on Libbie Custer's motives, 136; on Libbie Custer's reflected life, 135
Left side versus right side symbolism, 153
Legends, 3, 75; creation of, 49–50
Legend of Baby Doe, The (Burke), 65, 97
Letters from Silver Dollar, The (Minich), 69
Lewinsky, Monica, 108
Life Magazine article, 94
Life-writing, 209
Limerick, Patricia, 68
Linear autobiographies, 209
"Little bundle," 54, 210
Little Pittsburg mine, 12
Lives of the Saints, The (Butler), 32
Living dead, 119, 147
Lizzie. *See* Tabor, Elizabeth Bonduel (McCourt) Doe
Llorona, La, 129
Love, Waldo C., 57, 72
Love letters, 100; lovers' correspondence, 18
Love triangle, 19

Machebeuf, Joseph, 24
MacLane, Mary, 150
MacLennan, (Mr.), 161
MacMahon, Aline, 58
Madness, causes of, 125, 126, 213
Madwoman in the Attic, The (Gilbert and Gubar), 127
Madwoman in the cabin, 36
Madwomen, 129
Magical realism, 99, 205
Male dominance, 88
Malnutrition, 185
Marriage-wrecking wanton versus determined pioneer woman, 41
Marvelous realism, 205–206, 208
Mary Magdalene, 202

Masculine power, 83; of H.A.W. Tabor, 83; idol of (dying), 104; money enhancement of, 86

Matchless mine: Baby Doe's tireless defense of, 123, 130; cabin reconstruction, 59; in Dreamworld, 186; early rewards from, 12; fire/smoke in, 96–97; guardian of, 136; as hope, 186; as metonymic for Widow Tabor, 109–10; owned by J. K. McMullen, 123, 130, 135; press enters and exposes, 43, 44; replica of, 71; sold to Baby Doe's sister Claudia McCourt, 31; symbolism of, in Dreamworld, 151; as symbolism of Motherhood, 104; vandalism/destruction of, 45–46, 146. See also Tabor, Horace Austin Warner (H.A.W.)

Matchless Mine Girl, 142, 151, 195

McCourt, Claudia (sister of Baby Doe): blamed for stealing Lily, in Dreamworld, 117; Lily moves to live with, 32; secures Matchless for Baby Doe, 31; Silver Dollar writes to, 149; woos Lily to Chicago, 187

McCourt, Elizabeth (mother of Baby Doe), 7

McCourt, Peter (brother of Baby Doe), 22–23; acknowledges Silver Dollar's death, 36; Baby Doe appeals to, 28; blamed for stealing Lily, in Dreamworld, 117, 119; appears in Dreamworld, 165; as Horace Tabor's manager, 22; moves Lily to Denver, 33; woos Lily to Chicago, 187; woos Silver Dollar to Chicago, 187

McCourt, Peter (father of Baby Doe), 7

McCourt, Philip (brother of Baby Doe): arranges for Baby Doe's funeral, 42; blamed for stealing Lily, in Dreamworld, 117, 119; on deathbed edict claim, 103–104

McCourt, Stephen (brother of Baby Doe): corresponds with Baby Doe, 117; visits Baby Doe in Dreamworld, 162, 164–65

McCourt, Willard (brother of Baby Doe): arranges for Baby Doe's funeral, 42; on Baby Doe's sanity, 42; claimant of Baby Doe's belongings, 46; document cleansing by, 232n17

McKee, David, 63

McMechen, Edgar C.: on Baby Doe name, 76; on Baby Doe's beauty, 94; battle with C. Bancroft, 52–55; death of, 53; denies access to Tabor papers, 52–53; on H.A.W. Tabor, 84; inventories belongings of Baby Doe, 45; on Matchless mine destruction, 46; praises 1935 Tabor exhibit, 56; protects image of Baby Doe, 53, 201; role as Gentleman Historian, 55; Silver Dollar photo in Tabor Story, 173; spring auction of Tabor goods, 70; writes The Tabor Story, 94; booklet of on Tabor history, 53–54

Medea as Bad Mother, 109

Medieval mystics, 141, 183, 203–204

Memoirs: Denver Post article on, 141; drafts of, 141–42; role of, 209

Miller, (Mr.), 149

Milwaukee Journal, 90

Mindful Mother: Furman's book reveals Baby Doe as, 66; guarding daughters, 136; helps with Silver Dollar "problem," 157; heroism of, 115; of Lily, 115; stillborn sons, 170; subconscious work on behalf of Silver Dollar, 175, 178; supports Silver Dollar, 190

Minich, Jan, 69

Mining frontier: Baby Doe conversion to individualistic miner, 132; extramarital socializing in, 77; female sexuality during, 65; sex and power on, 73; womanhood on, 86

Mink, Louis, 211

Minor, W. C., 126

Miracles, 204

Miscarriages, 172, 174

"Mistress of the Matchless Mine" (poem), 131

Misunderstood woman, 55, 189
Moffat, David, 150, 237n9
Moffat, Mary Jane, 182
Molly Brown: Unraveling the Myth (Iversen), 91
Moore, Douglas, 60, 87
Moral climate of feminized Denver, 98
Morality tales, 83, 116
Moral lessons, 96
Moral standards versus social class standards, 98
Mormons/Mormonism and infidelity, 21
Morris, Edmund, 74
Morris, Ernest, 45
Morrison, Toni, 75
Mount Olivet Cemetery, 39, 57
Moynihan, Betty, 66, 88, 89
Mullarkey, Mary, 68
Mullen, J. K., 123, 130, 133
Multiple interpretations, 184
Mysticism: defined, 205; in Catholic Church, 201–202
Mythic biographies, 114
Myth of American exceptionalism, 230n4
Mythologizers' motives, 75

Names, agency of, 76
Nast, Thomas, 24, 49
National Enquirer, 138
National Women's Suffrage Association, 113
Neocolonialist language versus ex-centric discourse, 206
Newspaper coverage. *See specific newspapers*
New York City Opera Company, 62–63
New York Times, 23, 68
Nightmarish dreams as omens, 116
Night Owls like Us (Iversen), 69, 121
Nin, Anaïs, 183
Noel, Thomas, 68, 72
Not-language, 87
Numinous experiences/visitations, 204, 207, 213

O'Brien, Theresa, 96, 109, 130, 184, 215

O'Connor, Richard. *See* Burke, John
Oliner, Stan, 67, 71, 230n21
O'Mally, James, 96
Onassis, Aristotle, 137, 138
Onassis, Jacqueline Lee (Bouvier) Kennedy ("Mrs. John F. Kennedy"): compared with Baby Doe, 139; death of, 138; eschews Widow Kennedy role, 133, 137; goes into isolation, 138; as gold digger, 137; "Jackie O" nickname, 137–38; lessons from her mother, 137; transforms to "Jackie O," 136
Operatic home meters, 83, 86
"Our Lives Together" (Bonnie, S.), 216, 232n24
"Out-law genre" (Kaplan, C.) 188

Painter, Charlotte, 182
Paramystics, 204
Parkhill, Forbes, 100
Patriarchal society: disciplining strong women in, 92; efforts to control unattached women, 136; madwomen who rave against, 127; traditional language as trap for women in, 207; women as colonized subjects of, 206; women's surnames in, 76; world perception of, 206
Perkins, (Mrs.) (Leadville benefactor), 217–18
Petrik, Paula, 77
Pets, symbolism of, 185, 192
Pioneer women, 66, 182
Pitkin, Governor, 15
Pizan, Christine de, 147
Pleasant dreams, 196
Popcorn Venus, 94
Pokigo, Patty, 141, 177
Political power of men's wives, 86
Polyvocality, 184
Popular history, 54
Porgy and Bess, 63
Postmodernism, 99, 209
Powerful women: androcentric culture intolerant of, 105; colonizing other

women, 206; power and security through a rich husband, 137; power through beauty, 108
Predictive synchronicity, 197
Private writing, 142
Professional historian versus popular writer, 54
Professional widowhood, 132–33
Professor and the Madman, The (Winchester), 126
Prostitutes, 15
Public discourse, 112
Public opinion on Tabor divorce, 23
Publishers Weekly, 68
Punishment: films, 95; versus authority of experience, 92
Pure Child, 197

Racial anxieties, 198
Rags to riches, 101–104
Rape, 176
Rational and irrational behavior, 126
Rebecca (cousin to Libbie Custer), 134
Rebirth symbol, 197
Recollections versus memories, 104
Recurring figures in Dreamworld, 142
Reflexive biography, 74
Religiosity, 125
Religious mystics. *See* Mysticism
Religious women, 111
Reluctant wife, 202
Re-membering process, 41
Renouf, Jeanette, 196
Revisionist biography, 89
Reynolds, Debbie, 114
Rich, Adrienne, 183, 206
Riley, Marilyn Griggs, 91
Rita, Saint: as Baby Doe role model, 203; enters Dreamworld, 151; life of, 202; saint of impossible cases, 203
Roaring Camp (Johnson), 77
Roberts, William E., 93
Robertson, Clyde, 131
Robinson, Edward G., 58
Rocky Mountain News, 46; Augusta Pierce depiction in, 86; on Baby Doe's life and death, 103; fought sealing of Baby Doe papers, 49; illustration on Baby Doe conversion, 106–107; illustration on H.A.W. Tabor wives meeting, 106; McMechen worked for, 54; on Mormonism, 21; on Tabor triangle, 87
Roediger, David, 198, 236n8
Room of One's Own, A (Woolf), 146
Roosevelt, Theodore, 148–49
Rosen, Marjorie, 94, 95
Rough drafts, 141–42, 143, 185
Ruthless woman versus sincere person, 69
Ryan, William ("Billy"), 178

Sacred Heart, 71
Saints, 183
Sandelowsky, Jake ("Jake Sands"): appearance of, 80; Baby Doe in company with, 10; Baby Doe's involvement with, 77; Baby Doe visits, 13; Doe couple befriends, 10; and Doe divorce, 78; familiarity with Baby Doe, 81
Sangari, Kum Kum, 206
Schizotypal personality disorder, 215
Scrimegeour, Andrew, 202
Second-wave feminist movement, 97, 127, 207, 208
Secrest, Clark, 100
"Secret to Be Burried" (Temple), 183
Semiotics, 207
Senile dementia, 215
Sensational Designs (Tompkins, J.), 74
Serial autobiography, 182
Sex and power: assumptions about, 90; on mining frontier, 73
Sexual abuse, 200
Sexual icons, 108
Sexual revolution, 95
Shadow self, 198
Shunning: of Augusta Pierce Tabor in Dreamworld, 89; by the Denver Thirty-Six, 22; of Baby Doe by other women, 75; of female

Shunning (*continued*)
   troublemakers, 109; impact of on
   victims, 108–109, 120; to the point
   of stoning, 93
Signifiers in women's writing, 141
Sills, Beverly, 62
Silver Dollar (1932 film), 4; Baby Doe
   rejects action against, 38; H.A.W.
   Tabor depicted in, 83; political
   power of men's wives, 86; reissued,
   40–41; revival of, 58
Silver Dollar (Karsner), 4, 59, 61, 114
Silver Dollar Tabor: The Leaf in the Storm
   (Furman), 65
Silver Dollar Weekly, 34
Silver Queen (Bancroft, C.), 6
"Silver Queen: Baby Doe Tabor's Life
   Story as told to Sue Bonnie"
   (Bancroft, C.), 49–50
*Silver Queen: The Fabulous Story of Baby
   Doe Tabor* (Bancroft, C.), 52, 59, 90,
   91
Simpson, Nicole, 74
Simpson, O.J., 74–75
Sinor, Jennifer, 145, 211
Sisters of Charity of Leavenworth, 128
Situated knowledge, 189
Six Racy Madams of Colorado (Bancroft,
   C.), 54
Sleeping Beauty myth, 102
Sloninger, Claire, 178
Slotkin, Richard, 6, 230n4; on
   mythogenesis, 40
Smith, Daniel Scott, 86
Smith, Duane A., 64, 101; on deathbed
   edict claim, 103–104; on H.A.W.
   Tabor, 83
Smith, Sidonie, 206–207
Snakes, 150, 223; image of, 192–93
Social activism as unfeminine
   aggressiveness, 91
Social invisibility, 127
Social outcast, 22
Sporting girls, 14
Sprague, Marshall, 84
St. Louis, Mo., 21
St. Mary's Cathedral, 71

St. Patrick's Church, 96
St. Vincent's Hospital, 146
Star of Blood (Tabor, Rose Mary Silver
   Dollar Echo), 34, 65, 120
Starvation, 124, 204, 215
Stereotypes versus verifiable stories, 69
Stevenson, A. M.: dream of, 199; funds
   Silver Dollar's "health" needs, 158;
   power of, 176; receives blackmail
   letter from Silver Dollar, 175
Stillborn sons, 78, 79, 80, 170
Stone, Irving, 102
Story of "O," The (Réage), 138
Strategic madness, 124, 126
Strikes, 15
Subversive writing, 208
Suffrage, 113
Symbols/symbolism: in Dreamworld,
   181; left side versus right side, 153;
   of Matchless Mine, 104, 151;
   meanings of, 210; of pets, 192; of
   rebirth, 197. *See also* baby
   symbolism
Synchronicity, 197

Tabor, Augusta Pierce: depiction of in
   Baby Doe opera, 86; charities of,
   89; diary of, 88; eastern connection
   claims, 88; financial success of,
   after divorce, 87; as frigid and
   frugal, 85–86; Furman's biography
   of, 67; as gold digger, 91;
   interviewed by *Denver Republican*,
   23; lives in Denver, 15; marital
   name importance, 66; marries
   H.A.W. Tabor, 11; Moynihan's
   biography of, 66; opera's treatment
   of, 61; sexual availability of,
   230n17; social acceptance of, 22;
   socially ill at ease, 13; sues H.A.W.
   Tabor for divorce, 18, 19; support
   and drive of, 12; tragic flaw of, 87
Tabor, Elizabeth Bonduel (McCourt)
   Doe ("Baby Doe"): from abject to
   Warrior Mother, 206, 212; as
   actively predatory versus passively
   predestined, 100; as adulteress

versus faithful guardian, 94; Baby
Doe name origins, 76–77; baptizes
a drunk, 202; as Belle of Oshkosh,
8; birth of, 7; books written about,
56; calendar (1915) secrets, 151,
167, 168, 169; as Cassandra figure,
193–94; Catholic faith of, 32, 187;
codreamers in Dreamworld, 120,
148, 150, 171, 179, 191; as
colonized subject, 206;
commodification of, 40; compared
with literary giants, 205; date and
time details in "Dreams and
Visions," 145; daughters of, 115;
death and burial, 3, 38, 39, 42;
denies/acknowledges Silver
Dollar's death, 35, 105–106, 121,
215; dream of sailing, 188; early
childhood of, 7–8; exclusion of
Baby Doe, from Dreamworld, 210;
as floozy and freak, 89–90; as
former wanton, 90; "Foster" note
in 1915 calendar, 168; as Good
Widow after death, 108; on H.A.W.
Tabor in Dreamworld, 84; harasses
Silver Dollar's lovers, 120; haunts
Denver financial sector, 37; as
hero's widow, 134; interrupts Silver
Dollar's party, 155; and Jake Sands,
10, 78; as Jungian dreamer, 198;
Leadville residents' reminiscences
of, 96–97; letters to Father Guida,
96; library privileges, 132; Lily
born, 24; loyalty to H.A.W. Tabor
after ruin, 28; as manly-hearted
woman, 111; marriage to H.A.W.
Tabor, 14, 20, 22, 100; marriage to
Harvey Doe, 8, 11; as Merry
Widow, 109; midlife photo of, 96,
97; miner's costume of, 133;
mother-love for Silver Dollar, 186;
moves to Matchless cabin, 36, 110;
as mystic, 203; negotiates with
creditors, 28, 30; as "one
daughter's fortress," 91; opera
treatment of, 61; as "other
woman," 15, 86; personal items

dispersed after death, 43–44;
personalized purgatory of, 105;
portrait of by Waldo C. Love, 57,
58, 72; Public penance, 41; as
redeemed through her deference,
103; relationship with brothers
Peter and Stephen, 20, 28, 33, 117,
158; religious state of, 110; rescues
Silver Dollar from "miscarriage,"
120; as resistive postmodern life-
writer, 209; rift between Silver
Dollar and Baby Doe, 151; second
stillborn son, 26; sells Isabella
diamond, 32; as a sexual being, 95;
as sexual predator, 90; Silver Dollar
as dutiful daughter in
Dreamworld, 122; Silver Dollar
born, 26; Silver Dollar corresponds
with, 35, 162, 166; sinful seductress
versus irresistible beauty, 89; as
sinner involuntarily converted,
103; stereotypes of, 69; stillborn
pregnancy of, 10; as temptress, 78;
true-love conversion of, 103; vision
of Ed Brown's villainy, 153; vision
of Lily's "sad and living grave," 119;
visits Lily in Chicago, 118; visits
Silver Dollar in Indianapolis, 172;
voice of, 92, 207; wears crucifix
about neck, 36–37; as weeping
woman, 184; from whore to
heroine, 41. *See also* Widow Tabor
Tabor, Horace Austin Warner (H.A.W.):
1932 book on, 4; associates David
Moffat with mine failure, 237n9;
baptized into Catholic Church, 30;
as bipolar spectator, 214;
Chrysolite mine of, 15; Committee
for Safety, 15; as Croesus of the
Rockies, 13; deathbed edict of, 30;
early career of, 12; early Tabor
courtship, 100; Eugene Field on,
12–13; as everyman, 84; financial
ruin after crash, 27–28; Freudian-
inflected magnetism in movie and
opera, 83; funeral of, 30–31; as
gambler, 82–83; generosity of, 101;

Tabor, Horace Austin Warner (H.A.W.) (*continued*)
gets job as Denver postmaster, 30; Hubert Bancroft biography of, 54; as lieutenant governor, 13; marries Augusta Pierce, 11; masculine agency and financial potency of, 83, 84, 87; masculine fantasies, 82–83; meets/courts Baby Doe, 14, 100; memories regarding, 135–36; mock trial of, 67–68; moves to Colorado, 11–12; opera treatment of, 61; political aspirations, 19; praised by *Denver Post*, 41; reburied in Mount Olivet Cemetery, 57; as Silver King, 12; as speculator, 27; as strikebreaking capitalist mine owner, 83; sued by Augusta Pierce for divorce, 18, 19; Washington wedding, 20; works as day laborer after ruin, 30; Tabor, Maxcy (son of H.A.W. Tabor), 11, 15, 28, 89

Tabor, Rose Mary Silver Dollar Echo ("Silver Dollar"): accused of theft, 171; acts in movie, 159; affair with Leadville stable owner, 33; arrested but cleared of charges, 34; as artifact of Old West, 122; attracted to wildness, 150; as Baby Doe in Dreamworld, 196; becomes reporter for *Denver Times*, 34; birth and early life of, 26, 148; character development of, 65; in chorus line, 171; as codreamer in Dreamworld, 148; considers convent life, 35; corresponds with Baby Doe, 35; creates *Silver Dollar Weekly*, 34; death of, 35, 69 105, 121, 179, 215; delivers song to Theodore Roosevelt, 33; as dual being in Dreamworld, 195; as dutiful daughter in Dreamworld, 122; as Ed Brown's victim, 154; endangerment dreams, 172; good Silver versus sexual Silver, 150; hospitalized for "blood poisoning," 172; as Honeymaid in Dreamworld, 148, 174; as kept woman in Chicago underworld, 35; leaves home, 152; lost babies in Dreamworld, 179; medical problems of, 177–78; mine cabin life, 32; miscarriage, 172; moves to Chicago, 34–35; moves to Indianapolis, 171; name and address changes, 174, 177; as nymphomaniac and self-destructive victim, 122; offers body to be dissected, 166; opera treatment of, 61; pregnancy, 154, 168; purported rape by Stevenson, 175–77; receives marriage proposals, 149, 157; relates religious state of Baby Doe, 110; reporting on death of, 121; revue performer in Denver, 171; rift between Silver Dollar and Baby Doe, 151; scandal as sin and punishment, 120; seen as bold, 69; sexual promiscuity of, 192; as spirited young woman, 55; threatens suicide, 34; transformed to innocent child in Dreamworld, 190–91; as viewed in 1932 book, 4; visits Lily in Chicago, 118; as wild party girl in Dreamworld, 191; writes "A Statement" to Baby Doe, 151–52; writes song for Theodore Roosevelt, 32–33; writes *Star of Blood*, 34; writes to Aunt Claudia, 149; writes to Baby Doe, 172, 174, 178; writes to Father Guida, 110, 203; writes to Harrison Dewar, 154–55

Tabor Association, 46
Tabor Block, 15, 63, 71
Tabor Center (mall), 71
Tabor estate sale, 46
Tabor exhibits, 56, 57, 67, 72
Tabor Family photographs, 47, 48
Tabor Grand Opera House (Denver), 16–17, 71, 101
Tabor Latin theater, 63
Tabor Light Cavalry, 13

Tabor mansion, 71, 115
Tabor memorabilia, 70
Tabor Opera House (Leadville), 27, 37, 63
Tabor papers. *See* Documents
Tabors as quasi-saints, 56
Tabor Story, The (McMechen), 94
Tabor triangle, 82, 87, 88
Taylor, Elizabeth, 108
Teller, Henry, 21
Tempelsman, Maurice, 138
Testimonio of wrongs, 142
Theresa of Avila, 202
Third-wave feminists, 208
Titanic sinking, 113, 114
Tompkins, Jane, 74, 87
Town Talk newspaper, 9
Traditional language as patriarchal prison, 207
Transgender costume (Baby Doe's), 134
True Story, 49–50, 79, 92
Two Lives of Baby Doe, The (Hall), 64, 95, 116

Uncreated grace, 204
Underwood, Ollie, 171
Unlucky princess sagas, 102
Unsinkable Molly Brown. *See* Brown, Margaret Tobin
Unsinkable Mrs. Brown, The (Bancroft, C.), 54
U.S. Senate, 20

Vendome Hotel, 153
Vernon, John: on Augusta Pierce, 87; on Baby Doe's character, 98–99; creates drag queen version of Baby Doe, 68; depiction of Silver Dollar's death by, 121; on H.A.W. Tabor, 84; on Jake Sands's involvement, 79; on Silver Dollar, 122
Victimized Daughters (Jacobs), 199
Victorian attitudes, 41
Visions: of Blessed Virgin, 116, 221; drawing of, 144, 223; of Jesus, 222

Voice of author: Baby Doe's in Dreamworld, 140, 207; use of first person in C. Bancroft's work, 92

Wages of Whiteness, The (Roediger), 236n8
"Walking Woman" (Austin, M.), 127
Wanton into the Good Widow, 105
Warrior Mother: helps with Silver Dollar "problem," 158; as the Hero, 196; rescuing Silver Dollar, 193–94
Washington Evening Star, 19
Washington Post, 20
Washington wedding, 20
Waters, Frank, 128
Watson, Julia, 207
Wedding, dual, 191–92
White, Theodore, 137
Widow Kennedy, 139. *See also* Onassis, Jacqueline Lee (Bouvier) Kennedy
Widows, 136
Widow Tabor: appearance and apparel of, 112; changes in appearance of, 36; correspondence from suitors, 81; corresponds with Ida Doe, 77; enemies of, 211; growing strangeness of, 124; mine cabin life, 32; moves to live at Matchless mine, 31–32; seizes agency in her fate, 110; sexual liberation of, 98; shunned as widow, 31, 93; sympathy earned from spectacle as, 128; Sue Bonnie befriends, 38; visitors to Baby Doe's cabin, 97; writes to Stevenson, 158. *See also* Tabor, Elizabeth Bonduel (McCourt) Doe
Wilde, Oscar, 13
Wildest of the Wild, The (Parkhill), 100
Wild West: androcentric stories of, 65; anti-language, anti-woman code of, 92; assumptions about, 90; as safety valve, 8
Wilmoth, Dick, 219–20
Winchester, Simon, 126
Wolcott, Ed, 30

Woman/women-centered approach, 68, 104; mother-daughter love story, 186
Women: as colonized subjects of patriarchic society, 206; as hysterics, 207; as victims, 197
Women's agency, 104
Women's rights movement, 118
Wood, Geraldo, 203–204, 214
Wood, James, 213–15

Woolf, Virginia, 146, 182
Wright, David, 69
Writer's Diary, A (Woolf), 182
Writing materials, 146

"Yellow Wallpaper, The" (Gilman), 127

Zaitz, Mr. (Leadville grocer): on Baby Doe's sanity, 42–43; visits to Baby Doe's cabin, 97